THE BOX WINE SAILORS

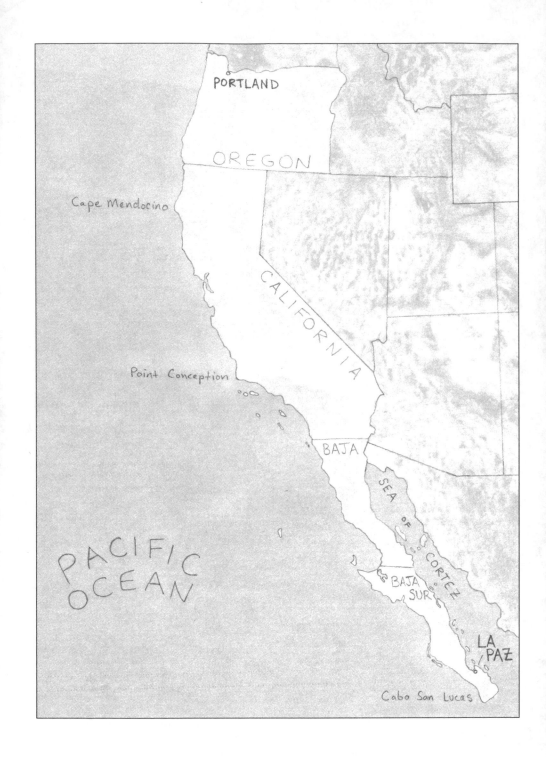

THE BOX WINE SAILORS

MISADVENTURES

OF A BROKE YOUNG COUPLE

AT SEA

AMY McCULLOUGH

ACADEMY

CHICAGO

Published by Academy Chicago Publishers
An imprint of Chicago Review Press Incorporated
814 North Franklin Street
Chicago, Illinois 60610
ISBN 978-1-61373-348-6

A section of this book previously appeared in
the January 2015 edition of *SAIL* magazine.

Library of Congress Cataloging-in-Publication Data
Are available from the Library of Congress.

Cover design: Natalya Balnova
Interior layout: Nord Compo
Interior design: Jonathan Hahn
Maps by Jimmie Buchanan and Amy McCullough

Printed in the United States of America
5 4 3 2 1

For Jimmie

To me the sea is a continual miracle,
The fishes that swim—
the rocks—
the motion of the waves—
the ships with men in them,
What stranger miracles are there?

—Walt Whitman

CONTENTS

THE BOX WINE SAILORS

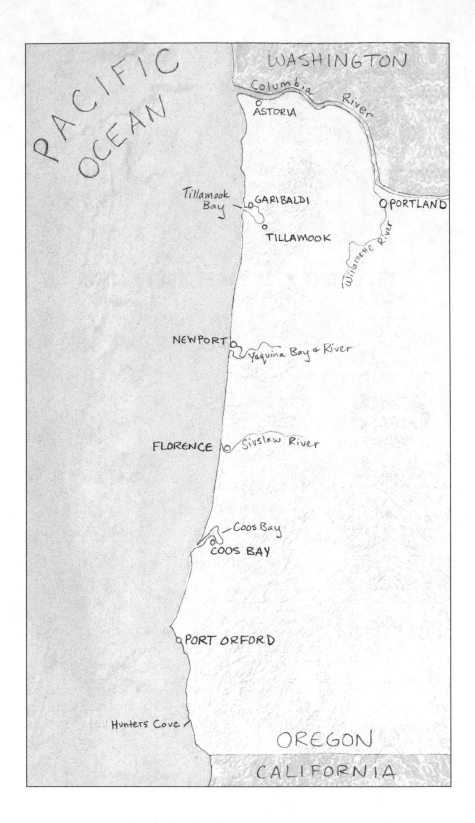

I

OREGON

"SENSIBLE" CRUISING

"Wow. I Wish I Could Do That."

It was gutsy, sure. And there were dangers. "We're quitting our jobs and sailing to Mexico," we'd say. "No, neither of us is a sailor. No, we didn't take lessons. No. We haven't been on the ocean before." The naysayers would remark: "You can't do that." "You need a bigger boat." "You'd better take a few classes." Or the ever-encouraging, "You're going to die." But, in truth, most people said, "Wow. I wish I could do that," or "You're so brave."

It turns out the only difference between bravery and stupidity is a happy ending. If we had died, if our soggy carcasses had washed up on some Californian beach months after our departure, everyone would have said that we were foolish. Or at least they would have thought it. *Sailing the Pacific on a twenty-seven-foot boat, with no experience? Figures . . .* But we lived. And so we are brave.

Jimmie and I did do something extraordinary together, but figuring out what the hell we were doing and the actual doing of it happened simultaneously. We were determined to be cheap—the only way a young, middle-class couple could see such a scheme through (thus skipping the expensive sailing courses)—and we were determined to do things our way (thus skipping the expensive sailing courses).

The extent of our experience upon leaving can be summed up as follows: we had read a few books, rented two low-budget instructional VHS tapes—one starring Flash Gordon and an actress from *Dallas*—and practiced sailing once a week for about a year before departing. Most people assume one of us was a sailor who convinced the other to humor his or her fantasy. But it was *our* fantasy. We dreamed it together. And neither of us had more of a clue about what we were doing than the other.

In fact, neither of us had ever been on the ocean in a boat until after we had quit our jobs, sold all our belongings, given up our apartment, taken the bus from Northwest Portland to our shabby Multnomah Channel marina, and crossed the notoriously dreaded Columbia River Bar. Before deciding on sailing, we had discussed building a cob cottage and living a self-sufficient, remote country life; we made plans for running a food cart or opening a small bar together; we considered canoeing to South America (from Oregon; we had our sights set high).

But a sailboat, we realized, could be purchased for only a few thousand dollars—if one's standards are low. And, once purchased, it can be lived on and traveled in indefinitely. As is often noted by sailors, the wind is free. Of course, there was the lack-of-experience obstacle, but we figured we'd deal with that in time. As it was, I had spent a handful of summery days aboard my stepdad's thirteen-foot racer (as a mere passenger) in my early teens. He sailed it on a small lake in Wisconsin.

Jimmie, for his part, grew up in the Cascade Range east of Portland. His family was poor, and luxuries such as family vacations were few and very far between. When he was twelve, a rather extravagant outing was arranged in which he was taken to the Oregon coast by his mother and paternal grandmother. Though he had spent his entire childhood a mere two-hour drive from the Pacific, Jimmie had never seen the ocean. Once on the beach in Seaside, he shit his pants with excitement.

"Welcome to the Jungle."

Our first day on the ocean was mostly beautiful. I had cried the night before, frying thin-sliced potatoes in oil on our two-burner stove while rocking on the wakes of fishing boats returning across the Columbia River Bar. Giant seabirds I later identified as brown pelicans were dive-bombing the water all around us, filling their flexible beak pouches with tiny fish and gulping them down; they'd rise up thirty or forty feet in the air, then tuck their wings and plummet so quickly that the subsequent splashes had us frequently popping our heads out of the cabin to investigate. We weren't yet used to the sound.

We were anchored right near the entrance to the Pacific, behind Clatsop Spit—perhaps a precarious spot, but we had never done this before, and we wanted to have as much time as possible to get from Astoria, at the mouth of the Columbia, to Tillamook Bay, our first scheduled stop along the Oregon coast. And we wanted to do it all in daylight. The opposite, north side of the mouth is called Cape Disappointment; let's just say Clatsop Spit had a better ring to it. We had made a dish of lentils and canned corn sprinkled with Tony Chachere's Creole Seasoning the night before and set it aside so we wouldn't have to attempt cooking while underway the next day.

The Columbia River Bar inspired many of the cries against our trip. "Not just anyone can cross the Columbia River Bar," people would tell us. "Special pilots are flown out to incoming vessels just to guide them across." "It's called 'the Graveyard of the Pacific,' you know." Yes, we knew. We'd taken a field trip to the Maritime Museum in Astoria earlier that year. There is a giant map in the entry corridor with little red lights marking all the historical shipwrecks in the region. And though we said many times later that the bar was the least of our troubles, we took it very seriously.

As such, we waited for a light forecast to make the crossing and were rewarded with a whitewash of fog and relatively calm seas. Rather than giant breakers and boats careening up waves at terrifying angles, our seascape was filled with bored seagulls, an impeccably opaque grayness, and the white stern lights of fishing boats speeding past us.

Eventually, the fog blew off and a lovely Oregon August day took over, bringing fifteen-knot winds on our beam. We set the sails, engaged the autopilot (a robotic arm that adjusts the tiller to keep you on course), and sat on the deck in the sun. The waves were long and low (for Oregon), but we both felt better sitting up high, rather than in the cockpit closer to eye level with the four- to six-foot swell.

I had never been too prone to motion sickness; Jimmie's history with it is, shall I say, on a par with how his body handled its first ocean encounter. At some point midday, we ate our lentils and corn, I hungrily and Jimmie begrudgingly. As afternoon came upon us, the winds picked up, as it turns out they often do, and the sea became an instant mountain range, its peaks and valleys growing more dramatic with each gusty whip. We maintained a facade of coolness, taking deep breaths and looking around with calm, collected expressions on our faces. We felt thankful it was sunny. We wondered if there was anything we could do.

We deliberated about going farther out to sea as the waves built up, thinking the deeper water might dull their height to some extent. As the distance between the water's surface and the seafloor diminishes, ocean swell begins to bump against the bottom and grow taller as it approaches the coast, ultimately resulting in breakers. But, as we later learned, such an effect doesn't materialize until the water is shallower than the waves are tall (duh). Even at a mere five nautical miles from the coast, a line we'd been riding most of the day, there were more than thirty fathoms (180 feet) of briny water under our turquoise hull. The queen mother of all tsunamis *might* have bounced back off the seafloor at that depth, creating the horror breaker of Laird Hamilton's wet nightmares. But, no, these waves were being caused by the wind. In our ignorance, we did venture slightly further out, only to find (ahem) no difference in the sea state. As we approached the entrance to Tillamook Bay, 55.7 nautical miles from our Clatsop Spit anchorage, we angled back toward the shore.

We were now sailing with a "following sea," which is just what it sounds like. The boat was yawing heavily, and we probably had too much sail up for the increased (and increasing) strength of the wind. We became more proactive about sail management as the trip went on, but in the beginning, we would have seemed downright lazy to a casual onlooker.

We had hank-on headsails, which meant we'd have to go on deck and unhook an entire sail to change it, pulling it down against the force of the wind (or turning into the wind to depower it), then bagging it before "hanking on" and raising its replacement. There were no shortcuts. Many boats have what's called a roller-furling headsail, which works like a giant window shade: you tug on a string and it winds up or lets out, all from the convenience of your cockpit. On a craft like ours, switching sails was a lot of work to get involved in if you weren't sure of the necessity. You might also, perchance, not feel terribly comfortable crawling all over the deck of your tiny boat, sail bags and ropes and hardware in tow, as it rides up and down seven-foot swell on your very first day on the mighty Pacific.

Each wave would lift our stern up and thrust us forward at a forty-five-degree angle, after which we'd slide down its face and then counter-steer to correct the spin it gave our rear end. During this repeated torture, I was holding on as fiercely as I could to the metal railings around the cockpit while Jimmie steered with all his might. (This was to become a familiar scenario in the face of intensifying conditions.) The autopilot, which we'd named Jeeves, had taken to seizing up and calling for help via a solid electronic *BEEEEEEEP* once we'd turned inland. Jeeves wasn't up to the task.

Neither, it turned out, was Jimmie's stomach. The lentils and corn were rearing their ugly heads just as the Pacific's waves grew white and dark in repeating, mesmerizing patterns in the dimming evening. Crest and valley. Foam and black. Over and over. We'd hooked up some marine speakers for listening to music in the cockpit, and our first coastal landfall was soundtracked by Guns N' Roses.

Jimmie, tiller in hand, leaned over the gunwales and yacked, the sea writhing beneath us and Axl Rose wailing in his ears: "Welcome to the jungle / Watch it bring you to your sha-na-na-na-na-na-na-na-na-na-na knees, knees." He threw up and steered simultaneously—*steady down the hill of water, keep your stern squared up to the waves*—and just when all the lentils and corn had vacated his system, we crossed the bar into Tillamook Bay. Huge lumps of swell smashed into the jetty tips behind us, creating salt geysers against the poo-speckled rocks. "It's gonna bring you down! Huh!"

Once inside the jetties' rocky embrace, I took over steering, the boat powered by our outboard. Jimmie brought down the sails as we entered a large, calm body of shallow water bathed in clear moonlight. Sitting across from me at the dinette after we'd anchored in the tiny crescent of Crab Harbor, Jimmie looked exhausted. I made clam chowder from a can and we slept. When I closed my eyes, I could see wave-shaped patterns of white and black shifting against the backs of my eyelids.

And even if I dressed them up in curry and stewed tomatoes, Jimmie was never again very enthusiastic about lentils.

"Oboete Imasu Ka?"

I met Jimmie in a Portland theater-pub where I tended bar. He came in one evening and ordered a Terminator Stout, taking a seat next to my soon-to-be-fiancé, Ben. A scruffy, gregarious fellow with a loud mouth and a penchant for gin, Ben was waiting for my shift to end and struck up a conversation with Jimmie, as he might with anyone who happened to belly up in his vicinity. After several more Terminators and gin and tonics for them and a fair amount of citrus squeezing and bar scrubbing for me, the night ended with drunken karaoke at Chopsticks, a nearby Chinese restaurant–cum–late-night hot spot. (Jimmie sang "Love Me Tender," a performance which, I can now admit, made my heart feel inordinately heavy.) Numbers were exchanged, and eventually Jimmie was added to our cadre of friends, being invited to group concertgoings, birthday parties, and an "orphan" Thanksgiving hosted at my and Ben's house.

Eventually—rather, simultaneously—my relationship with Ben deteriorated. We had become the type of couple who very much enjoys each other's company but rarely has sex. We were friends, roommates. Though it was bright at the start, the spark was gone, and the engagement was a last-ditch effort to preserve something we both knew (or would soon realize) was fading. It would be a lie to say Jimmie had nothing to do with my relationship's rapid demise. He had very much to do with it, because I knew him intimately from the start. And I loved him almost immediately.

I got to know Jimmie more than anyone else cared to during those initial social gatherings. He expressed interest in me, and I reciprocated. Jimmie struck me right away, and even though I wasn't ready to admit to any romantic attraction, I knew he was worth knowing. He was a bit of a loner and had sharp, deep blue eyes, black-rimmed glasses, and a uniquely curled upper lip—like an archer's bow. He was frequently clad in a threadbare black sport coat, collared shirt and tie, and Converse All-Stars. He lived in a one-bedroom apartment in Northwest Portland. I knew it was useless to resist when I started to fantasize about being there with him, about stretching out before him, naked and white. I imagined his solitary place (which was a lot less gloomy in reality than I'd pictured it), his lips and skin and tender blue eyes exploring me. His touch (like his apartment) was far better in truth than in fantasy.

Before I knew that, though, I knew simply that Jimmie made computer chips for Intel and that when he went out to shows he danced his ass off. In addition to tending bar, I was a freelance music writer for the local alt-weekly newspaper (Portland's *Willamette Week*), and I would often invite Jimmie as the "plus one" to whatever concerts I was attending that particular week. Ben, also a bartender, worked nights and usually couldn't accompany me. That's when I really met Jimmie. We would drink whiskey before the shows and talk, and listen. And we would walk all over Portland afterward, something I once told my college roomie was all I wanted in a mate. Concert "dates" led to more. We carved pumpkins together on Halloween and sat on his living room floor listening to records, eating fancy cheese, and drinking wine. We put the jack-o'-lanterns in the park across the street, lit up with tea lights.

I leaned out his kitchen window, blowing smoke into the cool, damp air as we drunkenly talked till 4:00 AM, even on work nights. We discovered that we'd both loved someone who had died in the same way.

Together we watched Jimmie's favorite anime movie, *Do You Remember Love?*, sitting on a makeshift living room camp of sleeping bags and pillows. We drank warm sake from little ceramic cups I stole from the sushi place on the corner, while poufy-dressed pop star Lynn Minmay sang the main theme, asking, "Do you remember the time / When our eyes first met?" Yes, I did. My belly hot with the liquory essence of rice, I mouthed along with the Japanese lyrics: "Oboete imasu ka / Te to te ga fureatta toki?" ("Do you remember the time / When our hands first touched?") Yeah, that too. I was beginning to know I'd never forget.

⚓ ⚓ ⚓

A few months later, one totally average night at the theater-pub, Ben and several friends, including Jimmie, were drinking and waiting for me to finish work. It was then that Jimmie looked at me dead seriously and mouthed "I love you" across the bar. I was rushing about with a bleach-soaked rag, turning over chairs and wiping things down. But I saw him. I read his lips. I knew I was in trouble.

Later that night, in response to my distress—my this-changes-everything, this-is-about-to-upset-every-aspect-of-my-life distress—he said it again, out loud: "I just love you," adding "just" as if there were no choice. And there wasn't. And it did change everything.

In a dramatic sequence of events—move out and stay with a girlfriend, move back in, second-guess moving back in, find a not-too-depressing-but-barely-affordable one-bedroom on West Burnside, scrawl my name by the X—I finally left Ben. And I consumed Jimmie. I learned all about him: that he had an often good-natured and charismatic father who also happened to be a manic depressive and self-destructive drug abuser; that his mother was a sad, and resultantly mean, woman during his childhood; that his brother—eight years his senior—had been his idol. His brother was also relatively unavailable beyond a certain age; he'd long had his eye on the prize of getting out of Dodge (a trailer court in Welches, Oregon) and did so, enlisting as a trumpeter in the US Army Band and marrying young.

As such, Jimmie was left to his own devices, which (fueled by a desire to emulate his brother and to simply rule at something) materialized in a near-obsessive dedication to practicing and playing trumpet. Side interests included directing friends in amateur videos laden with secondhand clothing, over-the-top stunts, and '70s funk music; attempting to craft homemade Cheez-Its on the stovetop; mastering original Nintendo games; and singing Queen songs in his room at the top of his lungs.

The more I learned, the more I loved him. The more it also became apparent that having someone care for him wasn't a feeling he'd experienced often, if ever. He responded to affection as if it were a foreign thing, and he returned it with such strength that it almost made me feel the same way.

I had often been a sort of girlfriend martyr. I would go for these guys I thought were great, awesome people but who didn't necessarily feel that way about themselves. I thought that with my love and attention I could convince them of the truth and make them see their own worth. I don't think it was very different, initially, with Jimmie. I thought he was entirely worth celebrating, and I wanted to show him. But he threw a wrench in my plan: he gave it back. He celebrated me, too. He did for me what I did for others, which, from an amateur psychology perspective, is probably what I'd always wanted, why I was the girlfriend martyr in the first place. The question Minmay asks is, "Do you remember love?" I did. Or, rather, I discovered it. Because of Jimmie, I learned not just how it feels to love but how it feels to *be* loved—to be really, truly loved exactly as I am. We celebrated each other. And that's the difference. That's why it stuck.

Jimmie got out of Welches, too. He moved to the city, Portland, as soon as possible. When his father died, Jimmie stopped playing trumpet. But he redirected his efforts. He went to school (first for video production, then for microelectronics), rented an apartment downtown, delivered many pizzas. He is, in every sense, a self-made man. And he's the type of person whose coworkers and friends weren't surprised by what he was doing, going sailing with no experience. They figured he could, and I guess I did, too.

⚓ ⚓ ⚓

Over three years—from meeting across that pint of beer to moving in together to gradually becoming disenchanted with "regular" life—it became apparent that all we wanted was to be together. Obligations like work became more and more inconvenient, unwelcome obstacles to that precious goal. By this time, I had earned the very demanding position of music editor at the paper, and though it was initially a dream job, it had become a monster eating all my time, keeping me from my love.

I began to wonder why my hours were spent staring at a screen instead of at that bow-curved smile, those tender eyes. Rather than go to shows and interview musicians, I wanted to stay in, talk, make love. Nothing else seemed important. I started working from home as much as possible. I even altered my schedule to allow for more days off together—six a month instead of two. And Jimmie used every bit of "personal absence" time he had, the instant he had it. But it wasn't enough.

So we dreamed up this plan to sail. It wasn't the obvious choice, but it's what we came up with after trying every way we could to think of how to do something adventurous together and not work, not be obligated to anything, for at least a year. And each of us knew we could count on the other to do whatever it took to make it happen—to be just crazy enough to see it through.

"We're Like Kids in a Dickens Novel."

Two weeks after arriving, we were still anchored in Tillamook Bay, an hour-and-a-half drive from Portland. It had taken us over a week to get there, and we were already worried about the season getting on. The North Pacific High—the weather system that makes passage along the northwestern coast of the United States doable (or at least less dangerous)—is a temporary, summertime phenomenon. Once it subsides, the Aleutian Low takes over, bringing, as any good meteorologist would know, the totems of low pressure: storms, rain, inconsistency.

We'd departed from Portland on August 2. Fall was sneaking in like a storm-carryin' fiend, and we wanted nothing to do with it. If we took too long, if the Aleutian Low descended while we were still in Oregon, we might not make it out. We were not on a daring adventure, really; we simply wanted to hang out together and not work for a while. Neither Jimmie nor I had a death wish. We would sail when the weather was good, and we'd wait when it wasn't. But we could wait only so long. As it was, an "unseasonably wintry gale" was blowing freezing air and rain through the region, so we were stuck.

The gloom wasn't doing our power situation (solar only) any favors, so our entertainment was reading with the little daylight we had, then living in darkness after nightfall. The inside of the cabin was hazed in a cold, dripping sweat, and mold had started to grow on the woodwork. We sat under damp blankets and drank tea. Jimmie likened us to the sorry-ass children of Dickens novels. All we needed were fingerless gloves and sullen eyes. On second thought, sailing gloves *are* fingerless, and we *were* looking rather dour; lack of sun will do that.

Then, to make matters worse, on our first excursion to shore (to explore the small coastal town of Garibaldi and perhaps buy some Doritos at the local grocery), we accidentally left open the self-bailing ports on our dinghy, a bright orange blow-up kayak we'd named Johnny Inflatable, and the frigid bay seeped in up to the waterline. When I tried to hang our wet jeans out on the safety lines one particularly breezy day, the thirsty sea salt now inhabiting their threads eagerly drank in the moist Pacific wind, leaving them more damp than they'd started. Our entire world was clammy.

We took a field trip to the beach one day, packing a thermos of vanilla tea and rum and a few granola bars for lunch. We hiked the hairy dunes, like giant knees of sand covered in thin whips of tan-and-green fur, until we were faced with the Pacific. The mist and wind were so unpleasant we retreated back to the lee side of the dunes to sit on logs, finish our drinks, and chat. At that moment, I could feel time stretching out before me, and it seemed that all of Bayocean Peninsula, the skinny strip of land separating Tillamook Bay from the sea—the entire coast, even—was ours. One leg of the trip under my belt (or, rather, my rain pants' elastic waistband), and my cup was already brimming. We were both wearing big, industrial-type rain boots from G.I. Joe's, Jimmie's black with his green raincoat and I entirely in blue, and I felt like a true adventurer. Not a Sir Francis Drake, necessarily, more like a kid with a really sweet portable fort.

A good forecast had come through, and we were building our confidence to leave. In fact, we were so excited that we celebrated with an innovative dinner of rice Alfredo with peas and onions. (Most of our meals revolved around pasta or rice, and being fridge-less and poor, we were quickly exhausting our sauce and mix-in combinations. In short: Alfredo on *rice* = innovative; peas *and* onions = celebration dinner!) We also celebrated with plenty of rum and some sort of generic Kool-Aid. Consequently, we were too hungover the next day to eke out another chunk of the Oregon coast—not for lack of trying, however.

We did go out the next morning, but we might as well have been an empty bottle bobbing, listless, among the waves. The weather proved a little *too* gentle. The windless clattering of the boom and the snapping of our limp sails atop the sea's tall, smooth swell sent Jimmie into dry heaves, and the Dramamine we'd both taken as a preventative measure nearly knocked us unconscious.

So, we turned around and entered Tillamook Bay a second time, just as the thick, heavy drops of an afternoon thunderstorm began to make vibrant cerulean circles on our otherwise faded blue deck. This was about halfway through our two-week stint at Crab Harbor.

The unseasonable gale, in addition to depriving us of light and warmth, had brought to our attention a number of leaks in the cabin. Though Jimmie had removed and furiously caulked the portholes as one of our many predeparture fix-ups, there were apparently several screws under the vinyl ceiling of the V-berth (our bedroom) that were letting water drip down from the deck and, ultimately, into our customized triangular bedding (which I'd industriously created by cutting regular bed sheets diagonally into two triangles, flipping one half, and re-stitching the pieces into a big V).

The rain was over, however, and we were now simply waiting for some lighter, more manageable wind. Waiting, in our damp, damp cabin. Garibaldi was extremely small—a Dairy Queen, a neighborhood grocery, and a bait shop—and we were itching to stretch our legs and see something besides the backsides of dunes and gray water. So we broke out the charts and came up with a plan to walk Bayocean Road to the next-closest town, Tillamook (of cheese fame), in order to find a laundromat where we could pop our soggy bedding in a dryer for a while. You might assume we weren't all that far from Tillamook, being anchored, as we were, in Tillamook Bay. Measuring by foot, however, you'd be wrong.

Jimmie made peanut butter and jelly sandwiches for the road, and, like a cartoon runaway with a polka-dotted bundle on a stick, I threw our dark green hamper bag over my shoulder, and we walked.

Twenty miles later, Jimmie's hamstrings were cramped so badly he could barely take a single step, but we'd achieved the goal of getting to Tillamook, about ten miles from our Crab Harbor anchorage, and our bedding was dry. We'd even eaten hoagies from a gas station and splurged on those cheap caffeinated malt-liquor beverages that taste like liquid Smarties (Tilt and Sparks—the stuff of college kids and bums). They'd become a hit with us during our extremely budget-conscious trip-prep period, when late nights of working on the boat made the later-outlawed combo of booze-plus-caffeine sound like a great idea.

So, preceding the muscle breakdown, we were buzzed and fed and relatively happy. Even the midday break we took to enjoy our PB&Js was wall-calendar picturesque: we sat on a lovely countryside dock, a rustic affair with bright red paint peeling off to reveal gray wood, like fresh skin under a sunburned back; a nest of baby barn swallows was tucked under a nearby roof; and a collection of black-and-white dairy cows hovered in a field of long green grass in the distance. At that point, our excursion had been going well. We didn't feel doomed at all.

But ten miles each way is a long walk for anyone, let alone two people who've hardly set foot off a tiny boat for three weeks. There's not a lot of walking space in the cabin of a twenty-seven-foot boat—hell, there's only one little area either of us (at six feet and five ten) could stand up straight in. What we'd been doing, primarily, was sitting, and our legs were not cut out for Tillamook. Jimmie considered lying down in the bushes on the side of the trail and just resting till morning. But it was cold, and the dampness of sundown hinted that our sheet-drying excursion would all be for naught if we didn't continue on.

My feet, plagued for years by a bone spur, bunions, and inherited flatness, ached throughout every joint. Jimmie was employing a strange hunch, walking in an almost seated position, hoping, perhaps, that the familiarity would bring comfort to his muscles. For the last few miles, the road became rocky and pitted, a fearsome combination in complete darkness. Even the surrounding woods, beautiful in the light of day with their gnarled and wind-twisted pines, seemed ominous and full of ill will. Like a couple of Tiny Tims, we lurched on, now with subpar appendages to match our tired eyes and sodden wool.

"Nothing's Gonna Stop Us Now . . . Except a Small Craft Advisory."

The sail to Newport, our next stop along the Oregon coast, brought with it our first experience of night sailing. This trip was long enough (68.5 nautical miles) that it was unavoidable: we would still be out at sea when the sun set. Sailboats are slow, and the smaller the slower, so for us, traveling even fifty nautical miles at an average speed of four knots (if we were lucky) meant a twelve-and-a-half-hour sail (one knot = one nautical mile per hour). Add the shortness of boreal Oregon's late-summer days, and the prospect of covering such distances in the warmth and comfort of sunlight becomes an unattainable fantasy. So we accepted our scary night-sailing fate.

It turned out the worst part was the cold. It was August, but August in Oregon—especially on the coast at night—is far from tropical.

It was also boring. Practicing on the Columbia and Willamette Rivers leading up to our trip, we were constantly tacking to avoid barges, other recreational craft, and, well, the banks of the rivers. Under those circumstances, sailing seemed a pretty active endeavor. But for sixty-some nautical miles of heading south on a great big ocean, one really has only to set the sails and then sit there, barring any notable changes in weather, of course.

And if the wind dies, as it did that night, it's unbearably slow.

But we were very determined to *sail*, and so we did. After all, the cheapness that our trip was tightly budgeted around—the cheapness that can be credited with the very genesis of our choosing sailing as a means of achieving a brief early retirement together—didn't have a luxurious gas fund. That, and we *wanted* to sail. It's what we'd set out to do. As such, any taking down of sails and starting up of "James Brown" (our outboard motor, which turned out to be the "hardest working motor in sea business") was weighted with an unspoken guilt.

Truth be told, we probably would have sat for hours that night, our limp sails lilting and snapping with the western swell, the deck and ourselves glazed in a shiny patina of dew, waiting for any slight hint of wind, had it not been for the whales.

We couldn't see them, but we knew we were not alone when a shocking noise began to interrupt the banging of our boom and sails: *FLOO! FLOO! FLOO . . . SH!* A moment after, we could hear countless speckles of liquid flotsam rejoining the massive Pacific in a tiny symphony of splashes and plops. A giant bowl of Rice Krispies.

Stinky Rice Krispies. It smelled like what, essentially, it was: a whale burp. Oceanic, salty, fishy, damp. Suddenly, they began to go off all around us: *FLOO-FLOOSH!* We were surrounded by spouting whales we couldn't see. Night whales. That was it. We lowered James Brown's propeller into the sea and away we went, motoring at a steady four-to-five knots the last two hours to Newport's Yaquina Bay.

The entrance channel was shrouded with fog when we arrived, and as we puttered under the city's landmark art deco bridge (something from the cover of a *Fountainhead* paperback), a chorus of sea lions barked and yelped along the waterfront, echoing "Who goes there?" in their native tongue.

⚓ ⚓ ⚓

A few days into our stay, we realized we could use some supplemental groceries. We had packets to make spaghetti sauce, but no noodles; peanut butter but no bread. We took the boat to a transient dock. The signage seemed to indicate that no fees would accrue unless a boat were tied up overnight, but our incredibly economical ways made us paranoid, and we resolved to hustle. We felt much more comfortable at anchor, our only contact with earth being some discreet patch of underwater rock or sand—a mere square foot or two of earth clung onto by anchor and rope and chain. Otherwise we were floating, untouchable by man's rules and prices and pestering.

Nevertheless, we tied up and ascended the riverside hills below the Yaquina Bay Bridge's majestic supports. And as we emerged through some brush onto the side of the highway, I suddenly felt as anonymous to the world as I had to those sea lions. *Who goes there?* Strangers.

It occurred to me that no one cared who we were, where we'd been, where we'd come from or how. It didn't matter to the drivers of cars along Highway 101 that I, only a few weeks earlier, had been the music editor of a Pulitzer Prize–winning newspaper. It didn't matter that Jimmie could very well have had a hand in making the Intel processor running your computer right now. We were polite, educated people. We had good manners and degrees and rental and work references that any property management company or prospective employer would be thrilled with.

But, right then, we were scruffy kids crawling out of some brush onto the side of the road. We were sea bums with intent to buy box wine and macaroni and cheese. It didn't matter who we had been. Ever. It was as if the instant I was living, my *now*, was the only real thing in the world. That's how it was the whole trip, really. It's the only time it's ever been that way.

⚓ ⚓ ⚓

Just as in Tillamook Bay, we made one failed attempt to leave Newport and found ourselves reentering now-familiar jetties and re-anchoring where we had so recently already spent too much time.

We had formulated a plan to leave around midnight and sail the ambitious (for us) ninety or so nautical miles straight to Coos Bay, skipping the potentially sketchy small entry at Florence. We had heard about Florence from someone who knew it well. When loading up some furniture we were passing on to my assistant editor, Casey, his father (whose van we were using) warned us about the area. He was a carpenter from England who'd lived in Florence most of his life, so we were inclined to listen to him. Plus, he had white hair and a mustache; he wore sweaters and looked salty. We believed he knew things. He did not warn us about the Columbia River Bar. He warned us about the small river bars along the Oregon coast, the entries to tiny port towns where barges couldn't even fit. "Those lit'l river bars can get pretty messy," he cautioned in his lingering semi-Brit accent. And we took note.

So we dragged ourselves into the cold night air and left Newport, the wind picking up noticeably once we were outside of the jetties. A north wind had been forecast, but we were getting a southerly, and a good brisk one at that. Heading out, we were pointed west to get offshore a bit, and we were hauling ass. It was strange to be sailing so fast at night. The white froth on the water displaced by our hull stood glowing blue-white against the dark sea, each midnight ripple capped in snow like downy fluff edging the hems of a deep blue Santa suit.

Glow-in-the-dark plankton, too, flashed through the water as we raced across the surface. It would blink—aqua, mint, electric teal—as if the sea were a giant Lite-Brite, a million living lights flickering across the world's largest piece of black construction paper. It was exhilarating, and we were confident at the start, so much so that we broke into a spontaneous rendition of Starship's "Nothing's Gonna Stop Us Now": "And we can build this dream together! / Standin' strong forever! / Nothin's gonna stop us now!" we chanted into the night, to the whales, to phosphorescence, to no one. "And if this world runs out of lovers / We'll still have each other / Nothin's gonna stop us now!" Yeah!

But once we turned more aggressively south and were forced to tack, repeatedly, into the ever-growing headwind—the boat heeling strongly and I barely able to pull in the jib, even with the assistance of a winch—our boisterousness waned. Wondering what the hell had happened to the forecast we'd counted on, we tuned into the National Oceanic and Atmospheric Administration (NOAA) weather broadcast on our VHF. They'd issued a small craft advisory. Still unsure if we were aboard what they'd deem a "small craft," we opted not to chance it. Defeated, we turned north and rode the long swell back into Yaquina Bay. So much for Starship.

"This Is Gonna Get Hairy."

I tried to think of the trip only a portion at a time. It was too daunting to be sailing "from Portland to La Paz," though that was our ultimate, semi-unspoken goal. In the beginning, I felt we were sailing for California; then once in Northern California, to San Francisco; then L.A.; then Mexico.

The aspiration to sail directly to Coos Bay was still in the back of our minds, but on our second departure from Newport, we were forced to admit that baby steps were our forte. We decided, officially, to play it by ear. If things went well, we would continue on toward Coos Bay, even if it meant a nighttime arrival. If things tended toward the shitty, we would use Florence as a bailout escape route.

Most of the day was pleasant. A light northern wind pushed us along from behind, and the blue, cloudless sky, warm sun, and cool air were pure Oregon September. It was the first, and we'd already been gone a month. Eventually the wind was so perfectly behind us that we sailed "wing on wing," with the headsail and mainsail out to opposite sides, our boat transformed into a great blue-bodied bird with thirty-foot-tall, billowing white appendages. It was a technique that we'd read about in our sailing books, and we both got a kick out of actually doing it.

As usual, the winds began to build as afternoon approached. The warming of the land throughout the day causes the heated air to rise, which beckons the cooler ocean air to rush in and fill the vacancy. It's essentially a sea breeze, but the North Pacific is pretty freakin' cold, and the September sun still warms the land considerably, so what we often found ourselves in was a rather strong afternoon sea *wind*—and on this particular leg it was blowing both the waves and our hair-trigger anxiety into a fury, enough to scare us inland.

In retrospect, we may have been better off staying on the Pacific and heading farther south, but you never really know, and when you're us and know even less, being anchored in a river or bay sounds much more inviting than staying at sea while the waves build. So we turned east-southeast and started making a diagonal toward the Siuslaw River Bar, the entrance to where Florence sits a few miles upriver.

The thing that makes these small river bars "messy," as Casey's father put it, is the fact that not only is a whole ocean-full of water meeting a whole river-full of water and tangling at the entrance, but the depth of the water drops rapidly as you approach land. The result is those beautiful coastal waves, aquamarine curls dressed with sudsy white topsides—waves suited for surfers, not sailors, and especially not amateur sailors.

It was becoming apparent that we'd soon be surfing these breakers ourselves when Jimmie placed a death grip on the tiller and said, "This is gonna get hairy."

As we neared the entrance jetties, everything logical told us we'd be pushed to the south. The wind and waves and current were all rushing at us from the north, and the last thing we wanted was to crash right into the south jetty once in the throes of the river bar. So Jimmie aimed just inside the northern jetty in order to give us some leeway. What we didn't understand—the thing sailing experience would have told us—was that our sails were set in a manner that, coupled with our fin keel, was turning us even farther to port. In other words, we were turling much harder than intended toward the jetty we were already barely skirting.

Both mainsail and working jib were up, their sheets pulled tight to harness the wind, but each gust that filled them spun us hard to port like we were on an axis (which we essentially were; what a fin keel provides in maneuverability it lacks in turning resistance). As if working in tandem, the seawater running quickly under the hull and past the rudder also gave a brisk shove to our port quarter, pushing our back end to the right and ultimately turning the bow northward.

Jimmie, sitting on the high, windward side of the boat, his sneakers pressed against the opposite cockpit seat—practically standing—was now trying desperately to counter-steer against all this natural power. Cringing, he hugged the tiller tight to his chest, pitting every bit of might he had against the forces of wind and rushing water. Each gust was a tug-of-war.

I was holding on tightly to the stern pulpit and leaning timidly over the low side of the boat, watching the bow float over nothing each time we rose on a wave. Just as a surfer's board sticks out over the crest of the wave it is riding, the front third of our boat jutted straight out and over the water, surrounded by 360 degrees of air (as opposed to its usual air-on-the-air side/water-on-the-water side arrangement). For a moment, I was detached from the situation, as if I were watching from some exciting documentary camera angle. It was a marvel.

But it was at the back of the boat, at the oncoming sea rushing toward our open transom, that I was staring when I heard it: the loud snap of wood, as if some coastal camper had busted a hefty branch over his leg to fuel a fire. And there sat Jimmie, with the majority of our tiller, now detached entirely from the boat, in his hands. Imagine being seconds from a car accident and having your steering wheel pop right off the dashboard. That's what it felt like.

Jimmie yelled for me to start up the outboard motor, thinking that we could use its throttle arm to steer, however poorly. I started it up. It died. I depressed the ignition button, held it in. Nothing. Tried again. Nothing. I realized I'd put it in forward the moment it had started and was now trying to fire it up in gear. I pushed the lever back to neutral and tried again. Nothing.

Meanwhile, we were still being pushed steadily toward the north jetty, its barnacle-crusted boulders close enough that you could sense the surge of the tide sucking down like a monstrous garbage disposal. Dotting the jetty rocks, beachcombers and fisherman stood, mouths agape, sure they were about to witness a shipwreck. A rotten stub maybe half a foot long was sticking up out of the tiller's metal housing; Jimmie sprung down from his seat and grabbed it with both hands. Putting his whole body into it, he swung it to the left, turning us slightly in the favorable, southward direction. In the interim, the boat had been sailing on its own.

"Pull down the jib and help me steer!" he shouted. He was low in the cockpit now and couldn't see a thing. For all he knew the rocks were already scraping the blue paint off our bow. They weren't, though. He had muscled us just far enough to starboard to avoid catastrophe. We were inside the channel. I loosened the jib halyard and leapt on deck, pulled the headsail down, haphazardly secured it with an orange bungee, and grabbed our little handheld GPS.

"Starboard a little. Good, good. That's close enough. It's still nine feet deep." I was simultaneously directing Jimmie, with his insanely small amount of leverage, along our preplanned GPS route while keeping an eye on the depth, assessing our surroundings, and managing the mainsail. To me, these were the acts of a superhero, yet only a mere sidekick compared to Jimmie's Amazing Rudder-Man! I was more like Panicgirl, his nervous yet helpful companion.

A bend in the river approached, and more breakers appeared along the shallow elbow of the turn, fanning out across the river. We were past the looming tip of the north jetty, but we still had to sail upriver with basically no tiller and definitely no outboard. If the sand dunes and jetties cut off the wind entirely at any point, we would have no power. Also, we had never sailed to anchor before, let alone sailed to a predetermined point of appropriate depth in an unnerving river full of shallow spots and "deadheads" (random pilings from old docks sticking up in rows perpendicular to the riverbanks or, worse, barely submerged and hidden from view, like little aqua mines).

Whenever we neared an anchorage, our usual technique was to drop the sails and fire up the motor. I would steer us to our desired spot and read off depths while Jimmie readied the appropriate anchor and perched at the bow, prepared to lower and set it. At least, that's how we'd been doing it so far, and it was, in fact, the only way we knew how to anchor. However unpracticed, this method had been hitherto effective, and a sudden, forced change of form was both unexpected and unwelcome.

Jimmie devised a plan: "When we get close to where we want to be, you say the word and we'll simultaneously drop the mainsail and the anchor as fast as possible. Give us time to drift to the right spot."

I love a plan.

When the time was as close to right as I could guess, I yelled, "OK!" For a moment, we were free-floating while I wrestled down a violently fluttering mainsail and Jimmie ran to the bow and lowered the anchor. The channel was choppy and windblown, and we were pitching all about. But the anchor seemed to set and the boat stopped. Stopped! Not by a wall of rocks or a deadhead or a sandbar, but by us, on purpose!

Once anchored, I made hot cocoa and handed a mug out to Jimmie, who'd gone to work on the tiller straightaway. It was wrapped in white-painted rope, a nautical look we had found aesthetically pleasing upon purchasing the boat but soon discovered to be a poor wood-preservation technique. As Jimmie unwound the rope, a waterlogged, rotten tiller emerged. With a flashlight in his mouth, a soon-to-be-common mode for him, he loosened and removed the moldering stub he'd been steering with; jammed the remaining end, which was less rotten, down into the housing; and tightened everything up. We again had a tiller. A not-very-confidence-inspiring tiller, but something.

⚓ ⚓ ⚓

It wasn't easy to just turn around and head back out through that channel, past those jetties where visions of our boat being destroyed were so easily conjured. At times like these, it was as if we were on autopilot. We weren't going to stop; that was out of the question. So we just moved ahead as if moving ahead were the only option. Tunnel vision. Don't think about it. Progress, progress, progress.

It was close to 11:00 PM the next night when we began motoring down the Siuslaw River. It was clear out, and when we turned a bend to face the ocean, the moon sparkled on the surface like silver glitter on a vast swath of black velvet. It was darker here, a scant two lights marking the jetties—green to the north and red to the south—and the glare of civilization nearly nil.

The waves are always steeper across a river bar, but we rode up and down, up and down until the depth of the ocean better absorbed them. Yes, we crossed it just fine. There was still a big swell running—there is always a big swell running off the Oregon coast—but past the bar it mellows. We aimed ourselves out between the next set of red and green lights, the signals that lead a vessel out to sea, marking the way until you're far enough to make your own.

"And I Could Be Your Fav-or-ite Gir-irl."

The thing I failed to mention about that entire debacle—from the potential jetty-ramming to our on-the-spot anchor drill—was that we had the pleasure of a Coast Guard audience for the whole affair.

Upon first sighting an orange and gray Coast Guard vessel floating inside the breakwaters, our hearts filled with a (totally unfounded) sense of hope. *Surely we'll be assisted!* we thought. Well, not exactly. They were no more helpful than the onlooking fishermen when we were nose to nose with the north jetty, and they seemed content just to skulk aloofly alongside us as we fumbled to navigate the channel with broken tiller and uncooperative outboard afterward.

Suddenly, in the midst of the latter portion of our trial, they signaled for us to pick up our radio. At this sign of life, I ran up on deck and tied what I hoped would be a tow line to our bow cleat, waving the other end desperately in their direction. When they didn't respond, I ran down and grabbed the VHF, attempting to hail them back, but it didn't seem to be transmitting. Jimmie, on his knees in the cockpit, simply thrust his broken end of tiller up in the air to communicate our situation. At this, they left.

By the time we'd sailed upriver far enough to be near our planned anchorage, the Coast Guard boat had reappeared. They tried briefly to beckon us over to a small station of theirs on the opposite side of the river, but we simply ignored them. (Two can play at that game! Ha!)

Once we'd actually anchored (triumphantly!), they whipped out a megaphone and asked us to pull in our fishing gear. We'd thrown out a trolling line in the hopes of catching a fish earlier that day, and the Coast Guard, piloting one of those little pontoon-style boats with the inflatable ring around the outside, were apparently wary of being poked.

Jimmie was wary of being busted for having an illegitimate holding tank for our toilet, and he ran quickly below to rig it up to look on the level. (A mere flip of a lever rerouted our head from its usual pump-straight-out path into a dummy holding tank—a tank with an "in" but no "out"—which we'd installed just for this purpose.) He switched the lever and zip-tied it in the appropriate position, a tactic we'd read was enough to please most inspectors.

I obediently pulled in our line but went slowly enough that Jimmie had time to reassure me things were in order below deck. We weren't sure why we were being boarded in the first place, but we wanted to have our ducks in at least the appearance of a row before admitting the Aqua Po-Po.

We were then treated to a safety inspection, because not answering your VHF radio is apparently grounds for suspicion. "A VHF isn't a required piece of equipment, is it?" Jimmie asked, knowing the answer. (Because we operated on such a bare minimum, we'd looked into and obtained only that which was absolutely required by law. Our VHF came with the boat, and it turned out to be extremely useful—essential, really—for receiving weather forecasts, but it was technically a luxury item. And we had no knowledge of its inability to call out until my first, ill-fated attempt earlier that day.) The officers agreed that the radio was not officially required, but they found us suspicious nonetheless.

That settled, we split up. Jimmie handled the in-cabin questions, which were administered by a steely-eyed man with dirty-blond hair and a mustache. Meanwhile, I worked on lashing down the mainsail and tidying up the lines. A baby-faced guardsman with dark hair and round, friendly eyes stayed outside with me and had me show him our foghorn and personal flotation devices. He also asked if we'd had any luck fishing. I mentioned that something silvery was on earlier that day but seemed to have been eaten off the line by a larger fish. "Probably a tuna," he conjectured.

The inspection didn't take long, and just about everything checked out, but we were found to be in possession of expired flares. The date on them was 1984. Our boat was a '72 and the year was 2008. Unable to help himself, Jimmie asked if it would really do much good to light off a flare if we were in trouble on the high seas, as in, would anyone (i.e., you guys) come to our aid?

Just then, the steely-eyed man's cell phone rang. The ringtone was Gwen Stefani's "Sweet Escape," that song with the horribly infectious "And I could be your fav-or-ite gir-irl" refrain, and he was obviously a little embarrassed. The call appeared to be from his wife. After he'd silenced it and engaged in some under-his-breath grumbling, he said,

"Flares are really more for signaling to a rescue party once you can see them."

Guess that makes them not entirely useless.

They wrote us a voucher for a ticket we were to receive in a few weeks by mail. They also informed us of a hotline we could call for bar conditions and mentioned that we should have checked those very conditions before entering; there had been a restriction for boats twenty-three feet in length and under that particular day. We told them our boat was twenty-seven feet long, but we noted the phone number regardless.

Both men were really rather pleasant and, despite the mustache and the guns on their hips, not terribly domineering. But we were tired and still miffed about their lack of help earlier, and—in conjunction with the issuing of a ticket (Really?! We almost wrecked right before their eyes!)—we were more than ready for their visit to conclude.

As soon as we were alone, I set to turning the boat from a sailing vessel into home for the night—putting the doors on the companionway, covering the sails, trading depth meter for anchor light and so forth— and, as I said, Jimmie jury-rigged our tiller (*almost* "straightaway"). The sun was down and a brisk wind was still whipping through the anchorage, lashing orange and purple streaks into the sky as if drawing from a giant palette just below the horizon.

We ate pasta with Alfredo sauce (reconstituted from a packet of dehydrated dairy and herbs and "thickened" with reconstituted powdered milk—what were we, astronauts?) and talked a little about the day. Jimmie jokingly proposed some vandalization of the Coast Guard station we'd been beckoned toward (in particular, rattle-canning the words "Doze Nutz" on it), and I broke into an insane laughing fit. Sprawled across a few of the blue vinyl pads that topped all our interior seating areas, I lay shaking like a jackhammer, tears rolling down my cheeks, my diaphragm aching for relief. It was damn near unnatural, but I think it made us both feel better. We never got that ticket.

"Headed for Mexico, Eh?"

Any time you look into whether or not you should try doing something, especially something bold or daring, there is going to be someone who says you can't. In the case of sailing a small boat on the Pacific with no sailing experience, the voices screaming "NOOOO!" were numerous. But who did these voices belong to? People sitting on the Internet, passing judgment; folks polishing their gunwales at the local marina and basking in the cred of being a "senior" member of such advice and discussion sites as SailNet.com; envious dreamers. I'm not saying these folks haven't sailed, or don't know anything about the topic, but what I have observed is that they, as a group, have agreed there is a "best way" to do certain things. Usually this means you need a newer, bigger boat, that you have to take some sort of lessons, that you must *spend more money!* Once they've made a decision, they then stick to their collective guns. Everyone agrees, so it must be true.

These are the same people who jointly agree you can't do what Jimmie and I did. They are "the Naysayers," and they are abundant. If we had listened to them, we would have missed out on the greatest experience of our lives.

The Naysayer comes in one of three types:

First, there are those who want to do whatever you're attempting—have considered it, dreamed of it, even casually thrown it out as a potential "someday" or retirement plan. But they never will. Deep in their hearts they know it, and they use "can't" as an excuse for themselves and a deterrent to others, all efforts pointing toward the grand goal of making themselves feel better. Not that there's anything wrong with preferring security, comfort, known entities, and a general lack of danger in your life; there isn't, but it is wrong to *pretend* to be a free-spirited adventurer and then disdain those who *are*.

Other Naysayers *have* done what you're attempting, but, in doing so, expended far more resources and feel superior for it. No one who's justified (to themselves, their family, their friends) spending hundreds of thousands of dollars on living a dream wants to hear that someone else could achieve a similar goal spending, say, ten thousand. Nor does someone who waited his or her whole life to embark on an adventure want to admit that two twentysomethings with nominal sailing experience can just quit their decent jobs, go gallivanting around on an old boat full of cheap wine and ramen, and then regain decent jobs afterward (which we did). It just isn't that easy, dammit!

Finally there are the Naysayers who truly believe certain goals can't be achieved, that they're simply too unsafe or even impossible. Their concern is perhaps more philanthropic—they just don't want to see a couple of quixotic young lovers die at sea.

Whatever their reasons, these people are all saying, "Can't," "Don't," "Stop," "No."

Look around your local library or bookstore, or do a quick Internet search, and you'll find that you *can't* sail the Pacific in anything less than a thirty-foot boat. That's the general consensus. Well, we did it in a twenty-seven-footer. That's the problem with taking someone else's word for it.

A few examples of someone else's words:

The first comment left on my farewell article, "High Seas, Low Wages" reads, "You're right on, Amy . . . BUT can you really learn to cross the Columbia Bar—the 'graveyard of the Pacific'—by watching a video?"

From the Hull Truth Boating Forum: "The smallest boat capable of safely [sailing an ocean] would probably be a 32' bluewater sailboat."

Here are some responses to a dummy post I added to SailNet's general discussion forum proposing the notion of sailing a Newport 27 (our boat) on the Pacific:

"You couldn't pay me enough to be in a boat that small, especially in the Pacific."

"I wouldn't do it in shorter than a 30, but personal preference plays a big role."

"I submit to you that the Newport is a great training sailboat but that you shouldn't put another penny into her, and start looking for something at 30 feet."

On a Yahoo! forum, in response to a question about the best size of sailboat for one or two people to sail around the world, readers voted this as the "best answer":

"The general rule of thumb is you need . . . 15 FEET OF BOAT for EACH PASSENGER . . . so for 2 people you need a MINIMUM of a 30 foot BOAT . . . but if you plan to use it off shore . . . you need ANOTHER 15 FEET of boat . . . so for 2 people to sail around the world you would need a MINIMUM of a 45 footer and THAT is just about MINIMUM SIZE."

The commenter went on to say, "These PLASTIC FANTASTIC [boats] that are lightly built today are NOT designed for DEEP SEA USE and every year, people who think all boats are the same get KILLED SAILING THEM AROUND THE WORLD."

And one more Internet expert: "Most boats under 30 feet do not dare to venture past 10 miles [from] land." Do not dare! You hear?!

Even folks who are optimistic about small craft would not champion taking our 1972 Newport 27—what most people would consider a "weekender"—on the mighty Pacific. John Vigor's well-respected tome *Twenty Small Sailboats to Take You Anywhere*, for instance, is a compendium of old fiberglass boats that are all small (from twenty to thirty-two feet) and all known to have crossed oceans. Such vessels exist. But you can bet your ass the Newport 27 is *not* on his list.

Clearly, we were not trying to get ourselves killed, and had we been able to purchase a trusted "bluewater" boat for around five grand, we would have been thrilled to do so. As it was, our 1972 Newport 27, which we named *Cotton* (after a favorite character in Glendon Swarthout's *Bless the Beasts and Children*), was the best we could find. It was for sale in the relatively nearby town of Everett, Washington; it was affordable; it seemed capable of feeling something like home. And, even though our opinion was unpopular, we thought it could get the job done.

Despite the enlightened discouragement coming at us from all channels, we were excited to see what our little boat—and our little selves—could accomplish. Suspicious that many of the Naysayers were happy to let "research" (a.k.a. whatever so-and-so-who-presumably-knows-about-it says) replace experience, we said, "Fuck so-and-so. We'll go out and see for ourselves."

The Naysayers also agree there's all sorts of gear that is "a must." You *must* have a roller furling (the aforementioned trim-from-the-cockpit) headsail, for instance, available new from West Marine starting at $999.99. You *must* have a CQR anchor (the best! the most trusted! from $360!). For your dinghy, you *need* a Zodiac, one of those small, hard-bottom crafts cradled in an inflatable U (on average, they run about $1,000, a quarter of what we paid for our actual *sail*boat). And of course you also *must* have newish sails. (Ours appeared to be 1972 originals.) Finally, don't even think about living without such creature comforts as heat, refrigeration, and some way to bathe.

We managed to do without all these things. We did invest a little (about $150) in a new storm jib, the very rigid and small headsail you put on when the shit is hitting the fan. Sailors like to call it a "postage stamp." Because it's so small! Get it?

Despite all the preliminary hubbub and cautionary tales, recommendations and so-called requirements that we never, ah, acquired, there were three things we encountered that actually encouraged rather than discouraged us. First was discovering a Thoreauvian book called *Sensible Cruising* by Don Casey and Lew Hackler. It said that not only *can* you take a cruise in a small vessel, you *should*—and soon! Basically, do it now and do it with what you've got, or you won't do it at all. And you'll regret it. This, obviously, spoke to us. *Sensible Cruising* also championed innovation and making do with the space and gear at your disposal, a philosophy we most certainly took to heart.

Second was happening upon a YouTube video uploaded by a fellow Oregonian named Cody Sheehy. He'd sailed from Portland to Monterey, California, mostly by himself, on a twenty-seven-foot sloop much like ours. (He even refers to it as "sketchy.") His video, besides being an example of someone else taking to the world's biggest ocean in a small boat, literally showed us what it might look like to be on Pacific swell in such a craft: How violently was his boat being tossed around? Did it look more like a cow in a midwestern tornado or an albatross confidently gliding among the waves? How terrifying (or not) did his world appear? These were things I wondered endlessly about, racked my brain trying to imagine, and fruitlessly sought information on. Having some idea of what was in store—regardless of how variable the conditions can be and how incredibly little his experience might have to do with ours—made me feel much more mentally prepared.

Third was Rob.

Rob was the Coos Bay harbormaster, an older man with thinning gray hair and skin that had the flaky texture of hard parmesan. Consistently clad in a heather gray sweatshirt (the kind with a V stitched in the center below its crew neck), his cheeks were pink with broken blood vessels and his lips were noticeably chapped. His boat was called *Summer Wind*.

Not long after meeting us, Rob said, "Headed for Mexico, eh?" It came completely out of the blue. We could have been headed anywhere, or nowhere, or, more realistically, someplace at least *sort of close*—say, San Francisco. But Rob called it without any clues: Mexico. And he didn't say it as if it were a possibility; he said it as if it were the nonnegotiable future. A given.

"Oh, Mandy. You Came and You Gave Without Tak-iiing."

When we met Rob, we'd been up for thirty-some hours, the last few of which we'd spent fruitlessly attempting to find an anchorage in what was the *largest natural deep-water port on the Oregon coast*. This was not a problem we'd anticipated.

Our overnight sail to Coos Bay (from Florence) had been intensely cold but enjoyable. To give you an idea, I was wearing two pairs of pants, two pairs of socks, a long-sleeved T-shirt, a sweater, a hooded sweatshirt, a wool overcoat, and a raincoat. I also had on gloves, a stocking cap, and a scarf. But the wind stayed steady and not too strong all night, and we were able to effectively sail (i.e., no motor) for hours on end.

A lot of sailors say they like to "motor-sail." We'd often think, *Whatever the fuck that means.* We surmised that it must be as simple as it sounds: motoring with the sails up. I suppose a few added horses of power might give the sails a little boost, but the way an outboard pushes a boat along doesn't really harmonize with the thrust of sails. So with very few exceptions, we did exclusively one or the other.

After a year at sea, we began to form the opinion that many sailors don't actually like to sail at all; they like to talk and act like sailors, hang out at yacht clubs, host cocktail hours, and spend absurd amounts of money—on their slips, boats, accessories, and gas (if "motor-sailing," mind you). They also like to claim to be really laidback and removed from society despite their radars and smartphones and weather faxes and satellite Internet. Perhaps those sailors like to motor with the sails up to create some semblance of real sailing, even though the motor's doing most of the work. Maybe it's different if you have a big, strong inboard. I couldn't tell you, as our motor had less horsepower (eight, to be exact) than most people have behind their dinghies.

Sailing all night, to us, was pure, concentrated accomplishment. It was the actualization of something we weren't even sure we knew how to do. So it was fantastic, despite the cold.

We listened to an audiobook (*Casino Royale*) and made coffee while underway. Making anything underway was an achievement as well, and we were very proud to have spilled only a few drops when pouring from the French press into our mugs while riding atop eight-foot waves. We ate granola bars and sucked on lemon drops (a seasickness preventative). We turned on a red light in the cabin when retrieving these things so as to not ruin our night vision. And all of it was just so incredibly fun—like we were a couple of kids playing "sailor"—and it was as close as we'd yet come to how we'd imagined it might be.

It wasn't until the sun began to rise over the Umpqua River basin that the wind lightened and our GPS-reported time to destination began to grow. This particular stat can really sink your heart, but we had come this far under sail alone and were determined to finish out the Florence–to–Coos Bay leg au naturel.

Eventually, the bluffs lining the entry to Coos Bay—sheer cliffs topped with mossy green so bright and consistent it might've been AstroTurf—became "conspicuous," as the *Coast Pilot* always described such things, and we were filled with anticipation. (The *Coast Pilot*, incidentally, is a ridiculously thorough publication put out by the Office of Coast Survey meant to supplement NOAA charts and "provide detailed information about US near-coastal waters"; we had the *United States Coast Pilot 7: Pacific Coast*.)

The sun was now a ripe, full lemon floating over the eastern horizon. We stripped a few layers off, feeling free and limber in only three shirts each. What looked like puffins were skirting the water in search of fish; I looked through the photos in my Audubon *Field Guide to North American Birds: Western Region*, aiming for positive identification. We'd been hoping to arrive in the early morning to avoid strong winds forecast for that day, but our dragging ass kept pushing that time back. Once inside the breakwaters, we finally dropped our sails and switched to motoring.

An hour or two earlier, we were sitting with near-limp sails, edging ever more slowly toward our destination, but now things were picking up. Suddenly, our bow was repeatedly riding up and smacking down over wind waves that were sweeping the huge bay with whitecaps, its surface a stiff-peaked meringue. Salty water splashed in over the bow and sides, stinging our wind- and sunburned faces. Worse yet, the rough water dared to mess with our anchorage plans.

We'd designed our trip to the Coos Bay/North Bend area (they're twin cities) around a Grocery Outlet, where we planned to restock our supplies as inexpensively as possible. We also hoped to replace our tiller and then move on toward California, lickety-split. But the area along North Bend where we'd plotted our anchorage was completely windswept. Also, there were private mooring buoys dotting the shoreline.

Jimmie piloted while I went into the cabin to reassess our options with the help of the Nobletec (our pirated navigational software). I plugged our GPS into the laptop, and it showed a lime green triangle where our boat was. There were two bridges on the way toward the town of Coos Bay, but both were tall enough for us to pass under, so we resolved to head farther in.

The wind was up to twenty-five knots at this point, and we were going directly into it. There was nowhere to stop. The whole bay was studded with wind waves, and much of it was too shallow to anchor in (outside of the channel). As an added bummer, the majority of the coast was an industrial wasteland that didn't bode well for our supply-getting goals. Heading deeper and deeper into the bay, we passed what looked like a public dock and followed a thin strip of water that quickly petered toward nothing. We came about and headed back toward the second bridge. There, we anchored in the only spot we could find that was both deep enough and not plagued by pilings.

We sat anchored there under the bridge, nowhere near the shore and with absolutely no shelter from the wind, for a few minutes before pulling up the anchor and heading back toward the dock we'd seen. This action might sound simple, but it so wasn't. It demanded that Jimmie pull the entire boat toward and over the anchor—the only way to dislodge it. That means dragging six thousand pounds through the water into a twenty-five-knot wind with only gloved hands, a three-eighths-inch rope, and the anchor's resistance. But it had to be done, so he did it.

En route to the dock we swung by a low island and tried out its lee side—anything to avoid spending money on slip fees. Still windy, still rough, still a poor anchorage. We weren't thrilled at the prospect of trying to land at an unfamiliar dock, and even less so in super-high winds. We weren't even sure this dock was open to transient boaters. But what choice did we have? We had very little gas left, not many groceries, and no water. And we hadn't slept since the night of the tiller breaking (unbelievably, only the night before last). We had to stop in Coos Bay.

Jimmie flipped a quick U-ie into the wind, hitting the gas hard to overcome the rushing wind waves, and sidled us up to the dock. I jumped off the bow with an anchor line. He threw it in neutral and did the same from the back, and we effectively tied ourselves up, the boat jiggling and tugging against its dock lines like an ornery puppy in sight of a cat.

You'd think relief would've come at this point, but the waves rushing down the side of the dock were so formidable that they kept bouncing our bumpers up out of the water, grinding the boat directly into the dock. I stayed to supervise while Jimmie went to find the harbormaster. Every time a wave boosted a bumper up onto the dock, I'd push the boat away and stuff it back down. We tried varying the length of the ropes and their placement along the hull, but the waves were persistent. At times it seemed the boat itself was going to leap right up onto the dock.

Jimmie found the harbormaster, Rob, and returned with the good news that we could, indeed, tie up there and that, lucky for us, it was incredibly cheap. (Coos Bay isn't exactly a tourist destination.) He'd also been told that once a small motorboat on the inside of the dock moved, we could take its more sheltered spot. While this was also good news, it meant more waiting, more time without rest, and, eventually, more dockside maneuvering in high winds.

Thankfully, a large fishing boat named *Mandy* housing at least four men and two dogs had arrived in the interim and taken the spot windward of us. For the time being, it was blocking the waves and preventing bumper trauma enough to ease our immediate worries. I was so filled with relief that I was tempted to serenade them, lowering to one knee, stretching a hand toward their dingy white hull, and belting out, "Oh, Mandy / You came and you gave without tak-iiing!" But I refrained.

"See, Nothing to It."

We couldn't hang out in the cabin while we waited for the motorboat owner's return—we'd surely fall asleep—so we attempted to kill a few hours discovering downtown Coos Bay.

Walking on land (so stationary!) was actually a little disorienting, not dissimilar to taking the first few steps off a Tilt-A-Whirl (minus the Lemon Shake-Up swirling in your belly). Our eyes were glassy and red, the skin on our faces enflamed with dryness. My naturally curly hair was whipped into wild, strawberry blonde ringlets about my face, and Jimmie, with his tan turtleneck sweater, black-rimmed glasses, and in-progress beard, looked like a sea beatnik.

We passed an old theater that was playing *The Breakfast Club* and listed Hitchcock's *Vertigo* as "coming soon." It was called the Egyptian, and its decor mirrored the name with hieroglyphic lettering adorning the facade and a neon sign featuring a pharoah's head. It was a welcome indication of culture in an otherwise ghostly downtown of mostly closed shops and vacant buildings. We later observed that everything seemed to have moved either south of the old downtown or up to North Bend, where big-box stores flanked the new Walmart along a commercial thoroughfare called Newmark Avenue. The Egyptian smelled like buttered popcorn and looked budget friendly. We liked it immediately.

Our dock area was officially the Coos Bay Boardwalk, and most of old Coos Bay sat across the main waterfront drag from it, a small courtyard in the center of the supposed action. We turned a corner and found ourselves confronted with a family-oriented pizza-and-burger joint called the Outdoor-In. The interior was painted to look like a forest, and the tables and chairs were wooden stumps coated in lacquer. There was a large plastic playground, and children were directed to remove their shoes before venturing into its tubes and down its slides.

⚓ ⚓ ⚓

Sailing is something intrinsically linked in people's minds to wealth, and we often got asked if we were independently wealthy. The answer is a big NO. Certainly not. Our boat cost $4,400. That's a lot cheaper than a year's rent. It's more about what we *didn't* have—cable TV, car and house payments, cell phones, credit cards—than what we did have.

We simply laid low for a year and saved up. I had inherited a few thousand dollars from a great-aunt (via my grandmother), and we used that to buy the boat. But certainly most people who are perfectly comfortable financing $30,000 vehicles and $200,000 homes could scrounge up five grand or so for an old '70s sailboat if that was their priority. Neither of us had super-high-paying jobs in Portland; what we did have was minimal debt and a goal.

In fact, sailing was settled upon for its primo combination of adventurousness, romance, and affordability—the whole "free wind" factor. If you spend $800 on a solar panel and a few grand on a boat, get rid of or sell all your belongings (the latter also *makes* money), and arrange your life so that there are absolutely no payments—rent, car, insurance, utilities, storage spaces, communications—while you're gone, you can be entirely self-sufficient.

When we left, we had $6,700 in the bank. With the occasional bump here and there—the security deposit refund from our apartment, Jimmie's 401(k), our respective tax returns, some minor overpayment refunds on final utility bills—we ended up with a total of about $12,000 for the year. Twelve thousand dollars. That actually sounds like a lot to me—more than I expected when tallying up our old check register. But $12,000 in this case means two adults living off an annual income of $6,000 each. Not much.

Besides gas and the very occasional toiletry, pretty much the only thing we spent money on while traveling was food, and we spent as little as possible on that. If we had put more effort into fishing, the fruits of the sea might have eliminated even our sustenance expenditures, but as it was, we ate simple, extremely inexpensive foods that required no refrigeration. Our diet consisted of so little variation it's easy to give a quick rundown of the rotating menu aboard Chateau Cheapo: instant rice with curried canned vegetables, pasta with either packet spaghetti or packet Alfredo sauce, canned soup (chicken noodle, tomato, or cream of mushroom—the three most affordable types), peanut butter and jelly sandwiches, mac and cheese, cereal (with very thin from-powder milk), potatoes, granola bars, and the dreaded lentils. Also, ramen—lots and lots of ramen. Always with Sriracha. Sometimes we added a can of green beans to the ramen to bulk it up, but that was about it.

We did not eat out. We couldn't afford to. The first time we went ashore in Garibaldi, we walked past the Dairy Queen and neither of us said a word as the smell of grilled meat filled our noses. We eventually splurged on the absolutely cheapest wine in existence and one bag of Doritos after those two long, cold, and depressingly soggy weeks in Tillamook Bay. We were attempting to be pretty darn hardcore about our asceticism, simply because it was necessary. Also, somewhere deep inside, past the cravings for fast food and potato chips, we thought that living "without" would add to our experience, do us some good.

The thing many people don't realize is that the only reason we were able to quit our jobs and take a year off from being "regular" people is because we were cheap, so very cheap. In a year of sailing and 2,450 nautical miles, we paid to stay at only six marinas. We nearly always anchored out for free. And we tried, whenever possible, to sail, sail, sail.

⚓ ⚓ ⚓

So, when we spied the Outdoor-In and our two sets of eyes fell on the marquee reading ½ OFF MEDIUM PIZZAS, we were hesitant to speak of it. A lot of small (and big) businesses were having trouble at this particular time in the United States (amid the 2008 recession), and throughout the trip we became ever so slightly more comfortable with occasionally seizing the impeccable value opportunities we were faced with. But this was early on, and neither Jimmie nor I wanted to be the "weak" one, the one to give in, to open that door. So we kept quiet, looking anywhere but in the direction of that marquee. Jimmie finally did it; he knew my inner desires, that I would support him, that I was just waiting for him to take that half-off pizza by the reins. "Wanna check this place out?" he asked casually. "*Yes*," my excitement betrayed me. "I mean, yeah, let's," I added coolly. We decided to at least look at the menu.

It was reasonable. There were places to sit and a salad bar. There were great big cups for ice water and large, clean bathrooms. We ordered a half-Hawaiian, half-pepperoni-and-mushroom and each got a "petite" salad bar, where we loaded up on pepperoncini, ranch dressing, tiny sliced pepperoni, and cottage cheese. It was heavenly.

We talked with wonder about the last couple of days, and even let ourselves be a bit self-congratulatory about turning right back around after our tiller broke and sailing on to Coos Bay. Talking about anything we'd done up to this point sounded just plain fantastic. Who were we? We were not sailors! We were average people! But look what we just did! Look what we'd done so far! We couldn't help but feel giddy.

The tab came to around fifteen dollars, more than a day's spending for the two of us, but we decided not to sweat it. After all, we were out of groceries and currently ostracized from our boat.

When we returned to the dock, the spot intended for us by the harbormaster was open. The wind was still fierce, though, and maneuvering from the bay side of the dock into a slim spot right next to the harbormaster's lovely ketch wasn't high on our list of desirable activities. We considered just staying where we were for fear of running into, well, a number of things, including the dock, other boats, the shore, the stairs leading down to the dock. But Rob wasn't having it; he assured us we'd be much happier in this new spot, and he didn't seem the least bit worried about Jimmie's capability when it came to piloting us in.

The dock was arranged like this: a stairway from the boardwalk led down to a short length of dock that was perpendicular to the shore, and it was along this short length of dock that we were to squeeze our twenty-seven feet of sailboat. The dock then took a ninety-degree turn to the right, where Rob's boat was anchored in the corner, and continued far enough to accommodate a few empty slips and several large boats. We were initially tied up to the outer side of this long portion, down at the end. Now, we'd have to back up or turn around and enter in between the long dock and the shore, a waterway that was neither very deep nor wide and that was flanked by piled-up rocks on one side and a series of tied-up boats on the other.

We were to travel up this waterway until we reached the stairs, then make a quick and tight right turn to point our nose straight bow-to-bow with Rob's. It was tricky, and would have been so for anyone in these conditions. The wind sure likes to bully the prow of a boat, and any faulty gust could sabotage our trajectory, send us into the dock, the rocks, or—worst of all—crashing right into *Summer Wind*. Ugh.

Jimmie fired up the outboard, untied our dock lines, and, standing on the dock, pushed off the nose of the boat. He then hustled down to the cockpit and jumped in, directing me on the tiller and throttle all the while. He always seemed to know what to do. We were both winging everything we did, but he was convincing!

Jimmie took over piloting while I ran on deck and got into position for leaping off the portside bow. He came about and headed into the shoreside channel. If only we could have pulled right up to a spot along there—an easy, straight spot you just glide on up to. But no, we had to turn the tightest corner and then stop on a dime, all into a good twenty-five-knot wind. Rob stayed on the dock and promised to stop our bow from slamming into his.

Jimmie gave himself some power as he neared the stairway, then swung the bow to the right and let our momentum slide us close enough for me to jump off with my rope. He threw the motor in neutral and jumped off too, pulling back on the rear dock line. We were in!

"See, nothing to it," was Rob's reaction to the whole incident.

"There Ain't No Buses Here."

We spent a week in Coos Bay waiting out a strong September gale, the threads of our nerves pulling ever tighter as the distance narrowed between us and the wintry clime of the Aleutian Low. Coos Bay was our first planned "resupply" port, and we spent much of our time there shopping, or trying to shop. Saying it was a pain to get groceries just sounds whiny, and sounding whiny is something Jimmie and I are both incredibly cautious about. We knew things would be hard—it was part of what attracted us to such a bare-bones operation—but at the risk of sounding like a you-know-what, let me say this: filling our decidedly iceless icebox (we used it as a pantry) was far more laborious than we'd imagined, especially compared to the visions of ease inspired by our originally plotted North Bend anchorage.

After some spotty Internet research, we decided to "Rock down to / Newmark Av-e-nue," which held the promise of Walmart, our precious Grocery Outlet, and a post office we'd handpicked to be close to our now-abandoned anchorage. We'd received a few checks—refunds from a contested parking ticket and our apartment's security deposit—and our mail handler, Jimmie's best friend, Shawn, had been instructed to send them general delivery to the Empire post office. The Empire post office was now more than five miles from our boat.

We walked along the waterfront, a route that led past several loading docks and bland concrete buildings involved with the area's numerous logging companies. Giant cranes and industrial landings took up much of the Coos Bay shoreline. It wasn't exactly scenic, but it was sunny and warm, and our side of the road was a wall of blackberry bushes. We snacked on them as we walked, our fingertips turning purple-blue as we kept an eye out for Newmark Avenue.

We took a left on it, ascending a great hill that, hours later, would cause Jimmie considerable grief. We'd purchased one of those wire "granny carts" that old ladies and other non-driving types use to transport goods (in our case, a great many heavy canned goods) home from the store. So convenient! But Jimmie had a hell of a time maneuvering its flimsy plastic wheels down the steep, bumpy grade of Newmark's sidewalkless slope toward the bay.

Our cart was loaded with cheap nonperishables from Grocery Outlet, just as we'd hoped, but we were irreparably downtrodden after discovering that the Empire post office, our farthest stop, was closed. It was a very small operation, and the posted hours were 10:30 AM to 1:30 PM. It was midafternoon when we arrived, having thought sometime before 5:00 PM would suffice.

We'd be making the ten-mile walk to and from Empire again tomorrow.

⚓⚓⚓

Before we left on our trip, we spent a lot of time working on the boat. Jimmie made several well-researched repairs that were crucial to our seaworthiness (such as installing new through-hulls, switching rusty old gate valves out for copper ball valves, and replacing our running rigging), while I focused more on creature comforts, readying the boat to be our home. I hand-sewed curtains for all the portholes, picked out decorative pillows and shark-shaped potholders, designed our custom triangular bedding, and looked into airtight food storage containers.

The fellows who wrote *Sensible Cruising* seemed to value the homey touch a rug could lend a sailboat cabin, and rugs also help keep your feet warm when otherwise there's only air and fiberglass between them and the icy ocean, which averages in the mid-fifties Fahrenheit off the Oregon coast. I made a point of selecting one that coordinated nicely with the rest of our interior and then doctored it to fit the weird shape of our cabin's "hallway." I cut a long wedge off one corner and then painstakingly wound heavy blue cord around the rough edge to give it a border matching the factory-edged portions.

During our clamminess-plagued days stuck in Tillamook Bay, I had hung out the rug (among other things) in an attempt to dry it. Upon retrieving these items, some play of wind and clumsiness sent the rug overboard, and I watched it sink slowly, fluttering to the bottom like an Arabian magic carpet, staying parallel to the bay floor as it descended. I considered jumping right in after it, but I hesitated too long. It seemed a lost cause, and the water was so very cold.

I had put so much work into altering the damn thing, though, and felt that it tied our little operation together so well, that I sat in the cockpit and shed a few tears at its demise. Jimmie, not being able to bear my disappointment, hopped in the dinghy and attempted to locate it. We were anchored in a mere ten feet of water, but it was still too dark to see anything. Finally, he donned his oversized and patchy hand-me-down wetsuit and dove in.

Though it was unspoken, we both knew me: I am stubborn and have an undying degree of hope when it comes to nearly everything. I knew it was down there, and I thought I had some idea where it had landed. I didn't, and Jimmie returned to the boat empty-handed. But he had tried. Even when it doesn't make sense, he tries. It still makes my heart feel heavy to think of him and that rug, which has probably been fully consumed by Tillamook Bay's murky bottom by now—that is, unless it's slowly made its way toward the entrance channel and been pulled out to sea, a ghost shrimp riding its crest like a toboggan.

⚓ ⚓ ⚓

One of the things on our list the next day was "replacement rug." I took some measurements of the cabin floor so we'd know what we were dealing with upon reaching the home decor section of Walmart. We tried taking a different, more diagonal route this time but found our shortening of distance compounded by a direct increase in hill climbing. It seemed any route from the docks to North Bend's main thoroughfare of consumerism was pretty awful. I hauled the empty granny cart on the "to" journey as part of an agreement that Jimmie would then roll it, supply-filled, back. As was often the case, he got the raw end of the deal.

Then, in another instance of my constant hopefulness, I came up with the idea that it would be both reasonable and possible for us to catch a bus back from day two of our Newmark Avenue shopping. We would walk there, retrieve our checks from the post office, load up on our remaining supplies, and then board a bus and ride back downtown. Talk about a plan!

While rich in the rug department, Walmart proved unhelpful on a few fronts. First, they have no paper bags. They're not available upon request, as in most stores; they simply do not have them. Our little cart was pretty useless without paper bags, as the gaps between its wires were spaced so that cans would just roll on through without some overriding structure. The clerk, a thin-haired middle-aged woman with leathery skin and tobacco-stained teeth, was not sympathetic.

Second, they had absolutely no info regarding the bus situation in the greater North Bend–Coos Bay area. I had noticed a bus stop near the public library downtown on our first day there, so it's not as if had I dreamed up the possibility out of the blue. We had even seen people waiting at said bus stop—you know, as if they expected a bus to eventually arrive there, of all things. We had substantial reason to believe that some sort of transit system existed. But when we asked the same cashier if she knew of a nearby stop, she scoffed, "A bus in Coos Bay?" looking around as if all heads would be wagging in agreed disapproval. "Pshh! There ain't no buses here." Guess those folks downtown must all be senile . . .

The only other issues we had with Walmart were all the usual things that suck about going to Walmart: crowded aisles full of customers who somehow manage to be both aimlessly wandering yet aggressively in your way at every turn, crazies talking to themselves, obese people zooming about in motorized carts, an inordinate number of children, the endlessness of it all—groceries, toiletries, stuff we want but maybe can't afford, this rug or that rug, guess we need a hardware store too, etc. We left feeling strung out, exhausted, and still in need of curry paste.

Curry paste was something that, remarkably, didn't go bad unrefrigerated, was relatively cheap for the amount of sauce it yielded, and had become a staple supplement to our abundantly rice-filled diet. So after Walmart we began hauling ourselves and our stuff toward Albertsons.

That's when we saw it: a scrolling marquee reading LARGE PEPPERONI FOR $6, NO WAITING. The sign referenced a nearby Little Caesars and an item we would eventually become *very* familiar with, the "Hot-N-Ready." Sure, we had just splurged on pizza two days ago, but six dollars! For a large?! We could not resist, and jointly decided it was time for a morale boost. Walmart had broken our spirits, but that tiny Roman pizza man, with his little sandals and laurel-wreath headwear and speared pies, built them right back up. I obtained curry paste and paper bags (imagine!) at Albertsons while Jimmie ordered. He dropped an extra quarter on a side of ranch for crust dipping. I met him in the dusty side lot next to Little Caesars; it was takeout only, but we were happy enough to feast in the hot sun, standing on a patch of baked gravel next to the restaurant's Dumpsters.

It's a good thing we ate, too, because not only were there no buses to be found but the "shortcut" we tried to take back led us up a small mountain, around a hospital complex, and back down to . . . wait for it . . . Newmark Avenue. Nothing like tacking an extra mile or so onto an already ridiculous trip that you're making for the second day in a row. Our resilient attitude toward the task of resupplying was unrelenting, though. We had to be ready. If the gale died down, we needed to leave. It was already September, and the impending demise of the North Pacific High was ever lurking in the back of our minds, urging us to *move . . . on . . . faster. FASTER!*

When we finally got back to the boat, toting numerous supplies and a handsome security deposit refund, we mixed up some rum and powdered fruit punch and tried to relax for a bit.

Jimmie leisurely unloaded bags upon bags while I played grocery *Tetris* in our icebox. Finally, we unrolled the new rug and placed it on the floor. We often remarked later what an improvement it was on the old rug, and it was true. It fit the cabin more fully and without any adjustments. Even the color scheme, more burgundy than the old slate and navy blue, was better. It was just right on its own.

We ultimately decided it would be dumb not to check out the Egyptian, so we sneaked a Nalgene of our ghetto booze mix into the evening showing of *The Breakfast Club* and shared a two-dollar popcorn. (Our stay in Coos Bay was full of extravagance.) The new projection guy accidentally played the last scene first. Good thing we'd both seen it before.

"After Conception . . ."

I wasn't sure how it happened, but the boat was grounded. Not just grounded, but sitting in a completely dry creek bed. The air had a weird quality—it was a hazy blue, but not smog or fog hazy, more as if a smoke machine were set up behind some backdrop, or as if the sky was made of blue gauze. The flat lighting made it feel like we were in a room rather than outside. It was dull, finite. Unlike the world we were used to, it had an end.

We were standing, hands on hips, looking at the boat and wondering how the hell we'd get it back afloat. The creek bed wasn't very wide, maybe twenty feet, and the ocean sat up over a ridge—a steep and sandy spit. We'd have to get the boat up and over that ridge, then somehow pull it out past the surf . . . or at least into deep enough water to fire up the outboard. It seemed impossible.

Jimmie shrugged and I knew what it meant. We each grabbed an end, I at the bow and he holding up the rear. It was a six-thousand-pound boat; that's three fucking tons. We lifted it. We bent our knees and crouched, our arms at ninety-degree angles and the palms of our hands turning blue from the hull paint. I grunted. Jimmie just stood.

I followed. What else could I do? And we carried it, like a canoe or something, down that cracked and furrowed creek bed, making sure not to trip on the dust-covered rocks. We were on our way, it seemed. Better to not think about it. We were doing something that simply couldn't be done. Two people with a combined weight of maybe three hundred pounds were carrying a three-ton vessel. What else could we do? Better to not think about it. Thinking about it too hard would surely make us drop it. Just keep going. Don't wonder if you can. Just keep doing it, and it will get done.

It wasn't the first weird dream I'd had about carrying the boat. And it wouldn't be the last. Jimmie had them, too—not just weird boat dreams, but dreams *specifically* about carrying the boat over land. The symbolism is rather obvious, yes, but it's still a little creepy that our psyches addressed the challenge not in merely similar ways but in the exact *same* way. Maybe it's just that obvious, that that's how our experience felt sometimes: like carrying three tons, which might as well be an infinite load.

⚓⚓⚓

On our seventh full day in Coos Bay, we finally heard a manageable forecast. The next day called for ten-to-twenty-knot winds (twenty knots being at the high end of our comfort zone), and we knew we had better take it. Before quitting town for good, we spent $2.50 each on showers at the public pool, where Jimmie used hand soap in place of traditional toiletries because I had them with me in the ladies' locker room. He had to run back and forth from the communal shower area to the hand soap pumps across from the toilets, among naked old guys rinsing off the chlorine from their morning laps. It had been over a month since either of us had bathed.

Earlier that week, Rob had said, "Come by my boat before you leave here, and I'll go over your charts with you, show you some alternate anchorages—little holes you can dip into if the going gets rough."

We were a little worried we'd be reprimanded for having only black-and-white, 11-by-14 office-paper printouts of the NOAA's "experimental" BookletCharts, a free, print-at-home resource meant to assist recreational boaters. (We'd illicitly printed them out after-hours at my workplace one night, using up a small tree's worth of paper and seriously depleting *Willamette Week*'s ink stores.)

Said BookletCharts urge boaters to "use the official, full-scale NOAA nautical chart for navigation" whenever possible. But no-color, reduced-scale BookletCharts were all we had as far as hard-copy navigation, a reality we weren't looking forward to sharing with our new mentor. "Go over [our] charts," he had said. What was he imagining we had? Respectable scrolls featuring the usual cornflower blue and butter yellow of water and land, dotted all through with numbers like the stitches in a quilt, ready to be spread out and examined at our nonexistent nav station? We didn't know, but he was just so damn friendly we couldn't help but say OK.

That night, Jimmie went over to *Summer Wind* and sat down with Rob, our shameful BookletCharts in hand. I milled about on the dock until they reappeared in the cockpit. Rob, apparently unaffected by our mediocre means of navigation, had circled places in stubby, unsharpened pencil all along the coast, places that looked too small to enter but where he said we could go in and anchor if need be.

Near San Simeon, California, his rough hand had written "CASTLE" in all caps. He said Hearst Castle, an attraction there, was a must-see. He had also circled Albion, a small cove in Northern California, and Hunters Cove just south of us in Oregon. He told us of our next stop, Port Orford, and marveled at how the boats there get put in and pulled out of the water via large cranes instead of being driven on trailers up and down a boat ramp.

With a mystical air, he indicated Point Conception, that corner where California turns and trends more aggressively to the southeast, the corner after which *Southern* California truly begins, also the corner that's known to sailors as the "Cape Horn of the Pacific." "After Conception," said Rob, "the whole world changes." There it was; the doorway to warmth and calm seas and a peaceful sailing existence—the doorway to fantasy—had been given a name.

"Stay Out of the Sunday."

Early the next day, Rob stood waving, the numerous flags among his stays—the stars and stripes, a black-and-white Jolly Roger, one with a martini glass—mimicking his motion in the morning breeze. We waved, too, watching him and the docks at the boardwalk shrink into the distance as the sprawl of Coos Bay widened before us. We were hoping to sail downwind (as forecast) around Cape Blanco, the westernmost point of Oregon (and second-westernmost point in the contiguous United States, after Washington's Cape Alava).

The predicted north wind did not pan out, and we eventually gave in to full-on motoring into a light southerly in the name of reaching Port Orford during the last bits of daylight. This would be our first true "cove" anchorage. All along the Oregon coast, we'd been crossing river bars and traversing entrance channels to anchor in calm bays or sheltered inland waters. The crossings weren't always so smooth, but once you're in, you're in, which is very comforting. Port Orford (like many of our planned anchorages in California) was more like a stop-off on the side of the ocean, a spot where you just pull over, tuck yourself behind whatever land you can, and drop anchor. It was another completely new thing for us, and we were nervous about it.

We never got to see the chalky namesake cliffs of Cape Blanco because, funnily enough, we were encompassed in a blanket of *blanco* ourselves. But fog is not funny, and neither is filling your gas tank while riding atop ten-foot waves, something Jimmie did twice in order to get us to our next anchorage. The wind was low, but the waves had not yet died down from the fury they'd been whipped into by the recent gale. That's the thing about taking off right after a gale: the sea is still high, even if the weather's lighter. But windows of pleasantness are small, and you have to take them, residual ten-foot waves or not.

The first refill demanded that Jimmie balance a completely full backup can in his arms and commence pouring it into our main tank without filling our cockpit storage with spillage. He precariously aimed the nozzle down toward the active tank, trying to line things up with some semblance of accuracy before tipping the can and letting 'er pour. The unavoidable slop, which was impressively minimal, worked its way down into the bilge, giving the cabin a faint odor of gasoline, an effect that was a bit nauseating and not exactly safe. And we did this while running the outboard off the active tank, another sketchy maneuver.

It was an odd feeling, being on such large waves with little wind. It's kind of like riding up and down a kiddie roller coaster: you're not going all that fast, and there's not much to truly be afraid of, but the sensation of rising and falling over and over keeps a slight thrill in your veins. And, on the sea, it allows for a crazy view. When in the troughs of the waves, we often couldn't see above the water to either side; we were literally sitting between long walls of sea. Then, when we'd lift up onto a crest, we could see endlessly, the whole landscape a vast, repeating tapestry of identical, blue-gray waves . . . until the fog set. Then we couldn't see at all.

Approaching Port Orford, we would have been happy just to see the bow of our own boat. As dusk overtook day, the sky turned from snow to mud, as if the scene had been washed in chocolate milk. It never rained, but the fog was so thick that drops of water coated the mainsail and flicked onto us when it would flap and snap with the action of the waves. It had gotten so cold that we mostly just stood staring, afraid to take breaks in the cabin for fear that returning to the cockpit would be too unbearable a temperature shock. Also, we needed two sets of eyes to keep staring at the nothing, just in case. After days like this, we would both have a strip of red running horizontally across the centers of our eyeballs. We eventually realized it was spot-bloodshotting; we'd been squinting all day, and only the blood vessels in the exposed areas of our eyes had swollen with red, leaving us striped.

The fog-wash was a deep taupe by the time we heard the green entrance buoy dinging its wave-activated bell only a few yards away. It had a flashing green light as well, but we heard it before we saw it thanks to the impeccable visibility. I took over at the helm and stuck to our preplanned GPS line like Gorilla Glue. Jimmie grabbed our claw anchor—twenty-two pounds of galvanized steel for use in rocky bottoms—and took to the deck, attempting to shackle it on in the waves and the dark as we approached our anchorage. (Our usual anchor up until now, a Danforth, had its own holder on the bow pulpit; the claw did not and was therefore stored in the cockpit until needed.) We were nearing the destination marked on our GPS, and I could hear the disturbing sound of surf washing up around us. It always sounds closer in the dark than it is . . . right?

There was a ring of rocks mimicking the shore here, we knew. We'd planned our spot to be as close into the cove as we could get while avoiding them. But we could have been off. Jimmie discovered once on deck that the shackle for the claw anchor was a different size from the one already prepped for the Danforth. He had to improvise, shackling a shackle to a shackle in a chain of ridiculous shackling that allowed for the claw anchor to be attached to our line. Amid this, he found his channel locks were busted, then lost his grip on his backup crescent wrench and dropped it overboard.

I was reading off depths and inching toward the shore when I spotted it: a rock roughly the size of a garage, looming out of the dark and the fog, far too close to us.

I swung around and reassessed. We'd have to drop anchor sooner. The rocks weren't where we'd expected! We re-approached the shore and set the anchor in the dark, farther to sea than planned. Then we sat, silent in the cockpit, peering into the blackness around us. Jimmie hooked up the GPS and connected it to our laptop. By the miracles of modern technology, a satellite showed us where we were, floating in the center of a half circle of rocks, the radius of our anchor line extending out to the fancy of wind and waves. Despite our shortage of solar power after the cloudy day, we kept the laptop on through dinner, watching as thin blue lines marked our movement over a screen of digital water. Bean and rice burritos sitting heavy in our stomachs, we eventually convinced ourselves it was safe enough to sleep for the night.

⚓ ⚓ ⚓

The only voice we regularly heard (besides our own and each other's) was that of the NOAA Weather Guy, who isn't really a guy at all but a computer that reads forecasts in a synthesized voice over NOAA Weather Radio. Because he's a computer, he sometimes makes mistakes—not big mistakes, like reading the wrong forecast, but jumping-to-the-wrong-conclusion linguistic mistakes. Back in Tillamook Bay, right before the onset of the unseasonably wintry gale that took us hostage, there had been something of a heat wave on land, oddly enough. Weather Guy directed overheated Oregonians to drink lots of water, check on their elderly neighbors, and "stay out of the Sunday." His voice was sometimes a comfort, often the bearer of bad news, and an occasional source of entertainment.

The morning after our fog-filled arrival and garage-rock scare, we found ourselves suitably positioned, with brilliant green water shimmering all around us, but the air was cold and a northerly wind whipped brutally through the anchorage as the sun climbed up to its midday perch. Tuning in to hear what our NOAA buddy had to say, we were greeted with the news of yet another gale. It was scheduled for that day and the next. And it was already so strong that we went ahead and set a second anchor.

When our weather service homie predicted low temps around forty degrees Fahrenheit on the leg following Port Orford, we made a mad dash for Hunters Cove, one of the tucked-away nooks Rob had circled. Unlike many cruising vessels, we had no dodger, a sort of windshield for the cockpit, so we were completely exposed to the elements all the time. My toes had taken to going completely numb whenever we were out, and our faces were so frigid on the way there, during the *day*, that we added "ski masks" to our shopping list in all earnestness.

Once in the misty confines of Hunters Cove, we were much more comfortable. There was room between the coastal rocks for probably just one boat, and it was ours. Despite the chill, we stayed outside the cabin until near dark, our windburned skin drinking up the damp air. I remember noting how coastal pines are always bent to the east-southeast—permanently molded *away*, away from the forces constantly pushing across the Pacific, pushing, too, against bark and needles and sap-filled veins. There were deer on the beach the next morning; we watched them make their way along the surf line, poking their cute noses into the seaweed and crud.

Tomorrow we would head for California.

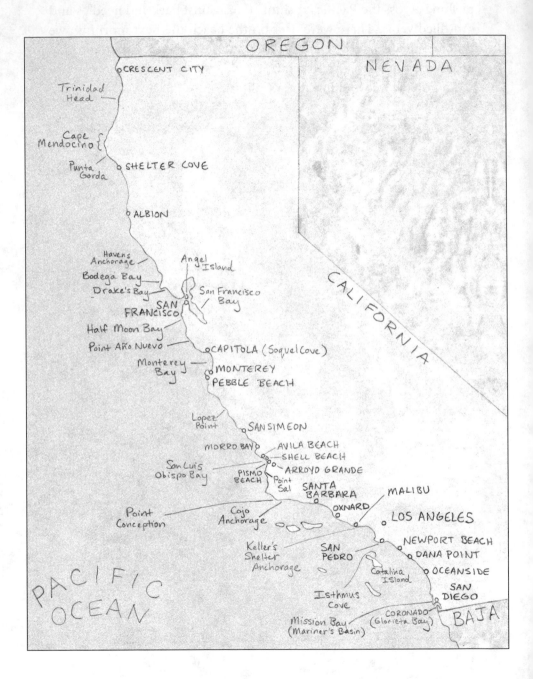

II

CALIFORNIA

DESPERATELY SEEKING SoCal

"You Two Look Pretty Salty."

The Oregon-California border and 42° north are one and the same. Armed with this information, I spent most of the leg from Hunters Cove staring at the GPS and giving occasional updates about how long it would be until we officially crossed into the Golden State. The moment we did, we snapped a commemorative photo. In it, we look far from Californian, our faces full of ruddy color like Bears fans after a late-season home game, our heads tucked into drab stocking caps, and Jimmie's glasses showing a hint of fog on the lenses. But our smiles are *explosive.*

Crescent City offered what I had dubbed a "snuggle harbor," an anchorage lovingly ensconced by a manmade barrier, in this case a massive hook of breakwater rocks. It was the perfect middle ground between Oregon's protected inland waters and the more natural pull-over coves à la Port O. No bar crossing necessary; no open exposure, either. It was as if the gods of anchoring had winked at us and said, "Just come right on in. The way is clear. And do enjoy the complete protection from wind and swell once you've rounded the entry and made yourself at home. Cheerio!" (Apparently the anchoring gods are British.)

Once settled in the awesomely calm harbor, we ate in the dark thanks to the cloudiness we'd experienced of late. It had been challenge enough for our solar panel to keep up with any laptop use and the nightly necessity of an anchor light. Entertainment was limited to reading with flashlights or playing Yahtzee by the light of an LED lantern. (Yahtzee, incidentally, was originally called "The Yacht Game" and was created— surprise!—by a bored couple living on a sailboat.) Still, we were feeling festive. I proposed the purchase of a very cheap bottle of champagne, should we come across one, in celebration of our arrival in California.

The next day, we weighed anchor and headed over to what looked like a gas dock. It was a pump-out station (for pumping poo out of one's poo-holding tank), but we tied up there anyway. The actual gas pumps, it turned out, were perched along an incredibly tall dock. If we had pulled up to it, we would've had to scale the mast just to talk to the attendant; apparently it was for larger boats. We took the stairs with two gas cans in hand and filled them up after a giant mega-yacht acquired (I kid you not) $600 worth of diesel.

We found the harbormaster's office and asked if we could stay tied up to the pump-out dock for a few hours while we grabbed some supplies in town. After getting permission, we immediately made for the Englund Marine Supply Company in the hopes of finding a new tiller. No luck, but I did secure a pair of "Goat Feet," intense water-resistant cold-weather socks, and Jimmie got some big, orange, fully waterproof gloves to aid in his anchor handling. He'd bare-handed it all the way from Portland to Astoria and made do with a pair of subpar "dipped" Atlas gloves since.

We stayed in Crescent City for five full days, doing laundry, exploring the giant hollowed-out trunk of a preserved redwood, and unsuccessfully looking for ski masks. (Halloween masks *were* available, however, which left us pondering the image of a couple of werewolves sailing the Pacific.) We also acquired that three-dollar bottle of champagne and a variety of fancy snacks at super-clearance prices. Fifty-cent Boursin and dollar-fifty Columbus Salame logs?! Thank you, Grocery Outlet! Because we had no refrigeration, we felt it necessary to eat all these perishables—plus additional blocks of cheddar and

Gouda—that very evening. The value of this extravagance was so irresistible that we did the same thing the next night. Yeah, really.

So, the good times were a-rollin' in Crescent City, but our upcoming trip around Cape Mendocino loomed in the near future, the reality of which had begun to frazzle my composure. We listened to the weather obsessively and discussed making a run straight from Crescent City all the way around that daunting headland. I could agree to such ambitious plans hypothetically, but, in truth, I didn't want to round it at all. Would I ever?

On our way out of our much-loved snuggle harbor, we stopped at the pump-out station one more time to drop off some garbage and fill our water tank. As I stood there, hose in hand, a sheriff approached us. Naturally, we assumed we were doing something wrong.

"You two been anchored here a few days now, isn't that right?" he asked.

"Yeah," Jimmie replied, his hand on the water valve.

"How d'ya like it here?"

"Oh, it's a really nice harbor," we chimed in different ways at the same time.

"You been doing any fishing or crabbing while you've been here?"

"Nope," said Jimmie.

"Only in Oregon," I added.

"OK," said the sheriff. "I'm just checking 'cause crabbing season just ended."

That seemed to suffice, and it was the truth. We hadn't acquired fishing licenses for California because the nonresident permits were just too damn expensive, at $116.90 annually. Our fishing days were done until we reached Mexico, where a license for the whole year is only about forty bucks.

A trim fellow with graying scruff, the sheriff added, "Some strong weather supposed to blow down in the next few days."

"Yeah," said Jimmie. "We're to hoping beat that south."

"Well," said the sheriff, giving us a once-over and glancing momentarily at the PORTLAND, OREGON, on our stern, "you two look pretty salty."

He wished us well and started back up the stairs. I know to this day Jimmie considers that last remark to have been made in earnest. But I couldn't help but think the old sheriff was poking fun at us. Even though we'd sailed all of the Oregon coast—a stretch much more experienced Californian seamen would later tell us you couldn't pay them to sail—I guess I still didn't feel too salty. Those same Californians told us after we'd made it much farther south, "You're here. At some point you're gonna have to stop saying you don't know what you're doing," and I guess they have a point.

But I'm still not entirely convinced that sheriff wasn't joking.

"I've Never Been So Pleasantly Terrified."

The tension over Mendocino came to a head over the next twenty-four hours, taking the form of tears, silence, debates, and surrenders. We had one available stop, an oceanside pull-off called Trinidad Head, en route to Mendocino. As we approached it, Jimmie suggested again that we just keep going and get Cape Mendocino over with, pull an all-nighter and arrive at Shelter Cove—the promised hideaway tucked in the lee of the cape—in the morning. As usual, I felt hesitant. I wanted to put off anything potentially frightening (which was everything) as long as possible.

I have always been a procrastinator, and in spite of taking this trip, I may not be very brave. I knew sailing around Mendocino was inevitable, but I still didn't want to do it. I couched my fears in a seemingly logical weather-based argument: "If we leave late tomorrow morning, we can get the afternoon winds out of the way *before* we're right across from the cape; then it will hopefully be settling down for the evening when we're in the worst spot." That was my theory, and it made sense with the forecast and our usual rate of travel.

Jimmie would have rather gotten on with it, but he was faced with the impossibility of reassuring me even though he had no idea how his suggested plan would turn out. This was a constant dilemma: Neither of us knew the best thing to do, and neither of us could fully commit to our own position for fear of the consequences (and the consequent blame). Neither of us wanted to be responsible for tragedy, or near tragedy, or even several hours of hell.

I deal with uncertainty by talking things to death and hypothesizing about every aspect. Jimmie, on the other hand, prefers to just do things and deal with conflicts as they arise. I can imagine it must be infuriating to have someone nagging you to go over "the plan" when there is no right plan. The truth is I was terrified.

Cody Sheehy, our YouTube mentor, was likewise psyched out by Mendocino, having said, "[It's] probably the worst cape on the West Coast. If the weather's bad it's gonna be really bad [there]. There's nowhere to anchor for miles and miles and miles." I wanted, more than anything, for Jimmie to just tell me things would be fine. I'm sure he would have loved to. But he couldn't. Because he didn't know. How could he ever know how things would be?

To make matters worse, the forecast wasn't, in my opinion, perfect. During our planned sail around Cape Mendocino, the NOAA's "out to ten" forecast (meaning the weather from the coast out to ten nautical miles) seemed manageable; the "beyond ten" did not. But, as Jimmie was wise (and accurate) to note, it was never going to be perfect, and we needed to be getting farther south. The longer we waited for "ideal" conditions, the worse our chance of receiving them became. Having a good-to-average forecast for "out to ten" might be the best we'd get.

We ate a dinner of canned chili and Saltines in stubborn silence, mulling things over and bobbing among the kelp at Trinidad Head, green orbs bonking against the hull with each swell. Jimmie was right: good-to-average might be the best we'd get. As the sky around us became striped heaven-to-horizon in mauve, apricot, coral, and violet, we resolved to take the chance.

⚓ ⚓ ⚓

When writing of a tornado in which he flew, Antoine de Saint-Exupéry said, "The cyclone of which I am about to speak was, physically, much the most brutal and overwhelming experience I ever underwent; and yet beyond a certain point I do not know how to convey its violence except by piling one adjective on another, so that in the end I should convey no impression at all—unless perhaps that of an embarrassing taste for exaggeration."

It is this that I fear in explaining what Jimmie and I came to call our "terror ride" around Cape Mendocino and its shadow cape, Punta Gorda. Did we almost die? It's hard to say. We didn't know much, and with our relative inexperience, we didn't even know that. How does one quantify such a thing? I do know I was very truly scared for my life. That's all I can be certain of: how it felt and what I thought about.

The thing you must understand about me, and about Jimmie, is that we are normal people. We didn't grow up tying bowlines and cleat hitches, tacking dinghies around yacht clubs, or yearning for the high seas. We climbed trees and rode bikes like most kids. We got older and went to high school and worked crappy jobs for a while. Then we went to more school and worked harder and got better jobs. We lived in apartments and houses in cities and towns. We broke bones and skinned our knees, took care of pet rabbits and hamsters, learned to drive and ate cheeseburgers. We made debts and paid them off, fell in love and had our hearts broken. We were not, presumably, unlike you, or anyone—until this. Only what we were doing, during the actual doing of it, set us apart. But we were still us: normal people. You know, just sailing a small boat on the Pacific Ocean.

What we knew about Cape Mendocino was this: It is, if not feared, regarded with respect by seamen. It is not just a point, it is a long swelling headland, a big, nasty mounded-up pimple on the Pacific coast, and the sail around it would be our longest yet (84.5 nautical miles). It is known as an area of "major climatic change" and is, according to our reference materials, the landmark widely considered to be the north-south divider of the Pacific coast, a reputation that apparently goes all the way back to the time of the huge Spanish galleons.

Punta Gorda is the point right after Cape Mendocino, which you have no choice but to round on the same trip. It immediately precedes the aptly named Shelter Cove and was described in our *Coast Pilot* as follows: "The winds, seas and currents off Punta Gorda are probably as strong as off any point on the coast." All of these things contributed to our general feeling of unease. But, after a "hearty" breakfast of two packets of oatmeal each—and our usual making and setting aside of peanut butter and jelly sandwiches (so lunch would be ready underway)—we were off. In fact, Jimmie made two sets of PB&Js this particular morning, just in case.

Our departure had an ominous air about it. It was the first official day of fall, and the cockpit was swarming with flies, like raisins on a coffee cake. We were surprised they stayed aboard so far out to sea, assuming they'd die making the flight back to land. We'd purchased a flyswatter in Crescent City, and an hour or so into the trip, our cockpit was littered with tiny black carcasses. Fly genocide.

The anchorage at Trinidad Head was shrouded in a silvery fog that morning, casting the world in a very believable black and white—the stuff of Ansel Adams photographs or computer desktop wallpaper. But a crisp blue sky emerged in the following hours, and the surface of the sea twinkled with diamond sun, blinding as a sparkler. Jimmie put on a favorite album, *Illinois* by Sufjan Stevens, just as the wind picked up. We were across from Eureka, California, heading straight southwest to get out beyond the far west tip of the cape.

We made a deal that, because of the length of the trip, we'd motor if our speed dropped below three knots, but as it turned out, we were already sailing much faster than anticipated. We had some reservations about getting across from the cape too early, during the peak afternoon winds, but we couldn't really slow down, and knocking a hefty chunk off such a long trip early on seemed serendipitous.

Things continued this way for several hours, the sun beaming, the sea sparkling, and *Cotton* hauling A. We would occasionally let the sails out a touch more—eased up on the gas, so to speak—but mostly we just picked another album on our trusty iPod (which we'd painstakingly stocked with some seven hundred albums before leaving) and sat there, hoping things would either stay the same or lighten a bit.

The farther out we got, though, and the longer the wind had blown over the water, the larger the waves became. They were, undoubtedly, the largest, tallest waves we'd seen thus far. But our boat was taking them, riding up and down their mountainous curves, pushed along by a steady twenty-knot wind. So we remained tensely taking it all in, watching as each giant approached and then disappeared beneath the stern, only to reemerge under and then in front of our bow.

The water was a brilliant blue-green, like liquid malachite, the sky clear and visibility splendid; the day *looked* beautiful. But there was, and always is, this feeling when you're sailing in a strong, and growing stronger, wind. It is the impending unknown: How strong will it get? How tall will the waves grow? Can we manage it?

Often, the thing that is the scariest is not the actuality of your situation but what your imagination sees as its potential amplification. The unknown. The unknown. The unknown. It haunts you. And it can never be answered until it is already happening. And then, an already worse unknown has formed in your brain. It is a special, nautical form of psychological torture, and on this particular jaunt, nature realized every gaudy intimation our twisted minds could conjure.

Once we turned more directly south, the waves began to tower over themselves in a manner that sometimes forced their crests to break. This is something we hadn't yet seen away from the breakers along the coast. They would occasionally shatter right next to us, but mostly they stayed a little behind or in front or over to the side. I recall Jimmie saying afterward that he kept thinking, *Sooner or later, one of those is going to do that right under us.* Maybe one did and it didn't matter. I'm not sure, but their white fizzy tops sizzling all around us were the first indication that conditions were reaching a new level.

Thankfully, it was still daytime, and our attitude toward any situation was always brighter in the light and warmth of the sun. Jimmie remarked, "I've never been so pleasantly terrified."

Not long after, he took a photo of me, bundled in a reddish-orange-and-black Pendleton "Knockabout" that had belonged to my mother in the '70s. I'm clutching our handheld GPS and smiling as an enormous wave towers in the background, well above the transom and my own head. Looking back at it, I don't appear as if I'm smiling through my teeth. I look rather happy, but I know I was very tense. Only Jimmie could make me smile so truly with that wave, a mammoth slab of Berry Blue Jell-O, jiggling at my back.

Amidst such conditions, you start wanting to talk about what's happening, or at least I did. I wanted to know what Jimmie was thinking, how bad he thought it was, what he figured might be the next logical step (as far as sail trim and heading), and so forth. But those of us who get this urge to talk do it only because we want to hear that the other person is comfortable—at least more comfortable than we are. But they aren't. Still, no one's gonna be the one to voice it, to actually say, "This is fucked. We're fucked." So you discuss your sail trim cordially, maturely. What else can you do? You have to rise to the occasion. You have to at least pretend you can take it.

In the course of day-to-day life, death is not a consequence. If you piss someone off at work, death is not the consequence. If you spill your coffee, death is not a consequence. If you don't pay your rent, water your houseplants, open your mail, keep your dentist appointment, death is not a consequence (well, hopefully). But here, on a violently windswept ocean, every decision bears the potential of being your last. Only what's necessary—only what's right—is allowed. One ill-informed move and you're dead. And it goes on like that for hours. *Hours.* It was still early in our day, and conditions would be getting much worse.

Sitting there, thinking all of this, I saw something shoot by the boat out of the corner of my eye. *Whoosh!* Again. *Whoosh!* A shot of blue-gray. Again. Dolphins! This was the first time we'd seen them the whole trip, and they were playfully darting through the water on our port side, Mendocino's False Cape looming in the distance. They'd shoot into the rear side of a giant wave, wiggle through almost too fast to see, and come launching out the front, right alongside our boat. They were the comic relief in our maritime tragedy, the chuckling gravediggers before Ophelia's burial. The thing about dolphins is they always look like they're grinning. So we smiled, too. Oh God, we smiled. We even laughed—tense, cagey laughs, but still! A wonder of nature had appeared just when we needed it, replacing our unspoken stress with a critical mass of joy. "OK," Jimmie said, "let's get this main reefed."

The less sail you have up, the less the wind affects your vessel, so in an effort to hold a reasonable speed, we lost sails correspondingly as the wind picked up. We had already dropped the jib, but we were still going quite fast, certainly at our hull speed of seven knots and definitely faster than we were accustomed. But reefing the mainsail was not going to be easy.

Reefing involves dropping the sail a little and then gathering up and binding the slack so less sail is exposed to the wind—essentially making a large sail a little smaller. Worried that we'd be swamped by the approaching megaliths of saltwater if we lost speed too suddenly, Jimmie thought to fire up the outboard and match us to the rate of the waves before we risked losing any sail power. Normally, you would turn into the wind to perform such a maneuver, since it's far easier to pull down a luffing sail than one that's taut with power. But we were *not* going to come about in these seas, so Jimmie climbed on deck and wrestled that bastard down.

During this reefing Jimmie recorded a vision in his mind. He says he remembers hanging on to this post, the mast, for dear life, being thrown side to side, back to front atop this little vessel and looking about him at what seemed like the apocalypse—waves crashing all around, their crests, like a million frosted mountain peaks, bursting into innumerable droplets, sliding to pieces, vanishing and reappearing all at once. The sun blazed down, lighting up the transparent, dolphin-filled, blue-green interiors of these living pyramids. And there he was, on top of it all, yet not necessarily the highest point. Although I was nearby, watching the whole mess from a lower vantage point, I cannot imagine what he was experiencing.

I was in charge of managing the lines (the main halyard has to be loosened for the sail to drop in the first place) and adjusting the outboard's throttle according to our loss of speed. This makes me sound capable, but that's not how I felt. The love of my life was balanced on the deck, and a good part of what he was trying to accomplish was in my hands. I could've cried, except that I couldn't have. As I said, any false step—crying included—might've gotten us killed.

"DANGER: Intermittent Waves of Unusual Size and Force."

We wound up approaching Punta Gorda just as the sun was vanishing behind the black horizon, at what was probably the worst time possible. We were happy to be mostly around Mendocino at this point, but we had no idea how bad Punta Gorda would get. Thankfully, Jimmie had dropped the reefed main in the last bits of sunlight, knowing it would've had to come down eventually with both wind and waves still increasing. We'd kept the motor running ever since initially reefing the main, and we seemed to be taking the waves as well as could be expected; we didn't want to mess with the formula too much.

When Jimmie took to the deck to pull down the last bit of mainsail, we were heeling and yawing so dramatically that the mast was within feet of skimming the crests of the waves to starboard. He was hugging the base of the mast the entire time, struggling to tie bungees around the sail and secure it, while I sat watching the whole ordeal, my hard, disbelieving gaze alternating between Jimmie and the autopilot. Jeeves had been performing like a champ, but I needed to be ready to take over if he failed, and he was up against an awful lot. Every time a wave rushed under us, it challenged the tiller, and Jeeves had to counter its push to keep us on course. I recall looking at our knotmeter around this time and seeing it pegged to fourteen, twice our hull speed. I'm not sure that's even possible.

The wind and waves had become furious. We were sliding down the faces of huge, built-up ocean swell while wind waves from a crosswise direction smacked into our side and blew froth and spray off their tops in every direction. It was mayhem, water mayhem. I recall looking to the east at one point and, in the dark of night, not being able to tell if what must have been mountains were truly mountains or oncoming waves. I turned away. I did not want to know.

Jimmie took over steering as the intense yawing had become too much for Jeeves and we were going to need some finesse to get us far enough to port to actually anchor in Shelter Cove. You see, the bullying wind, waves, and current were all forcing us south, south, south. We started to think we might have to go on to the next anchorage, fifty nautical miles beyond Shelter Cove, to even attempt a landfall. (That's when the extra PB&Js would've come in handy.)

We'd been pushed farther offshore than we ever intended and into (we were reluctant to admit) the conditions forecast for ten to sixty nautical miles off the coast—the hairy-sounding forecast that called for stronger winds than we ever deliberately sailed in. And the same forces that had pushed us out there were keeping us out there. So Jimmie, using the clear night's blessing of stars as his guide, stared ahead, gripping the tiller with his left hand and the frame of the companionway with his right, and steered.

There was no need to take stock of our situation by looking at the oncoming seas—we could tell just by listening what was going to happen. The howl of the wind was savage, piercing. Then, just as we prayed with all our heathenish might that it would back down, it howled harder. Louder. Sharper. It *screamed*. That's when the big waves would come. The big, big waves. We could hear them coming. The boat would half ride them, be half thrown by them. And after they passed, in that brief moment of time before the next one was under us—or into us—Jimmie would dart through the troughs a bit more to port, eking ever more eastward with the tiniest of ekes.

I sat, back to the oncoming waves, hitting the little light bulb button on the GPS and staring constantly at our course, at the distance and time to our destination. I also took note of how much farther to port we'd have to get to officially be (hopes! dreams!) in the lee of Punta Gorda, which is about ten nautical miles south-southeast of its big brother, Cape Mendocino, but still twenty nautical miles from our precious goal, Shelter Cove.

I would give Jimmie little updates: "Looking good." "What you're doing is great." "We should be in the lee of Punta Gorda in maybe [insert whatever amount of time or distance was close to reality but a smidge optimistic]. But, you know, any more to port you can get would be good." "Uh, huh. Thanks," he'd say. Or, "OK. Got it. Thanks."

A half hour later he might ask, "How's my heading?" It went on like that for hours. We were in the absolute worst of it for a good three, I'd say.

Rounding Mendocino was also the only time the entire trip that full waves came over the gunwales and into our boat. The first came from behind. I don't know if we slowed down for a moment or just fell out of sync with the waves or what, but I saw it coming, probably because I was constantly staring at the back of the boat, watching the approaching waves in the white stern light, waiting for just this thing to happen while trying my damnedest to will it from coming true. (How could I be staring at the GPS and the stern *both*, constantly? I don't know! But I was!)

A wave taller than the transom caught up to us, and over it crashed. We had two marine speakers—the same through which we'd listened to *Illinois* and several other albums earlier that day—sitting on the floor of the cockpit, and I watched them rise and float on the several inches of water now submerging our feet. The water quickly rushed out the back, through the cutout area surrounding our outboard, and we were left with no worse than soaked socks, shoes, and pant legs, and perhaps ruined speakers. But, again, it was the "What next?" that plagued us. Something we'd come to think might not ever happen had now happened. So what next?

I'll tell you what: two more. Two more epic waves howled with the wind right into and over our side, the port side, where I was sitting. The first one I heard coming. I quickly glanced over my shoulder, momentarily peering into a rushing wall of saline, but turned just in time not to get a face-full. Jimmie wasn't so lucky; he was already looking right in its direction. Smacked in the back, smacked in the front. Then came another. Again, I heard it first, but this time I didn't turn. I just braced myself and took the hit. We were now both completely soaked. Luckily, it either hadn't gotten that cold out or we were beyond feeling it, because the wetness seemed sufferable. Maybe it was just that our focus was elsewhere—on Shelter Cove, on survival.

⚓ ⚓ ⚓

Surprisingly enough, what I still think of as one of the most harrowing moments of the entire voyage took place during the first week of our trip, on a narrow stretch of the Columbia River. We were tacking along, sailing into the wind just as we'd consistently been doing since turning west toward the Pacific some forty nautical miles downriver from Portland. We were heading for an anchorage near Puget Island and entered the east end of a tight channel just as a large pleasure yacht entered the west end.

It appeared to be really booking it, as signaled by a pair of huge, menacing wakes. They spewed angrily forth, the product of several-hundred-horsepower dual outboards belonging to what, we soon noted, was called the *Casino Royale*. Figures. It looked like just the thing a scar-faced, high-class Bond villain à la Le Chiffre would be sipping cocktails and playing baccarat in, completely unaware of the small-boat neighbors about to get their balls rocked off.

Its wake was one of the *steepest* waves we encountered the entire trip. It wasn't the largest, or anywhere near the tallest, but it was a tremendous combination of high and brief. When we took it, our bow rose up and then slammed, hard, down into the surface of the Columbia. Water spilled across the foredeck, some of which forced its way under the V-berth hatch, showering our pillows and sheets.

The jolt shocked us to our bones and left me momentarily paralyzed. But Jimmie was up on deck seconds after the blow, frantically pulling the anchor, which had been knocked off the bow pulpit and into the water, back aboard. The main danger here—the thing that so effectively catalyzed Jimmie's on-deck hustle—is that our free, swinging anchor could have easily pierced the hull and begun sinking our ship.

The thought of our Danforth, the type of anchor made of two flat, dagger-like pieces resembling a steel-forged paper airplane, punching a hole in our fiberglass hull and sinking us right there on the Columbia, before we'd even reached the Pacific, aroused in us a sensation of disappointment we took very much to heart. The fact that the wake of a mere pleasure yacht could devastate us so thoroughly also had our imaginations reeling with the hypothetical effects of ocean waves on our humble craft. After securing the anchor, confirming that our bilge wasn't quickly filling with water, and continuing on, we resolved to devote the next day to ocean prep rather than progress along the Columbia.

Once anchored behind the "handle" of Coffee Pot Island, an offshoot of Puget Island, we took to weather-stripping the hatch and companionway, lashing down any loose hardware, and fantasizing about payback. We'd wait till dark, then dinghy over and float alongside the *Casino Royale*, that insolent fiend, spying on its passengers and making eerily informed *When a Stranger Calls*–type observations over the VHF. The horrible truth would soon occur to them: the calls were coming from *on* the boat!

Most important, Jimmie fashioned a drop-down half door for protection against high seas, an artful creation built from scrap plywood. (We did have full doors, but the half door allowed easy access to the cabin while still protecting it.)

We used that half door on our sail around Mendocino, and it (as well as the *Casino Royale*, I suppose) can be thanked for keeping the waves of Punta Gorda from flooding our home. Some portion of our two over-the-side giants did pour through. Our seat cushions and little two-burner stovetop got soaked, but those things eventually dried out. Our iPod, which was resting on the countertop nearby, did not. It displayed only a frowny face and a little caution sign forevermore. No biggie, considering.

⚓ ⚓ ⚓

The period of time when I really settled into myself and inhabited my head was after dark. With the horrific scene no longer illuminated, what else was there to do?

I thought about the motor quite a bit. As I stared at the back of the boat, watching the onrushing waves surge toward our home, our existence, our selves, I thought, *Our lives depend on this little machine. If it gave out on us right now, we'd be screwed, absolutely screwed. We would have to throw up a sail to get enough momentum going to not be swamped by waves. We'd surely be overcome by water. This little machine has both of our lives in its mechanical hands.* Jimmie must have recognized this, too, for he gave it an oil change while we were anchored at Shelter Cove. A little "thank you" maintenance. I stared at that motor—which earned the name James Brown that very evening— and knew it was running, knew it was humming. But I couldn't hear it over the wind.

I also thought, *This is why you never leave your boat.* When we were shopping for dinghies, we considered the need for a dinghy to double as a life raft, not just a means of getting ashore. But getting such a dinghy—some sort of hard, big, certifiable boat-type dinghy— is expensive and would have been cumbersome, if not impossible, to carry aboard *Cotton*. So we got an inflatable kayak, our trusty Mr. Johnny Inflatable, which we could deflate and store in the cockpit and which was easy enough to haul onto a beach and secure with a bike lock. I believe it cost around $150 at G.I. Joe's. It was great for everyday purposes, but it made the option of abandoning our boat in an emergency, well, a non-option—which was actually for the best.

It is said that you should never leave your boat, regardless of the circumstances—that sailors who abandon ship are sailors who die— and I can see why. French naturalist, philanthropist, and sailing badass Bernard Moitessier said a sailboat is like a bottle: "If you drop a well-plugged bottle in the middle of a hurricane, it will float just fine. The same is basically true of a boat . . . The rest is merely details and adjusting to circumstances." Chances are, you could close up all your hatches and hide under a table and, regardless of how much the sea tossed you about and flipped you around, you'd come out all right—as long as you didn't crash into a reef or the shore or take on too much water (and it would take a lot of water). As scary as it was on the boat, I would surely rather have been there than floating around on twenty-foot waves in a fucking *raft*.

And I thought about our tiller. I thought, *My God, I hope that thing doesn't break again.* It wasn't the most confidence-inspiring chunk of wood, and there was little reason to have faith in it after its performance in Florence, but Jimmie had secured it in its housing and tested it for rot, and it had held up. Through *a LOT* of force, it held up. I don't think it crossed my mind until later, but it's a good thing it did break in Florence because had it not, it certainly would have here. And that might have been the one variable that did it, that took us down.

Outside of these mechanical topics, I also thought about wanting to live and wanting Jimmie to live. Not long ago, as he was sleeping next to me, I thought, *I hate your mortality.* I do. And I deny it. If I have to acknowledge it, I think we will both live to be very old and die together. We'd better.

But I couldn't take it happening early, that's for sure. And I thought about that.

I also considered that I had to stay alive for my mother, and for my friend Ashley. My mother was so terribly scared for us. I know I kept her up nights and gave her nightmares and filled her with worry all the months we were at sea. Her hair even thinned. I wish I could have prevented all those things, but you can only control your own mind. Still, I figured the least I could do was stay alive.

I don't mean to leave out my father. My father is, in many ways, my inspiration. He is a helluva guy, a (now) septuagenarian ass-kicker if there ever was one. He's suffered from Crohn's disease since his early twenties and still rides a bicycle thousands of miles a year. He survived an eight-plus-hour surgery in which his entire bowels were rearranged. And he does all this with the most upbeat, go-get-'em attitude of anyone I've ever met. He taught fifth grade at the same grade school (in my hometown of Seneca, Illinois) for thirty-some years and loved a damn good portion of it. He's also a real sap; he'll tear up at any movie or song or poem with a dog in it, that's for sure. But he wasn't scared when I told him what we planned to do. He was excited, so I was less worried about him.

My friend Ashley was watching my dog for a WHOLE YEAR. That's an enormous favor, and I thought to myself, *I can't go dying and leave her with the responsibility of taking care of my dog for the next however-many years.* In retrospect, I realize she probably wouldn't have minded having Maggie; as it turned out, she was actually rather torn up about having to give her back. But she would have been pretty pissed if we had gotten ourselves killed. So I thought about that, and I held on, and I gave Jimmie little progress updates and general encouragement as I stared at the stern and the GPS and listened to the tormenting howl of the unrelenting wind.

Then, after hour upon exhausting hour of flexed muscles and pained concentration, focusing every bit of hope and energy on getting to Shelter Cove, and trying to coax the wind and waves to a reasonable level by the sheer force of our combined, desperate wills, things started to mellow out.

We were drawing near ten miles to our destination, and we were finally, apparently, in the lee of *something*. It didn't happen anywhere close to a time or positioning that we imagined it might, but at least it happened. Jimmie had muscled those twenty-seven feet of sailboat, inch by inch, to port and to port and to port, until we could see the lights of Shelter Cove sparkling in the distance. Our hearts fluttered lightly in our chests. But we didn't speak of it, of anything relenting, until after we'd anchored.

It was about 1:30 AM when we arrived at Shelter Cove. We could hear surf in the distance but couldn't see a thing; the magnificent view would have to wait until daybreak. We put all our underway gear into its various storage places, dried up the cabin as best we could, and changed into dry clothes. Jimmie's arms ached, his fingers bleached white from hours of death-gripping the tiller. Our eyes were shot. Our backs groaned with any shift of the boat. But we were alive. We would've rejoiced, but I don't think we even accepted our survival as a true thing until we woke up the next morning.

The anchorage itself was rolly. The boat pitched about in the remains of stormy sea still sweeping around Point Delgada, the long, narrow spike of land marking the cove. But we certainly weren't going to complain, and it was doubtful either of us would have trouble sleeping. A strange aura of what I think was astonishment filled the cabin—a faded sort of astonishment, beaten down substantially by exhaustion.

I made hot chocolate and chicken noodle soup, the easiest comfort foods I could come up with, and we ate. Our second round of PB&Js was still available, sitting in a plastic baggie under the stove (which was hanging, as usual, from Jimmie's homemade gimbal, an ingenious fusion of iron swivels, shelf brackets, and some scrap wood). But, for some reason, we passed. Probably something warm sounded better.

⚓⚓⚓

We awoke around eight the next morning to find ourselves surrounded by some of the most intensely steep cliffs I have ever seen. To the east were near-vertical walls of dark gray rock topped with spiky green pines. The water around the boat reflected the trees' bold emerald while, farther to the west, a vibrant turquoise mirrored the sky. The beach was black sand, something the area is apparently known for.

The sun was out again, calm and gleaming in the absence of yesterday's cold, harsh wind. It cast a soft white glow onto everything, like some hyperbolic scene of bliss replete with angels singing in operatic tones and ornately styled gates thrown open to reveal only a kind, blinding light. It sounds corny, I know, but that's exactly how it felt, like the most glorious, harmonious welcome back into the living you can imagine. We were alive! Oh God, the joy we felt in that crazy cathedral of nature!

Then we went ashore. Placed on a seaside cliff near an out-of-commission lighthouse, with craggy rocks and tide pools glistening below, was a sign that read DANGER: INTERMITTENT WAVES OF UNUSUAL SIZE AND FORCE. Yeah. You got that right.

"Punta Gorda? In *That*?"

Right away, we recognized Shelter Cove as home to a perma-party down by the boat ramp. Across from the anchorage was an arc of black beach with a short, steep road running down to its northern side. At the bottom, opposite the few moored boats in the cove, lay a stretch of pavement that, all three days we spent anchored there, was littered with pickup trucks, boat trailers, car radios blasting "Oye Como Va" and the like, and local men drinking beer from cans. Around the bend to the south were surfers in wetsuits, looking like seals among the surf. We rowed past them and slid easily up the boat ramp, dragging Johnny Inflatable to a fence near some trashcans and locking him up (hoping our habitual security didn't offend the locals).

We ascended the short road to find a small settlement of RVs and a general supply store perched on a level spot overlooking the sea. The store catered primarily to campers and passers-through with a small selection of groceries, a modest deli counter, and a variety of Cape Mendocino/Black Sand Beaches–related souvenirs. We asked where the closest gas station was, wanting to refuel before heading for our next stop, Albion. "Up the hill about two miles," they said. So we started hoofing it, both of us extremely exhausted from the perils of the previous day, but on task as usual.

It was the first truly warm day we'd experienced in a while, and I had donned a pink cotton halter top in celebration of the weather. The air was dry and toasty with sun and smelled strongly of eucalyptus, a ubiquitous tree along the Northern California coast. It was late

September, and leaves crunched under our feet as we took to the side of the road, spotting a few deer among the trees of Dead Man's Gulch, a deep ravine running between two of the area's most jutting peaks. We encountered a drifter, headed the opposite way down the highway's acute grade. He confirmed we were going the right way but assured us it was "quite a walk" up to the gas station. He also suggested we hitchhike.

We were not unlike hobos, we realized—we moved from place to place, had a general air of scuzziness about us—but we were not beggars, and we were not hitchhikers. Jimmie and I were both stubbornly against the idea of actively seeking assistance from others. We thought our independence set us apart. After all, we'd *chosen* to be jobless and live in this odd, nomadic fashion. We'd saved up what little money we could and were dedicated to doing everything for ourselves, by ourselves. We were proud, and requesting help, in our minds, surrendered some of that pride. We'd walk however many miles it took, straight vertical, before either of us'd put a thumb out.

Sometimes help came to us, though, whether we asked for it not, often arriving at the most opportune times and (thankfully) giving us little option to refuse. That was a constant throughout our trip; the people we met were incredibly selfless, helpful, giving, and kind—despite our stubborn allegiance to independence. Complete strangers offered us food, rides, conversation, directions. Although we had set out to be very much on our own, one of the main things we took away from our trip was this: People are nice! People are good! What a fantastic thing to have shoved in your face.

"Out of gas?" the passenger in the red pickup yelled to us, noticing the tank in Jimmie's tired grip. They assumed we'd been driving, naturally. "It's for our sailboat," Jimmie replied. The men were traveling downhill when they pulled over, but they quickly offered to swing it around and haul us up to the station, echoing the drifter's opinion that the walk was a doozy. We hopped in the back. It seemed pretty stupid to refuse.

I don't think they were really hauling that much ass, but the truck seemed to be going almost frighteningly fast. Perhaps it was the contrast to our usual creeping pace under sail (even our recent high-octane speed of fourteen knots only translates to sixteen miles per hour), or that we were in the bed of the truck with the wind whipping us, or maybe it was the effect of the crazy ascent up the ever-steepening hill—which, bit by bit, revealed a breathtaking, panoramic ocean view—but it felt like we were flying.

They gave us a ride all the way back down to the boat ramp, too, where they were received with familiarity. We thanked them zealously and made our way down to the water's edge with our dinghy. As we got ready to paddle away, we heard one of their buddies say, "Punta Gorda? In *that*?" We knew their eyes had been directed out to our little blue sailboat, sitting solemnly in the calmly rolling anchorage, looking completely miniscule in its majestic surroundings.

It made us feel completely awesome, that remark, as if we'd really done what we thought we had: rounded a crazy-ass landmark in a tiny-ass boat. It legitimized all we were doing, really, but especially what we'd come out of the night before. It *felt* impressive, what we'd accomplished so far, but now it had actually impressed someone, some random person who, we believed, understood what we were up against.

"The Kind of Person We Are."

It wasn't until our second day in Shelter Cove that all the emotional crap we'd been roller-coastering through came to an ugly head. The day had been good. We'd bought and written postcards, and Jimmie had reached his brother via our Internet phone (because nothing makes you want to reach out to loved ones like narrowly cheating death). We'd even purchased a few goodies (Pringles, potato salad, crackers and cheese, Rolos) at the camp store to enjoy with a special bottle of wine—one that had been riding up and down in the tip of our bow for over five hundred nautical miles, the word "Mendocino" all but written on it.

Despite being desperately afraid for us, my mom and stepdad had taken me to do some bon voyage wine tasting out in the Willamette Valley southwest of Portland. They're what you could call connoisseurs, whereas Jimmie and I might better be described as casual winos. But standards aside, we do very much enjoy wine, and my tasting excursion garnered us four bottles, as well as the suggestion that we might take them with us, so as to have something not completely ghetto to drink every now and again. We drank one before leaving, an Erath Syrah that smelled vaguely of cedar. The other three were packed into a cardboard wine box and stuffed very tightly into the pointy first of *Cotton*'s twenty-seven feet. We'd determined that we'd drink one after rounding Cape Mendocino, one after Point Conception, and the last after finally circling Cabo San Lucas and officially entering the Sea of Cortez.

So, one down. Upon returning to the boat from our Shelter Cove explorations, we corked the Deux Verres and dug into our treats. Once it was gone, we sought out a follow-up beverage, as is often our way. This time around it was sake, a drink we'd concluded was ideal for sailors because (a) Japan is a nation of sailors, right? and (b) it tastes good at pretty much any temperature.

For entertainment, we played *Super Mario Bros. 3* on the laptop. A main concern of ours before departing was having plenty of entertainment, so we'd copied about 270 movies onto blank discs using our Hollywood Video membership and some illegal DVD-copying software, filled the now-defunct iPod to capacity, and stocked every book we could fit on the custom bookshelf Jimmie built into the starboard side of the cabin (which was conveniently counter-weighted by our portside water tank). We also brought a few travel-sized board games (Scrabble, Yahtzee), and Jimmie made our laptop capable of playing just about any old-school video game you can think of. (As a result, I discovered my heretofore unknown giftedness at *Moon Patrol*.)

Why we began fighting, I'm not sure. I had been keeping a daily log of our experiences, and whenever we argued I often just wrote: "We argued." I didn't go into detail. I probably didn't want to write even that, as I have a tendency to want to ignore the reality of anything bad playing out between me and Jimmie. Yet, I am a stickler for accuracy.

I do know I was drunk enough to be smoking a cigarette in the cockpit, Jimmie standing in the doorway of the cabin, the boat riding up and down and occasionally rolling sideways on the ten-foot swell gliding into the anchorage. I also know that Jimmie doesn't want to be a hero, not mine or anybody's. He's a man of action, and he does what needs to be done, but he doesn't want to be labeled a thing, anything, ever. Maybe I'd called him a hero, and that's what had set it off. He most likely saved my life—saved both of our lives—but he didn't want credit for it. I think he also didn't want the pressure of that being his said-aloud job: "life-saver," "hero." I guess I can't blame him.

We don't fight much, but when we do it's torture. Jimmie is a very logical debater. His arguments are well reasoned, thoughtful, and infuriating. I'm not much for astrology, but he's an Aries, and he drives me nuts the way an Aries ought to. I'm a Scorpio, and whether it's a self-fulfilling prophecy or not, I get completely irrational, emotional, fired up. Jimmie makes sense while I cry. I get self-deprecating; he gets self-righteous. We both feel bad for making the other one feel bad. Then we both wish it had never happened.

The next morning, I felt almost as bad about the fighting as I did from drinking half a bottle of wine and a bunch of sake. I had a gross taste in my mouth from smoking a cigarette. (After ten years of sucking down Camel Lights, I'd quit cold turkey the spring before our departure, but I'd bought a pack on a whim—yes, a drunken whim—back in Coos Bay.) It should also be noted that a fairly large swell was still sweeping around Point Delgada and into the anchorage, bopping our home handily back and forth, our mast like the pendulum of a metronome. This did not, in any way, assuage the effects of my good old-fashioned hangover.

Jimmie made cream of mushroom soup with crackers for breakfast (we often ate soup for breakfast), and I began to come around. But the shadow of an argument always lingers, and any joyful, lazy embracing of our hangovers was tarnished by the recollection of our having been assholes to each other a mere eight hours earlier. Eventually, I fell asleep on Jimmie's lap. When I awoke it finally felt like we were friends again. I suspect a few culprits for the funk that led to our quick triggers:

1. We'd just been through the most terrifying experience of either of our lives. We lived, but we still had all these intense emotions built up inside us and nowhere to put them.

2. We couldn't stay in Shelter Cove forever. We'd made it to California, yes, but we had to keep going. That was the deal. Everywhere we went was temporary, until maybe La Paz, which at this point was still an untouchable fantasy.

3. The forecast hadn't been too awesome. Granted, we were tucked snugly in the lee of the great cape, the apex of which causes an ongoing storm, but let's face it, we'd recently dealt with some fucking huge waves. A few of them had come over the side of the boat and into the cockpit—something we'd started to believe might never happen—and we were freaked the fuck out.

4. Our next leg was fifty nautical miles. That was on the long side for us, and the trend of the upcoming coastline left us no choice in that matter at all. The anchorage at the end of those fifty nautical miles was Albion, a small cove we never would have thought to enter, except that Rob had circled it.

Like our "terror trip" around Mendocino, and every inch of sea that lay ahead, it was the "what-ifs," the unknowns, that taunted us. Every single thing we did was new, every place we went full of unanswerable questions, every forecast untrustworthy. Any buildup eventually reaches a breaking point, and the night of Deux Verres was it for us.

⚓⚓⚓

Outside of the very occasional spat, most of my relationship with Jimmie has been like an extendo-version of the early lust and romance you feel when you're first falling in love. Even now, we're super jazzed to have any time together; we cherish our common days off, and we plan most every aspect of our lives with togetherness as the paramount goal.

When it became apparent that doing something for the sake of togetherness could afford us the opportunity to do something *crazy* as well, we couldn't resist it. That's one way in which Jimmie and I are exactly the same. Once something becomes irresistible, it's over. In that, we are cursed. We have the ability to think things through, yes, but there is a point past which there is no returning, and talk of our sailing trip reached that point fairly early on. There was nothing we could do but do it.

From the start, Jimmie and I were plagued with longing; we were always pining for something. At first, it was just to be together, which was complicated enough.

Once *that* longing was satisfied, an urgent need to live together took over. We scanned Craigslist and e-mailed ads to each other from our respective workplaces, eventually setting our sights on a building called the Saint Francis. It had glass-enclosed balconies. That just killed us. It took dogs; it was right across from Wimpy's, our favorite Northwest Portland bar; and it was a ten-minute walk from the newspaper. It also had a waiting list, a long one.

I'm not sure how it happened, but Jimmie got us in there. He probably wouldn't admit it, but he can be rather charming when he wants to be. He got hold of the lady in charge of the rentals, and somehow we moved right up to the top of that waiting list. Perhaps it was our admission that we'd sign the lease and pay a deposit without even seeing the place. It's true. We would have. (Those balconies!) Sometimes we know what we want, and that's that. (Sometimes we also talk about ourselves in a weirdly unified manner. Jimmie recently used the phrase "the kind of person we are." Just like that. Seriously.)

So, cohabitation: check. Then, of course, we had to take it up a notch.

We'd already done one moderately crazy thing together, riding a motorcycle 967 miles from Bakersfield, California, to Portland in about forty hours. On virtually no sleep. It was a *Planes, Trains, and Automobiles*–level transportation catastrophe just getting there (I won't go into the details, but let's just say it involved a several-hours-late Amtrak, an abandoned train, a failed car rental, a bus to another train, and the extreme flexibility of the dude selling the bike). The return leg included such difficulties as having a hotel room we'd reserved just given away (due to our super-late arrival, which we'd foreseen and warned the front desk about) and our shelling out one hundred dollars to sleep for three hours (no late checkout allowed!) in a different hotel.

No time to stay an extra day and get some rest: the limited window we'd taken off work combined with the length of the trip necessitated extreme riding. Keep in mind, Jimmie had never piloted this particular motorcycle, and I'd never ridden farther on one than around town. At one point, Jimmie's hands were so frozen he wasn't sure he could properly operate the throttle and shifter. At another, I was literally falling asleep on the back of the motorcycle; I seriously considered bungeeing my hands around Jimmie's waist to be sure I'd stay upright. But, despite all that, we had the time of our lives. We enjoyed the challenge. We'd been bit.

And so, the longing. What had once been apartment hunting became sailboat browsing, which, when possible, became sailboat stalking. We'd go down to a dealership called the Sailing Life in Portland's Jantzen Beach area. They had an open house on Sundays, and we'd taken to snooping around their boats, making mental notes about the roominess and layouts and features of different models. We obsessively searched Craigslist up to Seattle and down to L.A. and skulked around low-security local marinas, sizing up different makes and rigs, trying to draw conclusions about the vessels we'd seen for sale online.

Then we found our Newport. It miraculously came to us without a name, the hull a blank, solid blue. So I made stencils in Heineken font and painted COTTON and PORTLAND, OREGON on it in white antifouling paint. Then came the final object of our longing: departure.

I remember a very orange day, a day bright with citrus sunshine spraying over the clear sky of Portland summer. It was hot, but not too hot, just nice. Jimmie was supposed to go into work around 7:00 PM. I was supposed to work a full eight hours at some point. Working Sundays was part of my adjusted schedule—only this one I was slacking, not working, and Jimmie had called in. We went to a bar: Crowbar, in North Portland. I ordered a Campari. I still remember its bright Maraschino-cherry red, distorted by a few ice cubes, gleaming in front of me, looking sweet but ready to taste bitter, and Jimmie, backlit with sun, facing me with Mississippi Street behind him and a whiskey in front.

A piece of notebook paper scribbled with calculations lay on the rough wood of our table. We were crunching some numbers, some data concerning money and time, trying to make sense of it all, trying to give our dream some reality. It must have been early on; there were a lot of "ifs." But we had our boat. We had it a year before we left.

Still, we were figuring things out right until we left, and we continued to figure things out once we had gone. We're still figuring some things out now. All I know about then, about that perfect red-orange memory, with booze and sun and not working when you're supposed to on a Sunday, is that it felt real enough to me. It felt real enough that I believed it was going to happen. And so did Jimmie. There was nothing else we could do at that point. It was hopeless. We were hopeless, in every romantic way the word's ever been used.

"Is the Ceiling Really High in Here?"

A mere 6.5 nautical miles outside of Albion, our next stop, we found ourselves enveloped in a thick white fog. It wasn't ideal, but at least fog was something we'd dealt with before. Our newest opponent, however, went by the name of kelp—dense, impenetrable kelp.

As we would later discover, a clear route through Albion's kelp beds does exist, and it is actually rather obvious once you've navigated it. But we lacked what the *Coast Pilot* referred to as "local knowledge," and we couldn't really see where we were going. So James Brown found himself at war with innumerable hard, round baseball-sized heads of Pacific bull kelp. They formed what appeared to be a completely solid net over the water's surface, and it seemed the only way to reach Albion Cove, our intended anchorage, was to motor right through them.

Naturally, we were concerned that JB's propellers might get irrecoverably tangled in the long green whips below the water, killing his engine. The potential for catastrophe by outboard failure was intensified by the fact that we were in very little wind and traveling ever closer to a narrow, rock-laden entry. We attempted to aim for thinner-looking kelp patches, but we had to be careful to avoid rocks as well. Sometimes a rock is only a foot or two under the surface; you can't see it, and the way looks clear, but it's there, lurking, and only the Nobletec knows. The only way to dodge the rocks with certainty was to stick to our planned GPS course, regardless of vegetation.

As always, JB was a fucking champ, his props miraculously slicing through the kelp's hardy-looking stems. I steered while Jimmie kept watch through the fog from up on the bow. Once we emerged from between the large boulders flanking the entry, the kelp dispersed dramatically, and we were able to cruise over and anchor behind Mooring Rock, which was crowned with a light and a foghorn, not to mention a complete icing of bird crap. Like Hunters Cove, the anchorage was only big enough for one boat, and we were it.

The enclosure was breathtaking, and despite the trying entry, both of us look back on Albion as one of the best stops of the entire trip. The wall of land to the north was chunky and salt-gray near the sea, with shrubby pines dotting its ridges; closer in were slopes the color and texture of busted-up pie crust, their surface crowded with the peeling trunks of towering eucalyptus. Narrow ravines were stuffed with giant grasses, light sage stalks topped with immaculate tan feathery tips, inspiring thoughts of dinosaurs. A light gray beach arced along the eastern curve of the cove, and the smooth, parched trunk of a dead eucalyptus lay vertically against the northern side of the river valley, a bright white slash against the gouged land. To the south, the beach terminated in sheer chestnut cliffs, the base of a grass-covered plateau.

Connecting the two sides was a magnificent wooden bridge, under which ran the shallow green waters of the Albion River.

The next morning, Jimmie did some relatively uneventful San Francisco–related research, calling marine supply stores via our spotty Internet phone and discovering that, even in the sailing mecca that is San Francisco Bay, a tiller for our totally average boat was going to be hard (or impossible) to come by. He also looked into the convenience of cheap grocers to various anchorages, affordable groceries being a prime goal of most of our urban stops. In the midst of this, we heard a man's voice say, "Hello? Anybody home?" It came from outside the boat. This was an unusual occurrence. We slid back the companionway hatch and peeked out. There was Bruce, the Albion River Campground host, bobbing alongside our hull in a dark green canoe.

Apparently, it wasn't every day that a sailboat appeared in Albion Cove, and Bruce, a brown-haired, outdoorsy man in his early forties, couldn't help but make our acquaintance. We asked him about the river, its depth and current; we were actually wondering if it would be possible to take our sailboat up it a little way, since the bridge gave plenty of clearance. No go. Swift and shallow, he said. Landing our dinghy on the beach and walking up to the camp was his recommendation. He and his wife ran a little café there during the summer, and it stayed open as a sort of thin-supply convenience store during the off-season. He tried to persuade us to stop in and take a look at some photo books documenting Albion's yesterdays. We said we might just do that, and he was off, paddling back toward the river.

⚓ ⚓ ⚓

Jimmie and I like drinking together; it's something we've done recreationally since we first met. That said, I don't think either of us imagined we'd be drinking *at all* on the sailing trip (besides our few special-occasion bottles of wine).

Then, at the going-away party thrown for us by the newspaper, we received a handle of rum as one of our parting gifts. Portland already has a rather annoying fixation with pirates (actual pirates were rapists, man; *not* cool), and my snarky-by-nature coworkers couldn't resist the kitschiness of getting two sailors a bottle of rum. We accepted the liquor graciously and found a home for it behind a built-in storage drawer, nestled against the curve of the hull in what came to be known as the "prohibition chamber." It was half gone before we even hit the Pacific.

Turns out, rum was actually a really good choice. It went well with hot chocolate (or even vanilla or orange-spice tea) as well as the sort of mixers we tended to have around (Tang, powdered fruit punch, etc.). Vodka worked similarly well with our dehydrated juices, but not so much with the mulled beverages. So, like a couple of clichés, we gravitated toward the buccaneer's choice. Quick to ditch our assumed sobriety (we felt we were sacrificing enough in other realms, OK?), we also drank copious amounts of box wine, a tradition that began at our very first Pacific coast stop, Tillamook Bay.

It was Monday, August 18, 2008, when we bought our first box. It was probably Vella Merlot, or perhaps Almaden Mountain Burgundy. We didn't care much at the time. Later, however, we became well versed in the options and made more careful selections. (For instance, Vella's button spout offers what we termed "passout protection," where Almaden's rotating tap could accidentally be left open if one blacked out mid-pour.)

Though Jimmie and I had shared plenty of low-dollar wines and had felt blessed in Portland to live near a Trader Joe's (home of the famous Two-Buck Chuck), we'd never sunk to the bottom shelf—the shelf on which box wine sits. I must, even now, have some pride left, because I feel it necessary to note that we never drank white zinfandel, or any other mom-keeps-it-in-the-fridge-style blush. We never sank quite that low. But we did sink, gladly, really. Perusing the aisles of the Garibaldi general store, we realized that box wine was the wine for us. It was the wine we could afford, and affording any was awesome.

We paired our first glasses with (what else?) cheese—macaroni and cheese. I also made "roasted" potatoes; I'd figured out a way to sort of "bake" them on the stovetop using Pam, several shakers of dried herbs, some patience, and a steamer basket. All in all, a very classy meal. And the last word of the log for that fateful day? "Magnifique!" But of course.

⚓ ⚓ ⚓

Our second morning in Albion, we were feeling less than magnificent. We'd consumed a four-dollar bottle of wine from the Albion Grocery (they must not have had boxes), followed it up with whatever remaining rum we had, and then indulged in some whiskey-spiked lemonade. The whiskey came from a plastic flask of "medicinal whiskey" we'd been keeping in the pantry, which, along with a bright blue canvas bag of Band-Aids and various pills, constituted our version of health care. The bag had a red First Aid cross on the front; it seemed pretty official.

Utilizing some superb hangover logic, we came to a couple of important conclusions: (1) We would, this day, allow ourselves the luxury of one item each from the Albion Grocery (which featured a tantalizing deli area), and (2) All-you-can-eat Chinese buffets seemed almost designed for our cheap-and-starving lifestyle, so we would seek them out and abuse them whenever convenient and affordable. That decided, we promptly lay around in the V-berth for a few more hours before dragging ourselves to shore in order to fulfill our deli promise. (So maybe we weren't the greatest ascetics.)

Passing the camp store (for the third time, counting our wine run the day before), we felt it would be too rude not to stop in. If two people can be a loner, that's what we are—antisocial, I guess you could say. But not unfriendly. Whenever we did get to talking to someone, we became a couple of Chatty Cathies. But, for the most part, we avoided outside interaction like the plague. Perhaps we'd become a little introverted from living in a tiny cabin together, just the two of us, for two months. We were used to dealing only with each other, and we liked it that way.

We bought a V8 and a Gatorade (hangover serums if there ever were any) and perused the photo albums. They documented the cove's urchin harvest, the town's old sawmill, and the time a semi drove off and wrecked part of the almost-completely-wooden bridge, the only of its kind left in California. Bruce's son was working the register, and we asked him about good pizza places in the area. Bruce came in while we were still mingling, and—bam!—just like that, we'd been invited to dinner. And I had accepted.

Jimmie, severely hungover and therefore feeling even less social than usual, was not pleased. To be honest, I was feeling pretty worn out and brain-dead myself, but I hadn't seen any way around it. How does one turn down a gracious offer from a friendly guy when it's obvious one has *nothing* else going on? This is the defense I spewed during our walk up the hill to the deli; if I couldn't get us out of dinner, I at least wanted out of the doghouse.

Jimmie tended to think such events would be painfully awkward and an expenditure of time he'd prefer to use differently. In retrospect, he often admits to enjoying himself. But my acceptance of Bruce's invitation had ruined his vision of the day, and I was backpedaling for all I was worth. "I'll just tell them you weren't feeling well and go by myself," I offered. "No. I'll go," he said, unwilling to cop out. So, we resigned ourselves to the reality of our dinner date.

As dinner-with-Bruce-time approached, we began to gussy ourselves up as best we could. I attempted to straighten my always wild bangs by drying them in bobby pins, and Jimmie went so far as to comb his beard. We both wore deodorant. I put on some makeup. It had been twenty-one days since we'd last showered, and attempting to look, let alone *feel* suitable for dinner in a normal family's home was pretty hopeless.

We trudged through the sand dunes and big, hairy patches of grass up to the camp hosts' door and knocked. Upon entering, we met Bruce's wife, Kim, and their two dogs, Buster and Bear. We were told to take a seat in the living room area; they were just finishing making dinner. While Bruce went to grab beers for everyone, Jimmie and I marveled at how enormous their house felt. "Hey, is the ceiling really high in here?" Jimmie whispered to me. "I don't think so," I said, but I knew how he felt. It could have been vaulted, but I don't think it was. It was normal and we were odd.

Bruce handed us each a brown bottle of beer and sat down across from us. Kim came over and announced that we were just waiting for some au gratin potatoes to finish browning. *Cheese!* I thought. *YES!* Jimmie and I took turns using their bathroom to wash up, and it felt strange to use a regular faucet with pressurized water. I also realized, suddenly, that I hadn't really *seen* myself in quite some time. They had a large mirror—or, rather, the size of vanity mirror most bathrooms have—and it was comforting to see that I didn't look too crazy. Or scummy. I dried my hands on one of their thick, fluffy towels and came out.

Dinner was a cornucopia of freshness, a major change of pace for us: breaded, baked cod; the au gratin potatoes, all crisp and browned along the top and oozing with melted cheese underneath; asparagus; an Asian-style salad with sesame dressing and slivered almonds (it's amazing how much you miss fresh greens when you never have them); and local abalones, which neither of us had ever had before, local or otherwise. Apparently, they're really desirable, and divers come from all around to harvest Albion's red abalones.

The conversation was easy, and Jimmie and I both felt really glad that we'd come.

After dinner, Kim brought out small ceramic mugs of coffee-flavored ice cream, as well as licorice tea. "I love the taste of these two things together," she told us. We hadn't had any dairy besides powdered milk for a while, and the ice cream seemed incredibly creamy. I liked the tea so much Kim insisted on giving me her last bags of it.

Before we left, we were also each given a sweet Albion River Campground hoodie. They were thick with blanket-like fleece and had serious hoods with ties for being snugged around windburned faces. They were exactly the kind of outerwear we could use on those misty Northern California mornings, and they had a totally cool old-school illustration of the campground silkscreened on their backs. We were overwhelmed with gratitude.

That's what struck us most about Bruce and Kim: their undiscriminating generosity. We'd been given food, beer, conversation, freakin' awesome new sweatshirts, bags of tea. And for what? Just for being there. Just for sailing into some random cove on the California coast (and even after a day and a half of stupidly avoiding the gracious folks who lived there). Their attitude was not uncommon, either. Like Rob and the red truck guys of Shelter Cove, most people we met wanted to help, to give, to participate.

The other thing that struck us about them was their last name. Before getting hugs and handshakes and well-wishes on the front porch, Bruce handed us his card. We said we'd send them a postcard from further on in our trip (which we did). Walking back through the darkness toward the beach, where we fumbled to change from sneakers back into our boots (we'd neglected to bring a flashlight), Jimmie squinted at the card. "Campbell!" he exclaimed hushedly. "His name's *Bruce Campbell*." Being huge *Evil Dead* fans, we were thrilled. "Go figure," Jimmie added. "That's awesome."

We told Bruce we planned to leave early the next morning, and we had a hunch he'd be drinking his morning coffee from their small wooden porch, which afforded an excellent view of the cove. We were really hoping the wind would be favorable for sailing off our anchor, because that was the coolest thing, and we wanted to be in top form in case Bruce was watching. The weather didn't disappoint. A nice, light morning breeze was coming off the land. Jimmie pulled up the anchor and I sailed us off. We couldn't tell, once we got going and glanced back, whether Bruce was standing there, steaming cup in hand, or not, but both of us had a feeling he was.

A badass day was shaping up. The sun was out, already warming the air; a dazzling blue sky began to emerge from the morning haze; and a maroon-purple starfish the size of a saucer had hitched a ride on our anchor! We unattached its little suction cup feet from the metal of our claw and set it flat on the cockpit. I looked it up in my Audubon *Field Guide to North American Seashore Creatures*. It was an ochre sea star. And its appearance made us both giddy, as if we really were living in the wild.

Much like the spirit-brightening dolphins of Mendocino, that little sea star made our day. But where the dolphins appeared in sharp contrast to their apocalyptic surroundings, our sea star matched the sparkling tranquility of Albion, the crown on an already magical stay. Cape Mendocino could have been a million miles away.

"I'll Keep an Eye on Things."

Next up was the stop that would ultimately earn the title of "Trip's Suckiest Anchorage." We didn't know it was the sucky-*est* just then (there was always the chance of things sucking worse in the future), we just knew it sucked. It was the only stopping point between Albion and Bodega Bay, just north of San Francisco, and it was what we had to settle for to keep our legs at their usual one-long-day time limit.

This most-sucky spot was, ironically, named Havens Anchorage—a haven, apparently, for kelp beds and outlying rocks, all being swept by a horribly uncomfortable western swell. ("Haven," I later realized from all my chart perusing, can refer to good fishing in an area, often due to an artificial reef—a "fish haven," as it were.) The approach was a clouded field of pink jellyfish, their lacy bodies *thunk, thunk, thunk*ing ominously against the hull. Wavy tendrils outlined in deeper pink and purple swayed all through the aqua-colored water, like shards of shredded chiffon, the aftermath of *Nightmare on Elm Street Goes to the Prom*.

After navigating the treacherous grounds and finding a spot we might narrowly feel comfortable calling home for the night, we set our bow anchor . . . only to somehow drift over its line and become caught, however implausibly, on our own keel. Jimmie tried swinging us this way and that, pulling on the rope while I motored per his directions, being careful not to run over the line with the outboard and scramble our propellers into the already perplexing mess.

We eventually got loose, but Jimmie lost a chunk of skin to the anchor line and was bleeding all over the cockpit, saltwater in his fresh wound, while deploying the stern anchor. He'd decided two anchors would be necessary if we were to stay in our tight little area just seaward of the surf and treacherous rocks, let alone achieve any sort of comfort (or sleep) there. With one anchor, you inevitably turn lengthwise to the waves and get rocked like a baby in a cradle of increasing discomfort. It's worse the larger and more frequent the swell, and the swell was pretty tremendous here. Anchoring perpendicular to the swell thwarts this effect, but it requires two anchors (or the appropriate wind).

Jimmie got them set, but the place already seemed cursed: the jellyfish-laden entry, the rocks and surf and wakes of fishermen zipping around in little speedboats, the blood all over the deck and cockpit. It was warm and sunny, and we were happy to be wearing T-shirts, but that's about all we were happy with.

Once inside, Jimmie wrapped some paper towels around his hand and we listened to a goofy San Francisco radio station called MOViN while I made dinner. It specialized in R&B faves of the '80s and '90s, and it cheered us up despite ourselves. A stew of peas and onions swimming in warm green curry filled the cabin with fragrant spiciness. Eating was good. Sitting was good. We felt a little better. But Jimmie was beside himself with exhaustion and clearly concerned about our anchor situation. Jimmie was always concerned about our anchor situation, even more than I knew.

⚓ ⚓ ⚓

The first night we spent off our boat (after the trip, in a hotel), Jimmie said, "That's the first good night's sleep I've had in a year." It was revelatory to me. He wasn't exaggerating. I could tell. And it was because of anchoring. I knew he'd felt deep concern over it, that the integrity of our setup at each and every stop was a big deal to him, but I didn't know it was like that. I didn't know he took so much personal responsibility for it. He bore that weight far more than I had ever imagined.

To me, once we were anchored, we were anchored. I did worry, and I did occasionally lay awake listening to and stressing about weird sounds (and sometimes I'd lay awake simply because the weird sounds kept me up), but I hardly ever investigated them. Jimmie did. Or he would when I'd say, "What's that sound?" But I almost always slept; I am a better sleeper than Jimmie even on land in a totally stationary, square bed. And he always let me sleep, keeping at least one nerve attentive in case something went awry. I just slept. And he let me. He bore the weight.

To his credit, we only dragged on our anchor twice: once during a formidable Newport Beach gale (in very poor holding ground) and once back in Oregon, in the silty bed of the Yaquina River. We were both wide awake, drinking box wine and eating macaroni and cheese, watching *Live and Let Die*. We simply paused the movie, re-anchored, and eventually moved on to *The Spy Who Loved Me*. It was a Bond double feature.

⚓ ⚓ ⚓

Ironically, the only other time Jimmie slept well was that night at Havens Anchorage. Seeing him look so tired, his grip all raw like a piece of Oscar Mayer ham, I offered to stay up after dinner while he slept; I offered to take the weight from him, though I didn't know how much it meant. "I'll keep an eye on things," I said, thinking little of it. I had some sewing to do, and he looked so very worn out. I promised I'd stick my head out of the companionway hatch occasionally to check our position, so he took to the V-berth and crashed.

I probably sewed for only a few hours: a button on my mom's old Pendleton; a seam on Jimmie's full-body long underwear (a red, lumberjack-ish number we called a "unitard"); the zipper on our teardrop jib bag, which was coming loose from repeated zipping and unzipping. I did check our position occasionally and was met with an enchanting dark and starry night and a relatively stationary boat. All was well in the Trip's Suckiest Anchorage.

I don't know if he woke up and only half slept after I eventually came to bed, but at least for a bit, he slept fully, well. It was the one time I took the weight from him, and I held it long enough for his head to lighten, for him to rest. I don't think he ever forgot it.

"Do You Still Want to Keep the Boat?"

If there's one thing we were always grateful for, it was having each other around, if for no other reason than to have someone *understand*. So much of what we did was a strange mix of magic and torture, as if performing the most inconvenient, trying tasks could somehow be infused with an indescribable wonder, even joy. Everyday events ranged from doing the hardest thing you've ever done *ever* to witnessing the most breathtaking sights imaginable. Jimmie often likened it to a game of "Bad News, Good News." For instance, bad news: you almost died rounding Cape Mendocino. Good news: Shelter Cove is one of the most stunning places you've ever seen. Bad news: you're stuck in Coos Bay and have to walk ten miles for mail and a cheap can of soup. Good news: *The Breakfast Club* is playing at the Egyptian. And so on.

We were constantly filled with awe—both at what we had to do and how fully we were rewarded—and we felt that we'd never be able to fully explain to anyone what our experience was like, so it was reassuring to know that someone else was there, living it, filing away the details in the library of their mind—most often in the "unbelievable" section.

Take San Francisco's Angel Island, deserted and deer-filled on a Friday afternoon. It offered a haunting desolation that made for one of my favorite days of the entire voyage, a perfect meeting of time and place. After a rather unpleasant into-the-wind crossing from one end of a very choppy San Francisco Bay to the other, we settled on an anchorage along Angel Island's Quarry Beach. It was on the east side of the island, in the lee from the prevailing winds and rather calm, except for the constant wakes of passing ferryboats.

We could see cool, decrepit old buildings from the water, but paddling to shore from our Quarry Beach anchorage, we had no idea what we were in for—or that we'd have it entirely to ourselves. We locked up our dinghy to a fence near the beach and hiked up a small hill to find a field filled with deer. We froze and stared at each other. The pair nearest us made their way over to a white-tailed party in a deserted baseball field. Beyond deer haven were the ruins of Fort McDowell, an army garrison used during the Spanish-American and both World Wars.

We explored them thoroughly, discovering hanging, broken staircases leading to floors never to be visited again, listening to our steps echo through the empty rooms, occasionally shuffling and crunching on loose plaster and paint chips broken off over years of weather and sightseers. Many of the structures were lacking not just windows and doors but entire walls. The effect was that of standing in a worn-out blueprint, or wandering through the scaffolding of a construction site that had somehow been dramatically advance-aged. The framework for everything was there, but the details had faded away, the remains only skeletons of buildings that once housed soldiers, nurses, immigrants, and POWs.

We decided to walk the path north to Ayala Cove, a popular anchorage that charges visiting boats to tie up to moorings (i.e., too popular a place for us). From there, we couldn't help but continue on, circling the island's perimeter as the setting sun cast an amber glow on everything west-facing. We briefly visited Camp Reynolds (the West Garrison), then rushed the last leg across the island's southern border in coming darkness, anxious to turn our anchor light on.

The day had been crisp and perfectly October: warm sunshine through a clear turquoise sky, a cool dryness in the air that hints of electricity on your skin and fingertips. Crunchy leaves underfoot, releasing the minty scent of eucalyptus with each step. And no one— not a single person besides the two of us—on the island. Other than the sound of our footsteps, a breeze through the browning trees, or the occasional bird or squirrel, the island was eerily silent. Standing inside the ruins of a hospital among the East Garrison buildings, a hidden deer scratched its hooves on the cement floor as it commenced to flee the room—and momentarily scared Jimmie's heart out of his chest.

It was the kind of day you dream of as a kid: coming across some empty wonderland in the middle of a beautiful, wooded place—on an island, no less! And it appears to be just for you, as if no one else even knows it exists. The only inhabitants are wildlife. Unthreatening, adorable wildlife—deer, small birds, fuzzy gray and brown squirrels. You're wearing your favorite sweater, and you're neither too hot nor too cold. The time of day just before sunset seems to last for hours. You look all around, past your immediate fantasy and into the distance, only to be reminded that you're in one of the most excellent cities in the world: San Francisco. White sails full of wind traipse around the bay; the Golden Gate Bridge in all its brick-red glory looms over the entrance to the Pacific, where you came from. Where you live.

⚓ ⚓ ⚓

But getting to San Francisco, even deciding whether or not to go, came with a lot of anxiety. Because of its reputation as a busy and significant port along the West Coast, and as a sailing destination, we were majorly intimidated by it, so much so that we'd almost passed on it entirely.

Little did we know we'd see only two industrial ships on our way in, and that—compared with the amount of traffic we'd seen on the notably slimmer Columbia and Willamette Rivers, where we'd briefly learned to sail—the entrance to San Francisco Bay would feel downright roomy. We were so comfortable, in fact, that we had an all-out photo shoot on our way in, taking turns posing on the bow, even going on deck together, leaving jeeves at the helm, for a couple's shot with the Golden Gate in the background.

So many of the things that had worried us—crossing the Columbia River Bar, our first day on the ocean, the traffic and sailing cred of San Francisco Bay, our cutout transom—turned out to be inconsequential. Looking back on our entire boating experience, I've come to realize that something we came close to doing *before* leaving was perhaps the most risky.

It was our attempted maiden voyage. When we found our sailboat, we were living in Portland; it, however, was in Everett, Washington, about two hundred land miles up I-5. This was a tad inconvenient considering we didn't know how to sail and didn't want to pay to have a boat shipped, but we were convinced this certain Washingtonian chiropractor's Newport 27 was the boat for us. So we decided to sail it down to Portland anyway.

We had a plan that, though strikingly incomplete and downright absurd in retrospect, seemed quite feasible to us at the time. We figured we would try to learn how to sail the boat on our way from Everett out of Puget Sound and into the Strait of Juan de Fuca. And, if we weren't getting the hang of it, we'd motor. We prepared in every way a person who knew nothing of the sea or sailing could prepare.

We were very thoughtful and organized. Every detail—our Amtrak-and-Greyhound trip up to Washington, our stopover at an area grocery store to buy nonperishable provisions, our purchase of a handheld GPS and downloading of the appropriate charts, considerations such as power usage and the toting of an extremely heavy backup battery in a shabby old suitcase all the way from Portland—had been taken into account. We looked into advice on how and when to cross the Columbia River Bar *into* the river, toward Portland. We'd each taken a total of four days off work. We did the math. Motoring at hull speed the entire time, we'd just make it.

We did not, however, think to check the weather off the Washington coast. I'm sure we looked at the weather in general via some normal resource like Weather.com (it was August and probably lovely), but the concept of an ocean forecast—wave height and period, wind strength, gale warnings, and small craft advisories—or the NOAA, for that matter, was still foreign to us.

Nor did we consider tides, currents, ports for refueling. We also planned on not sleeping—that's right, not sleeping *at all*—basically the entire time. The assumption that we could do this was not coming out of nowhere—Jimmie and I had both withstood impressive periods of unrest, in extreme conditions, even, throughout our lives, be they in the name of work, creativity, partying, travel, or sheer necessity—and we thought we could do it. And we had *so much* Red Bull. We also could only get so much time off work, so it had to be done in the time we had to do it in. It had to be done in *four days*. That was that.

We were, of course, concerned with safety, as much as we were informed enough to be. We considered that there might be times when one of us could sleep while the other piloted, but we were uncomfortable with the idea of leaving the other in the cockpit alone. To this end, we purchased whistles—P.E. coach–style whistles. The idea was if you fall overboard, whistle.

We made the chiropractor (a friendly, sophisticated man we'd met about a month prior) aware of our plan and indicated that, if possible, we'd like to spend the night before our departure on the boat, which was tied up to his private dock. When we arrived very late in the evening—after a cab ride during which the cabbie told us about a kid and his dad recently being killed by a "rogue wave" in the same body of water we were about to embark upon—we found a nice note from the chiropractor aboard the boat, along with a sales receipt and a couple of mints. *Nice touch*, we thought.

The next morning, we headed off, not even having any idea how to leave a dock. We accidentally took the doctor's bumpers with us, as they were tied to the boat. Maybe they were included? He'd left us directions out of the area, pointing out a channel marker to look for and indicating which way to head around it. Everything he'd noted matched up with our GPS, and we were motoring along just fine, rounding Whidbey Island, Useless Bay, and approaching Port Townsend, where the Point Wilson Lighthouse marked our passing from Puget Sound into the Strait of Juan de Fuca (apparently considered a rough sailing area).

We'd prepared peanut butter and jelly sandwiches for lunch, and I recall eating one while standing at the helm, steering. Weezer's *Blue*

Album was blasting on the cockpit speakers. Our meticulous planning prioritized the need for sea jams, and we'd purchased and brought along all the means for a rockin' marine system—this, mind you, from the same pair who deemed their record collection (in storage at Jimmie's mom's) their only worldly possession worth keeping. The sun was out, the sky blue, and things were generally going as well as could be expected.

As the day moved on, we realized that we were going to have to motor *a lot* in order to get to Portland (and work) in the time allotted. Because of this, we were going to need more gas. But before addressing this, we did attempt to sail, to see if we could. When we first tried, the wind was light, and we mostly just drifted around.

During this aimless drifting, we were almost swept by the current into a large cement-bottomed buoy. As we neared it, we fired up the motor and attempted to drive quickly away, but we were revving the throttle in neutral. I ran up on the deck, ready to reach out and push us away from the buoy (if possible), when Jimmie identified the problem, threw us into gear, and sped us off. Needless to say, our incompetence with the motor and our near collision rattled us a bit.

Motoring on, we began to face the reality that we'd have to stop soon for gas. We consulted the marina info included in our GPS software and discovered a gas dock near the entrance to Sequim Bay. We planned to pull in, refuel, and head back out. I had a cell phone at the time and called ahead; unfortunately, the John Wayne Marina attendant told me, they would most definitely be closed before we could get there.

We learned that most marinas (and their gas docks) hold rather slim hours, many closing by 5:00 or 6:00 PM. Our progress was already slower than expected, and we knew it would be hazardous to stop overnight, but we realized—as we would in regard to many, many sailing-related concerns—we didn't have a choice. It was still sunny and pleasant in the late-summer afternoon, and things seemed remarkably calm once we'd motored behind a large hump of land into Sequim Bay's outer waters. Since we had time to kill, Jimmie thought it a good opportunity to try sailing again. We raised the sails, which we hadn't bothered to inspect whatsoever before handing over $4,400 cash to the selling party, and gave it a shot.

A light wind was up, and Jimmie was pretty successfully tacking through the outer bay. (One had to traverse a small entry channel and skirt a geologic Q-tip to enter Sequim Bay proper.) We were feeling rather enthralled with these baby steps in our seaward education when . . . we grounded. A man had been waving at us from the shore, frantically trying to warn us that it was only a few feet deep, just seconds before our keel dug into the gravelly bottom. We hadn't been watching the depth meter. I'm not even sure it was on.

A mixture of pissed-offedness and embarrassment swept over us. But Jimmie recognized the urgency of the situation and was soon looking for a way to free us. He settled on poking through the water with our whisker pole, a long metal tube that holds out the clew of certain headsails, we'd later learn. He jabbed it into the squashy bottom while I accelerated the motor and experimented with different tiller positions. It seemed hopeless, and we didn't know if the tide was coming in our going out—or if it mattered this far inland.

Jimmie, ever-persistent as he is, managed to wiggle us off after what felt like a long time. We were free! And we shot through the water thusly, staring at the depth sounder and heading back toward the strait, into deeper waters. I killed the motor and we resumed our trial-sailing, our earlier confidence not completely dashed. Again, we were pretty successful at tacking around in the light wind, and we even experimented with sail trim, pulling in the jib sheets to go a little faster. The thing about speed on a sailboat is that it gives you the feeling of control. Too much wind and speed can become distressing, but full sails mean the boat is at your command.

Once past that bulge of land that had been causing such pleasant environs in the bay, however, the prevailing west wind—funneling in from the Pacific and shuttling down the huge artery of the strait— presented itself, and we began hauling ass. We were really sailing! Being powered by the wind alone! As our sails grew more taut with rushing air, I couldn't help but think, *If we can get going and sail overnight, we can work our way to Port Angeles, farther down the strait, and gas up there the next morning. We can still achieve our goal!*

Jimmie, steering and manning the mainsail, directed me to further tighten the headsail's sheets, reigning in the wind with more might, essentially stepping on the gas. I wrapped the sheet around the starboard-side winch, stuck the winch handle in, and gave it a crank. This is when we discovered that the ratcheting mechanism in our starboard winch was broken. The wind gusted. I attempted to hold the sheet by strength alone, but my arms were as faulty as our winch.

The handle spun out of my grip, the headsail instantly freed and whipping violently ahead of the bow, and the winch handle spinning ferociously—into my sternum. *Smack!* Every ounce of breath in my lungs shot out in one pounding *Thump!* Again. *Thwack!* I was being beaten, repeatedly, in the chest with the heavy plastic winch handle. Robbed of breath and in shock, I sat there, unmoving. Frozen. And, because I was frozen, I continued to be pummeled by the thick red handle, hard, right in the center of my chest. When I did breathe again I became tingly from hyperventilation. Finally, I moved . . . and took the tiller.

Jimmie had moved long ago. During the vast few seconds in which I lost the winch handle and incurred my beating, Jimmie had wrestled in the headsail and was struggling to bungee it to a bow that was now heaving up and down over insta-waves that had formed in the strait. He had never done this before. Jumping on deck in rough waters and keeping balanced while pulling in a wind-whipped sail was not something we were old hands at. It was instinct. Jimmie saw the root of the problem—the sail being pulled away from me with force—and he killed it. But neither of us could kill the wind, and we were shaken up rather badly.

Our next action, turning back toward Sequim Bay, was understood, a given. We would not be sailing on that evening. We would not reach Port Angeles by sail. In fact, we would not reach Port Angeles at all.

On the way south, toward the refuge behind that big bump of land, we donned the faded orange life jackets that had come with the boat, musty from cockpit storage and in disrepair. Each of us asked repeatedly if the other was all right.

"Yeah. I'm OK. Are you OK?"

"Yeah. Are you hurt?"

"I don't think so. My chest is probably bruised, but I'm OK."

"OK."

"OK."

I recall feeling an overwhelming sadness on that short trip motoring south across the strait. It wasn't at the knowledge that our maiden voyage would, ultimately, be a failure. It wasn't at the cruel reality that what we so assuredly thought we could take on in a few days, we couldn't—that our Everett-to-Portland escapade wasn't going to happen, not by a long shot. It wasn't even the now more serious question of whether we could take such a trip, our big trip, at all. It was sadness over the thought of something happening to Jimmie, and his sadness over the thought of something happening to me. He'd seen me get beaten by the winch handle, my face aghast, my body's sudden lack of breath, the fear in my eyes. I'd seen him get tossed up and down and pitched easily from side to side on the deck (by what weren't even very large waves). I saw, briefly, an early shadow of the sacrifices that would need to be made, of the constant demand on Jimmie that lie ahead, and just a hint of the unrelenting power of nature.

Once we got anchored (for the first time ever), past the Q-tip, past the lights of the docks at John Wayne Marina, in the very peaceful, deep green water of Sequim Bay, we sat down at the table, which at the time had a border like children's wallpaper of playful orcas. There we ate very salty sandwiches of dried beef with mustard on hoagie rolls. We weren't sure if we'd anchored correctly, or if it would hold, despite the extremely calm conditions within the bay. We attempted setting the "anchor alarm" on our GPS, which is meant to alert you if your vessel drifts farther than a set distance beyond its current position in any direction. We had a bottle of port wine (essentials, I tell you: we had them down), and Jimmie poured each of us a Dixie cup.

"Well, we have to go back, right?" I said, just a little afraid that Jimmie would still want to try for Portland in the face of our new, seemingly hopeless circumstances.

"Yeah," he agreed. (He is not beyond reason.)

Phew. "Do you still want to keep the boat?" I ventured.

"Yeah. Do you?"

"Yeah."

So it was settled. We weren't giving up. Not altogether anyway.

Moments later, as I was mumbling on about how I could call the chiropractor on the way back to try to arrange something—a brief holdover at his private dock till we could figure out shipping options or at least get a temporary slip at the nearby Port of Everett—I noticed Jimmie was asleep, sitting up at the table. Even though I know he hardly slept once we'd moved into the V-berth (bearing the weight, episode one!), he dozed heavily right then, a half cup of port in front of him and bright yellow mustard stains around his fingernails.

After we anchored but before dinner, I'd snapped his picture across the cabin from me, standing in the only place he could be completely upright. He looked absolutely exhausted. In the photo album documenting our attempted Everett-to-Portland sail, the caption reads:

REALITY SETS IN/REFUGE,

SEQUIM BAY, WA

AUGUST 2007

The next morning, after successfully acquiring gas from John Wayne Marina—our off-the-cuff navigating of an unknown marina and first time pulling up to a gas dock (*any* dock!) cultivating its own load of anxiety—we left Sequim Bay and turned back toward Everett. Later, huddled in the V-berth while Jimmie piloted us over choppy wind waves, I made a sheepish call to the chiropractor, admitting that we were on our way back. We didn't have time and it just wasn't realistic, I told him. I didn't mention the fact that I'd been pummeled by our winch handle or that we'd grounded on our way in *and* out of Sequim Bay or that we'd been battling clashing conditions for hours, motoring into the wind the whole way back, brackish water spraying across the deck with every slap of the bow on the waves, the salt stinging our sun- and windburned faces, over and over again.

He said we could tie up where we'd left from until we figured out a plan. We were aware of the fact that he'd priced the boat low to get rid of it easily, not wanting to show it to tons of prospective buyers. He didn't have the time, and he didn't need the money. (We later found out he'd gotten the boat himself for $300 at an auction.) Naturally, we felt bad about complicating the situation, but he was incredibly gracious. "I thought that sounded pretty ambitious," he offered. As we meekly unloaded our things from the boat and trudged up the hill toward his house, his wife offered to make us dinner and would accept nothing less than at least giving us a ride to a hotel.

We accepted the ride but had her drop us off at the closest chain hotel, even though we didn't intend to stay there. We walked to a highway overpass, where we caught a bus into downtown Everett, then walked some more to a cheap hotel by the Amtrak station. All the while, Jimmie dragged the battery suitcase (without the battery) on one wheel and a bald corner; a wheel had shot off back in Portland under the weight of the battery, and the remaining upholstery had ground off to reveal the metal piping underneath. Sparks now flew off down the sidewalk behind us, and when Jimmie resolved to pick the damn thing up he burned his finger on the fiery edge. Battle scars. Injuries of an absurdist mission.

Once in our room with Chinese takeout from a neighboring business, we realized how incredibly run-down we were. Our faces and necks and ears were bright pink and dry as sandpaper. Our ear creases were lined with coarse granules of salt. Our hands ached, our eyes stung. Our pride hurt. We were parched, hungry, beat. We'd been amply roughed up by the little old Strait of Juan de Fuca. The question loomed, *How bad a beating, then, could the Pacific deal us? Would we have to reconsider our plan?* If nothing else, we did have to reassess getting the boat to Portland (something we eventually accomplished via Marine Travelift; an overnight, Tilt-fueled session of de-rigging labor to prepare the mast for unstepping; and an eighteen-wheeler). Then we could tackle that learning-to-sail business.

⚓ ⚓ ⚓

Fifteen months later, we had sailed to San Francisco, a true sailor's haven. We anchored there and explored. We ate at a Chinese buffet and obtained a new iPod, a hefty but necessary expenditure for a couple of music fanatics. (Luckily, we'd thought to back up our music collection via external hard drive.) We hiked to the top of Mount Livermore, the highest point on Angel Island, and watched the Blue Angels' Fleet Week performance, followed by fireworks. We owned the ruins of Fort McDowell, if only for a day.

Crossing back under the Golden Gate Bridge and turning south toward Half Moon Bay, Jimmie made another decision: he declared he was no longer wearing his safety harness. It had tripped him up too many times on deck, times when he felt it would have been safer just to trust his balance and his firm resolve that "falling overboard is not an option." He took it off and never wore it again. Shortly thereafter, I did the same.

"I Look Pretty Put Together, Don't I?"

Not all of our choices were so stellar, however. Take a particular margarita-infused mission to get, ahem, more margaritas. Once we'd reached Capitola, on the north side of Monterey Bay, thoughts of stormy weather and brutal temperatures drifted further from our minds, the Aleutian Low's once-fierce cackle more a faint whisper, its fangs withdrawing rather than nipping at our heels. We started to think the occasional warmth we'd been experiencing might actually stick around. (We were even wrong.) After all, there were sunbathers on the beach! There were even swimmers in the anchorage, a Rob-recommended nook called Soquel Cove.

A string of hotel rooms called the Capitola Venetian, painted in almost absurdly beachy colors—teal, peach, salmon, canary yellow, robin's egg—sat along the waterfront like a handful of Jordan almonds flung onto the sand and topped with terra-cotta roof tiles. The scene looked tropical, the hotel vaguely Spanish, and, combined with people actually enjoying the weather, we thought, *Now we're in California for reals, baby.*

Naturally, we found this reason enough to paddle ashore for margarita fixins, tortilla chips, and—splurge-o-rama—a bag of ice! We also had some business to attend to at the Capitola post office, where we were expecting another check (from an overpaid final phone bill), sent general delivery via Shawn, the Dr. Gonzo to Jimmie's Raoul Duke. The post office was a bust (and we unhappily received a lecture about how general delivery is not for people like us, it's for people in the midst of relocating from one *permanent* address to another), but the little touristy esplanade made for a lovely walk, and we were still elated to be wearing T-shirts and enjoying the summery atmosphere.

Snacks and booze in tow, we unlocked our dinghy from one of the Capitola Pier supports and faced our first run-in with the Soquel Cove surf. Coming in that day, the back of the dinghy had spun out at the very end of our landing, and I actually stumbled and fell into the surf, but it was due more to my own clumsiness and slow-footed disembarkation than anything else.

Getting back over the surf that had tailspun Johnny Inflatable, however, was a bit trickier. Jimmie ended up having to wade out past the breakers—the supplies and me already aboard—and then slosh himself in and start paddling in one fell swoop. We managed, and neither of us really minded getting wet, impressed as we were with the natural drying properties of a clear, warm day.

Considering our diets consisted mainly of ramen, rice, and canned vegetables, it didn't take a whole lot to get us buzzing, alcohol-wise. Being an ex-bartender, I attempted to do us up right, with coarse salt and shaken drinks on ice, and boy were we celebratory! In fact, we had a dance party. Granted, a dance party aboard a twenty-seven-foot boat with minimal standing room is a tad challenging—as was keeping our balance in the incoming swell—but we managed, taking turns in the six-foot-clearance "hallway" and DJing on our brand-new iPod. Then the tequila bottle ran dry . . .

We seldom want the party to end, but in this case, keeping the party going necessitated going ashore. Rob had recommended a certain bar on the beachfront, Zelda's, and we figured in our reckless abandonment that we could afford a few late-night happy-hour margaritas (not exactly true) or at least make a liquor store run. We boarded Johnny Inflatable and headed in.

Whether the waves were more ferocious or our timing was off, I'm not sure. Regardless, once we neared the beach we were lofted atop the crest of an incoming breaker, teetering there insecurely for a moment while simultaneously rushing forward through the salty air. In a flash, we were sent tumbling into the water and pushed ashore, both of us finding ourselves completely soaked, our shore-landing boots full of sand and seawater, our exalted party-pride a wee bit crushed. We gathered our equipment and sat on the beach for a few minutes, reassessing the situation. It appeared the only thing we'd lost due to water damage was half a pack of cigarettes (the remainder of my Coos Bay impulse buy).

Jimmie, who tends to be more realistic than I, felt we should probably tackle the chore of getting back to the boat. A piece of kelp was draped down the side of his face whereas I, so far, was only wet (as opposed to being covered in seaweed). I was, however, drenched up to the chest and standing in soaking, sloshing rubber boots and jeans so heavy they threatened to succumb to gravity at any moment.

"I look pretty put together, don't I?" I said to Jimmie, smoothing the wild hairs around my face. My endless hope had me believing I could still make a liquor run. Only my bottom two-thirds were soaked. From across the counter, I rationalized, you might not even notice my salty situation.

"Are you serious?" he protested. "You're not going into a mini-mart like that." Grimacing, I reluctantly agreed. He was right: getting back was more important than getting more drunk.

We dumped the flooded dinghy as best we could and reloaded ourselves into it. We'd have to get going fast enough to make it over the crest of whatever breakers we met, but once past them, we'd be home free. This is not as simple as it might sound to, say, an experienced ocean kayaker—or any kayaker, in general. Our light, high-riding inflatable worked more like a dagger-shaped raft than a proper kayak, and it was easily bested by the rush of strong incoming waves. During the day, when we were also (usually) sober, we could watch the sets come in, look for the timing of the smallest waves, and make our launch accordingly. But Soquel Cove offered some of the biggest waves we'd dealt with as far as beach landing, and it was dark, and we'd been only slightly sobered by our first toss.

This time, we weren't just swamped and tossed. We totally capsized. The dinghy itself, our regular shoes, our bike lock, our oars, ourselves, all went tumbling into the white froth—upside-down, right side up, sucked under, spit out, tugged down by the weight of sand and water in our boots, toyed with by the overpowering surge of the tide, the briny taste of seawater filling our mouths and grinding out over our lips and teeth as we spit and gasped and lunged toward our belongings. Jimmie grabbed the dock line tied to our dinghy and slugged it ashore. I saw the oars and his shoes—a completely rad pair of white Adidas with green Velcro straps (he'd gotten Velcro specifically to have less to tangle on deck)—floating in a retreating wave. I flopped and slogged out toward them, grabbing a shoe and tucking it hard into my left armpit. I had hold of the oars. That was important. I had the oars. *Don't let go.*

I saw the other shoe! It was getting farther out to sea. I took weighted steps in its direction and got pummeled by a breaker and knocked on my ass, the first shoe dislodged from my pit's grasp, floating delicately away on a line of fuzzy white foam, toward its mate. Back on my feet, I considered making one last try for them. Jimmie loved those shoes, but that last hit really put me in my place. I often think I can take on anything, but I knew at that moment the next wave might be worse. I dragged myself toward the beach and joined Jimmie in the catching of breath. At least we had the dinghy. And the oars. And yes, it is worth noting that at least we hadn't drowned.

⚓ ⚓ ⚓

Looking back on it, I suppose this is another instance in which we *could* have died. That strikes me as a bit dramatic, but it is feasible. We were drunk, and the surf was violent. But we didn't die. And I don't think it can be attributed solely to luck—which is not to say our successes were entirely due to capability, either. They were due, more than anything, to attitude.

After I had put in my notice at the paper, the human resources lady asked me if I wanted COBRA, that circumstantial, temporary (and rather expensive) insurance option. I said no. "What if you fall overboard and get mangled by another boat's propeller or something awful like that?" she'd asked via e-mail. "I'll take my chances," was my response.

Like Jimmie, I had fully committed myself to never falling overboard. It was not an option. Neither of us, the entire trip, ever did fall overboard. A decision was made in each of our minds, outside the reality of whatever actual circumstances might be. We were careful, of course, but we were also committed.

In addition to determining not to end up in dangerous situations, our staying (relatively) safe was also largely achieved by not succumbing to any fear that was present. Riding the first steep waves we'd encountered on our way into Tillamook Bay at sunset, I thought, *This must be how it is. Other sailors have dealt with the reality of this situation, and we must, too. There is no changing the truth of these waves and the tilt of our boat, so we must face it. We must deal. To let fear prevail would be to lose.* And so we tried to assume the best. Around Mendocino, when we were terrified every second that things would get worse, we told ourselves, *This is clearly the worst it could get, and we're doing OK (read: still alive).* Then it would get worse.

Repeat previous thought. Keep doing OK. Keep telling yourself you'll make it.

I am not in any way saying we weren't truly scared for our lives. I know Jimmie was at least once (rounding Punta Gorda), and I definitely was twice—scared enough to try praying. We just didn't fully admit it, or talk about it, until far after the fact. Jimmie wrote a song on our trip called "Die Tonight," in which the refrain is, "I really might die tonight." (He later sings, "Turns out I'm alive!" which is how it felt, like a nice a surprise.) He wrote it once we had rounded Cabo San Lucas and were off the Pacific Ocean. I don't think it's a coincidence that he held onto that emotion until *after* a particular geographical point in the trip.

I don't really think you can *will* things into (or out of) reality in regard to the greater world—in regard to, say, weather—but I do think your attitude affects how you behave, whether you realize it or not. And how you behave affects what situations you end up in. It's a very important cause-and-effect relationship that has a for-real bearing on the course of your life. And it all begins with your outlook, with whether you think you're going to succeed or not.

We decided, when we set on the idea of sailing from Portland to La Paz, that we could do it. How could we think anything else? I mean, if we weren't yea-sayers, who would be?

I wasn't necessarily born with this outlook. I have tended to do well at most things—I am the intern who became the editor, I survived a crazy sailing trip, etc.—but I also second-guess myself plenty. Jimmie, on the other hand, believes anyone (including himself) can do anything at any given moment. It doesn't hurt that he's proven it time and time again.

He's the kind of guy who started his own cable access show, the "PWL" (Portland Wrestling League), complete with commentators, competitive posses full of creative characters, and a bona fide ring, just for fun—just because he loved old-school wrestling. He's the kind of guy whose best friend assumed he'd jumped overboard when our tiller snapped in Florence, that he'd latched onto our rudder and steered us from underwater. He's a little crazy like that—Jimmie, not Shawn. He just might do that, if it was necessary.

Jimmie wanted his own movie projector, so he built one. He also wanted an arcade machine, the stand-up type found in Pizza Huts and laundromats. So he hauled huge panels of particleboard up his apartment stairs, broke out a jigsaw, and went to work. Voilà! He had an arcade machine wired to play three-hundred-plus games. I painted a Space Invader on the side of it. Even with me, he got what he went after. He realized we should be together and he made it happen. And he was right.

Once, Jimmie decided he wanted to sleep on the roof. He was a student at the time, renting a big two-story house with some friends in outer-southeast Portland. The roof, like many, was an inverted V with slate shingles and a brick chimney. He didn't want to roll off in his sleep, naturally; when his roommates discovered him asleep up there, he had a rope tied around his waist at one end and lassoed around the chimney at the other. Sensible.

During the prep period before we left Portland, many hours were spent at Fred's Marina (Portland's cheapest!), sawing and painting, sewing and installing, measuring and fitting. One of these hours, Jimmie was working on switching out our main halyard (the line used to raise and lower the mainsail). Using a technique he'd read about online, where the new rope is attached to the old and fed through the cleats and pulleys from below, he had it nearly replaced. Then he reached for something a smidge too distant and the halyard escaped his grip. In a split second, the far end plummeted down, down, down, pulling the working end, the end he'd had hold of and needed to complete the job, straight up, swiftly. It was carried to the top of the mast, where it sat, stopped by the chock at the mast's tip.

Without thinking too much about it, Jimmie scrambled up the mast, hand over hand, Chuck Taylor over Chuck Taylor. He stopped on the spreaders, about halfway up, to briefly assess the situation. He had no rope around his waist this time, no safety line or harness of any kind, no bosun's chair. He decided to go for it. Up the remaining ten feet or so of mast he went. He was completely alone, figuring if he fell he'd try to aim for water. Atop, he sat there, collecting himself, feeling the strain of aching muscles in his hands and arms and calves. He put the halyard between his teeth and carefully slid back down. A live-aboard girl we often ran into, a hired hand working on a neighboring, piratical boat—all big and black with rope crow's nest ladders—must have observed the event. Passing him on the dock, she said, "We've got a bosun's chair if you ever want to borrow it."

That kind of can-do stuff really gets under your skin, especially when you choose to live with it, to be around it as much as possible. It is inspiring. It was love that inspired me to want to do the trip, but it was Jimmie, mostly, who made me believe I *could*. And, look, just like that, I did.

⚓ ⚓ ⚓

So, I'm not terribly surprised that we recovered our boat and oars and selves from the Capitola surf. Serendipity is a word that often comes to mind when recalling our voyage; things tended to go our way, at least when it counted. But I never underestimate the fact that we *believed* we'd be all right. We decided that was the truth, so it became true—drunken mouthfuls of saltwater notwithstanding.

I woke up the next morning with seaweed in my hair, a bed full of sand, and one hell of a headache. Lesson learned: you can't just run to the mini-mart when you get drunk on a boat.

"I Can't Tell You That Over the Phone."

Ever since I was sixteen, I've taken a birth control pill each afternoon at 3:30 PM, pretty much without fail. Three-thirty was an easy time to remember; I was in high school when it was decided upon, the qualifications being privacy and memorability. So I popped that pill each day on my way home from school, when I'd be alone in my car and doing the same thing at least five days out of seven. Three-thirty. Without fail.

I'd kept it up throughout my adult life. Three-thirty came along, and I'd rummage through my purse, push that tiny white disc through its foil backing, and swallow it down. Even if I was in the middle of wrapping a sub, taking an anthropology exam, or conducting an interview, I'd remember.

But living on a boat is weird, as is not having a job or a routine of any kind. So I missed a few pills. I couldn't plan to take it when I got up, as we'd sometimes embark on a leg of the trip at 5:00 or 6:00 AM, and while at anchor I'd occasionally stay in bed until noon. Which is why, when we ventured ashore the day after our dinghy-dumping to visit West Marine and (hopefully) pick up our mail, we swung by the Capitola Mall to find me a watch, one with an alarm on it.

Swinging by the Capitola Mall was basically swinging by the late '80s. It was a time warp. And we loved it. It was relatively empty, but not in that sad, endangered-commerce-species kind of way. Debbie Gibson's "Only in My Dreams" was playing over the mall speakers, and the amount of neon was, well, excessive. Naturally, we felt a Swatch was in order. Apparently, Swatches are very expensive, so we obtained a two-tone pink Armitron, which, to this day, I cannot set without the instruction manual. My mind is simply unable to recall the exact intricate pattern of buttons to press, hold, release, repress. Later, when traveling cross-country in a camper van (a post-sailing Amy-and-Jimmie odyssey) and frequently changing time zones, I still didn't memorize the sequence. It's that complex.

But the Armitron successfully kept my conception prevention in check, so, ridiculous instructions or not, it was a success. We continued (and still continue) our happy existence as a mere duo, leaving procreation to the less equipped (all you need is a watch and some pills!) and, you know, people who actually want children.

⚓ ⚓ ⚓

Our visit to West Marine was less fruitful.

When we couldn't find a tiller in San Francisco, of all places (I mean, WTF? It's the "City by the Bay"!), we gave up hope of ever finding one in stock at a marine supply store. What San Fran *did* have was numerous unsecured Wi-Fi networks, so, via the magic of the Internet, we ordered a brand-new tiller from WestMarine.com, to be picked up at their Santa Cruz location. We'd traveled 639 nautical miles without one—or without a fully intact one—and done fairly well, but we were looking forward to finally chucking our rotted old stub and moving forth with something resembling solid wood.

And, yes, the Santa Cruz West Marine had our tiller. But we'd also ordered a roll of "dry bunk," a mildew-battling absorbent liner that works wonders under sailboat mattresses, and it was that, we learned after walking two and a half miles from Capitola to Santa Cruz, they did not have. It had mistakenly been sent to the wrong store. We'd have to come back.

Of course, the salespeople at West Marine didn't realize that we'd walked from Soquel Cove, or that we'd just gotten dumped, hard, by the Capitola surf the night before. They didn't know what "coming back" entailed for us. It wasn't even easy for us to follow their suggestion to call ahead and see if the dry bunk had arrived before returning. We convinced them to e-mail us once the product had arrived, as e-mail required less stalwart Internet than Skype.

We returned to the boat a tad defeated, yet comforted by two very important discoveries. First, while purchasing beverages at a Circle K, I realized it was very much in my power to steal liquid creamer from the coffee bar—like twenty little cups' worth (we always counted my booty). We'd been using powder the whole trip, which is OK, but liquid creamer in French vanilla and Irish crème was far more exciting. While I would never steal something that's actually for sale, I have no problem lifting, say, a coffee mug from Denny's or a neat glass ashtray from a hotel room or, in this case, complimentary condiments in uncomplimentary amounts.

The other discovery redefined our stay in Soquel Cove. Upon returning to the dock, where we'd haphazardly secured our dinghy to a dock support using the impromptu combination of a safety line and auxiliary padlock (our usual bicycle lock had drowned in the preceding night's wipeout), I spotted a crucial gateway. It was used, during the day, by Capitola Boat and Bait, a business that rents motorized skiffs and kayaks to tourists. They had a small hoist that pulled the boats out of the water, coupled with a ladder and landing for patrons to climb from water to pier. On a whim, I walked down the pier and pushed on the gate to find it *unlocked*.

There was a bar at the end of the pier, just a short distance from the gate, but we hoped neither the bartenders nor customers would notice a bright orange dinghy being hauled past and stuffed down the stairs. Launching from farther out seemed such an appealing option compared to battling the surf again, so we walked with Johnny Inflatable, as if we were supposed to be there, down the pier, through that swinging doorway, and onto that most precious landing below. Jimmie, holding Johnny's dock line, dropped him over the side and down into the water, a shifting distance of five to ten feet below, depending on the waves. Then, we climbed down the ladder with our oars and boarded him. We were out past the breakers! Beyond the curling tunnels of foam that had handed us our soaking wet asses the night before! We were paddling, easily, atop the rising and falling swell toward our main vessel, toward home. We were thankful. And dry.

⚓ ⚓ ⚓

Drinking our coffee with liquid creamer the next morning, we naturally began to ponder what other quality-of-life-improving items I could thieve from convenience stores. That's when the potential of mayo packets struck us.

Up until now, for about two and a half months, the only sandwiches we'd eaten were peanut butter and jelly. Given our restrictions of refrigeration and money, it was our only option. Tuna, we knew, is canned and cheap, but we had nothing to mix it with. By the grace of the 7-Elevens and Circle Ks of central California, however, we would soon have individual, non-spoiling rations of mayonnaise, as well as pickle relish! Our underway lunch menu had literally doubled. "Oh, thank heaven" is right.

We'd yet to receive the "dry bunk: go!" e-mail, so we focused on our other main goal. Jimmie secured a decent Internet connection and got the Capitola post office on the horn. Here's how the exchange went:

POSTAL WORKER: Capitola post office.

JIMMIE: Yeah, I'm expecting a letter general delivery from Oregon. I was wondering if you could tell me if it's arrived. My name's Jimmie Buchanan.

PW: General Delivery? Uh, yeah. Hang on a sec. I'll check.

DISTANT VOICE: You *can't* inform someone of general delivery status over the phone!

DISTANT PW VOICE: Why not?

DISTANT VOICE: That's the rule. General delivery can only be dealt with in person. And it's only for people who are relocating from one *permanent* address to another. Got it?

DISTANT PW VOICE: Yeah.

PW: Thanks for holding. I'm sorry, sir, I can't tell you that over the phone.

JIMMIE: Really?

PW: Yes, I apologize. I can't give the status of general delivery post over the phone. You'll just have to come in. [*Then, hushedly*] It's here.

JIMMIE: OK. Thanks a lot!

⚓ ⚓ ⚓

And so we left Capitola, up one roll of dry bunk; down one pair of shoes; a newly deposited check in our account; a pink plastic watch, with alarm; one 43½-inch-long ash-and-mahogany tiller, type B; a replacement dinghy lock; several cans of tuna; a new handheld VHF that could transmit *and* receive (a splurge); and about thirty assorted mayo and relish packets.

"How Long's Your Boat, a Twenty-Nine?"

At San Simeon, we not only missed Rob's "CASTLE," I didn't even get off the boat. The waves sweeping around San Simeon Point blasted forth as if a Bunyanesque gun were firing cannon-sized bullets underwater. And their breaking on the beach looked impassable. Jimmie took to Johnny Inflatable and paddled over to a nearby pier, but there was no ladder, no stairs, nothing. As intriguing as William Randolph Hearst's former estate sounded—the magnificent pools! the dismantled private zoo! the wine cellars and grand rooms!—we would have to pass. Had we realized adult admission was twenty-five dollars each, we wouldn't have gone anyway.

But San Simeon was not entirely uneventful. We met our first in a line of really likeable sailors here. The rest were Californians; these were Canadians.

We'd seen their boat before, a small red-hulled sloop named *Ladybug*. It had a matching dinghy painted with black ladybug spots, and soon after Jimmie returned from his investigative loop around the anchorage, it paid *Cotton* a visit. A fair, balding man probably ten years our senior introduced himself and his brunette wife, sitting behind him with a laptop in a large Ziploc bag on her lap. "How long's your boat?" the fellow asked, quickly adding, "A twenty-nine?"

"Twenty-seven," Jimmie responded.

"No kidding," the man scratched his head, butterscotch-colored wisps lifting in the breeze. "Well, that's too bad," he said genially, explaining that they hadn't encountered anyone on a boat smaller than their own twenty-nine-footer thus far.

We saw them again, en route to Morro Bay the next day. They were sailing along, using a spinnaker in the extremely light wind, just as we were debating throwing on the motor. We gave in. And it's a good thing, as the anchorage was a confusing mess of moored boats and the entry was narrow, rough, and fog-shrouded; we needed that waning daylight. Several hours later, we noticed *Ladybug* motoring into the anchorage, its running lights fuzzy in the smeared, pitch-black night. *Those Canadians are hardcore*, we said to ourselves.

Morro Bay, coincidentally, is the hometown of our favorite know-no-limits small-boat sailor, Robin Lee Graham. Graham had sailed around the world in a twenty-four-foot boat, *Dove*, beginning at the age of sixteen. He took five years doing it, stopping all along the way and really experiencing the world he was rounding. And he did it all with only himself to rely on. Unlike these modern circumnavigators, teenagers aboard ever-more-ridiculous boats competing to beat each other's records, Graham took his time—and he did it without technology. He navigated entirely via sextant, and he was damn good at it. No smartphones, no weather faxes, no satellite Internet, no easy escape routes. And he did it first, as far as teenagers go. No one can ever be him again.

Though our journey was admittedly *much* smaller in scale, and we did rely on satellite technology for navigation, Graham was the sailor we felt most like. He was someone who sailed just because he wanted to do it, despite odds and means. He was very young, he had an incredibly small boat, and his main source of currency was trading Mickey Mouse T-shirts and Bic pens with Americanophilic islanders. Also, our spirits were similar—our open-minded approach and our belief in possibility. We all wanted to see the world we were traveling, and did. And there was love: he met the love of his life on his voyage, and we made ours because of it. His intentions were innocent and good. And he succeeded. He was our hero.

Bernard Moitessier, the French sailing guru who competed in—and bucked—the first ever solo, nonstop, round-the-world race (the *Sunday Times* Golden Globe), was perhaps more our idol. He was someone to look up to more than relate to, a man so spiritually connected with the sea that it was his home more than any other place. He left that historic race in 1969 not because he was losing—in fact, his odds for winning one or both titles (for first and fastest completion) were quite good—but because he became disenchanted with the concept of a sponsored competition. And he wanted to keep sailing.

In contrast, Robin Lee Graham, by the time he was finished, wanted nothing more than to be done. He moved to Montana, a landlocked, mountainous cathedral of land. He was over it. He used the sea to do what he wanted, to challenge himself and to travel. And then he moved on. That's how we felt. It wasn't a love affair, it was a means to an end.

It was in the youthful spirit of Graham—and on a pretty wholesome task—that we spent much of our time in Morro Bay: preparing for Halloween. We acquired plastic jack-o'-lanterns, an array of miniature candy bars, and autumn spices for mulling wine. We began making plans for a horror movie marathon. We bought pumpkin beer and plastic "skele-mugs." We didn't plan on spending Halloween in Morro Bay, but it was our favorite holiday and we wanted to be prepared.

Little did we know when we sailed out past Morro Rock, a 581-foot volcanic plug rising out of an otherwise flat coast, we were headed for one of the longest and most disheartening stops of our trip: San Luis Obispo Bay.

"Don't Worry About It."

After our experience rounding Cape Mendocino, we took Point Conception's nickname as the "Cape Horn of the Pacific" severely to heart. As legend has it, conditions are always "plus-ten" at Conception. The fifteen-knot wind we might be perfectly comfortable in would become twenty-five knots or stronger once we were actually rounding that conspicuous elbow in California's nether half, where a geologic cookie monster had taken a big, fat bite out of the Golden State, leaving the Channel Islands as crumbs floating nearby.

As anxious as we were, we also wanted very much to get it over with. In fact, we initially tried to depart close to twenty-four hours after arriving at Port San Luis, a harbor on the western side of San Luis Obispo Bay. So you can imagine the gloominess that swept over our twenty-seven-foot world as we spent more than two weeks—eighteen days to be exact—stuck at the stop right *before* Conception.

We planned to leave SLO (as the locals say) in the late afternoon so as to arrive at Conception in the dead of night, when wind and sea are often calm. The forecast agreed: the next day called for light northwest winds throughout the day and afternoon, dying off and switching to even lighter winds overnight. Perfect. If all went well, that'd leave us having to motor a bit around the point itself before arriving at San Miguel, the northernmost Channel Island, in the early morning. Then we'd anchor and hit the hay. That was the plan.

I prepared some rice and canned veggies with Kung Pao sauce for dinner, and we took our antsy selves to bed. We would refuel and re-water the next day and depart around 5:00 PM.

We woke to thick fog in the anchorage, which might have been in our best interest, as we seemed to be anchored in the middle of a mooring field, where we probably weren't allowed. The boats next to us were almost all teeming with sea lions—huge, brown, blubbery bodies lazing about on the decks of sailboats and in the large cockpits of fishing vessels. They were in the water, too, menacing flotillas prowling in spirals and figure eights all around the anchorage.

It became obvious, looking around, that sea lions were an epidemic here. Many boats had bright orange netting stretched around the perimeters of their decks, all along the safety lines. One large troller, the *Eleanor Marie*, had a fisherman "scarecrow" of sorts, a stuffed pair of rubber overalls strung up on its pilothouse, complete with fishing hat and blaring radio, but the sea lions were not deterred. They hung about the *Eleanor Marie* as if it were their own, basking on its decks and pushing their flab up against its side rails and pulpits.

An angry seaman, presumably the owner of Miss *EM*, came out in a motor dinghy at some point and shooed them off, yelling and waving his arms in desperation. The sea lions reluctantly dove into the surrounding water at a leisurely pace, as if to indicate their complete lack of respect. Only a few hours later, several had reboarded.

Later that day, when we dinghied to the gas dock, we met another perturbed mooring-field tenant. He said thousands of dollars of damage had been done to his boat thanks to sea lions on a rampage, and he was furious with SLO port officials for not reimbursing him for the damages. He invited us to share a whiskey with him aboard this fantastically demolished vessel, but we declined. He seemed a smidge crazy, and we needed to get going.

Something on the charts covering our next leg had been bothering us, though. Throughout the waters leading up to Conception and its smaller, preceding point, Arguello, were areas marked as "Vandenberg AFB Missile Testing 'Danger Zones.'" Imagine sailing along, approaching the door to Southern Californian paradise, when, out of the blue, your boat is shot to pieces by an air force missile. We pictured this grotesque sight in our minds and sought reassurance that it wouldn't become a reality. The scruffy young clerk at the gas dock shrugged and said, "Don't worry about it."

Apparently the missile tests are pretty carefully scheduled; he said we'd know if there was an upcoming launch planned. *How we would know?* we were left to speculate. We stopped at a pay phone and tried calling a 1-800-Vandenberg-type hotline we'd found online, thinking there might be an informational recording like those for movie times at a theater. No such luck. We'd have to take the gas station guy's word for it.

At around 4:30 PM, we pulled up anchor and motored over to a small, free-floating "work dock," the perimeter of which was discouragingly decorated with chain-link fence. Ever paranoid about doing something wrong (or illegal), we'd asked while ashore if it was all right to refill our water there, and the same scruffy attendant told us to "go for it." As we approached this floating concrete hub of numerous hoses, a vacuum, and power outlets, I saw none other than a giant brown sea lion lounging right where I planned to hop off and tie our dock line.

A sign came into view: HELP KEEP SEA LIONS OFF THE WORK DOCK. REMEMBER TO CLOSE THE GATES. At least the inner area was sea lion–free.

This was already a complicated landing, as I usually jumped off the port bow, but here we were forced to approach from starboard. I already felt a little ambidextrously challenged, and the surrounding chain-link fence didn't really offer anywhere *to* jump. I could try to clear it and land in the middle of the dock (a rather ridiculous notion) or cling to the small area outside the fence while cleating us off. To be fair, there was about a foot of dock outside the fence, but that one foot, at the moment, was completely filled with shiny, whiskery, potentially violent sea lion.

Thankfully, as Jimmie veered our bow toward the landing, our looming foe was startled into the water, and I leapt onto that foot-wide perimeter. No prob. All we needed to do now was ward off the threatening wildlife long enough to top off our water and get out.

"I *Steel* Don't See Why You'd Wanna Travel This Way."

We set out in a crisp breeze listening to one of our favorite Portland bands, Graves. The sun was on our starboard quarter, and we were comfortably sailing along as it dipped below the horizon and sucked its warmth down with it.

A heavy fog also rolled in, leaving us motoring toward Point Arguello in a strange, dark blankness. We strained our eyes to see anything, a buoy, another boat's running lights, an offshore oil-drilling platform. Nothing. Just blank, dark drab. So we put on the audiobook version of *Live and Let Die* (we were in a serious Bond phase) and exercised our patience.

This was fine. The wind was low to dead, and we were motoring, on schedule, toward Point Conception. If we had to round it in dense fog, so be it. As time and some twenty nautical miles passed on, the wind picked up. We killed the audiobook right after CIA agent Felix Leiter told Bond in a thick Texas drawl, "I *steel* don't see why you'd wanna travel this way."

It was time to check the weather again.

Our pleasant overnight breezes had become a "gale watch" beginning at 7:00 AM. It was currently about 11:00 PM. We'd been sailing for nearly six hours. We were only about two-thirds of the way to San Miguel but at least halfway to Point Conception, probably closer, which was a lot to give up on. *Could we outrun the weather?* We began crunching numbers, hoping we could arrive at San Miguel before 7:00 AM, or perhaps cut the trip short and duck into Cojo Anchorage, right behind Point Conception.

In an added bit of complication, we weren't sure exactly when 7:00 AM was, as far as the NOAA was concerned. Time was set to change for daylight saving on this very date, and our GPS, which is obviously fed info via satellite, was in conflict with the weather reports. Had the NOAA not yet "fallen back"? Was 7:00 AM to them really 6:00 AM to us? That would give us even less time to beat the imposing forecast. But we were halfway there! What's more, it was only a gale "watch," not a warning, making it even harder to enact that heartbreaking U-turn.

But we did enact it. We had vowed not to end up in another life-threatening mega-cape fiasco, and we meant it. When we came about, we were thirty nautical miles from SLO and fifty-eight from the Channel Islands. Just turning around isn't as easy as it sounds, though. Our return trip, because it was aimed *into* everything, made for six hours of pure, wet, body-aching hell.

Sailing into the wind, when it's heavy, is always worse than sailing downwind in the same conditions. Once we turned, we had to reduce sail, struggle more with steering, and put up with waves constantly splashing in our increasingly salt-crusted faces. Our progress was also slower thanks to the onrushing waters; going four knots over two knots of current equals six knots in your favor, whereas the same setup in reverse (i.e., sailing upwind or against the current) leaves you making only two measly knots per hour. We were also heeling heavily to starboard, which makes everything, even something as simple as sitting, hard. To remain upright and stable, every back muscle must be flexed—in this case, for six hours.

Eventually, the wind picked up even more and we decided to bare-pole it, taking our last bit of sail down and motoring the rest of the way. Jimmie had the unfortunate job of pulling down and securing the mainsail on a very wet, very tilted deck. In the midst of doing so, he lost both his San Francisco Giants ball cap and his hold of the main halyard.

Jimmie watched in horror as, with each lashing movement of our boat on the waves, the blue-and-white line proceeded to spin circles around the mast, like red on a barbershop pole, inching its way ever upward. Wearing his treadless, beat-up old Converse (reinstated after the loss of the beloved Velcro Adidas), he leapt up toward that dangling shackle and miraculously grasped it before it flew out of reach.

It was just then that the oncoming wind caught under the bill of the aforementioned hat and sent it sailing right off Jimmie's shaggy head. With the mainsail shackle in his mouth and a death grip on the mast, he reached out to starboard and snagged it in midair, saving it from a soggy demise on the ocean floor.

Back in the cockpit, he took on the crummy job of hand-steering against the mounting wind waves. Jeeves had basically given up the ghost after Mendocino, joining our iPod on the list of "terror-ride" casualties. We'd still hook him up and occasionally get some cooperation in light conditions, but we'd been steering mostly by hand since Shelter Cove, and Jimmie was our rough-sea helmsman.

Jimmie did everything hard. He took care of sail changing and sail reefing. (I changed the headsail on my own only once, and not until we were on the Sea of Cortez.) He was always the one to pull out the dinghy, inflate it, deflate it, pack it up, put it back. He filled the gas while underway. He deployed and pulled up the anchor. He maintained the outboard and was the one who crawled down into the hull when the water filter had to be changed. I contributed, don't get me wrong. I cooked and sewed and kept a positive attitude. And I did cut a giant fish's head off with a hacksaw and then gut it. That was the one hard thing I did.

⚓ ⚓ ⚓

I recall going down to pee once on this depressing return and looking, in the half light of the head, at a corkboard collage I'd made of our friends and family. Wall space is slim in a twenty-seven-foot boat, and the collage ended up behind the toilet simply because that's where there was room. So we saw our loved ones—smiling at the camera from mountaintops and forests, eating cotton candy in front of the Space Needle, playing Rock Band in a suburban basement—every time we hit the head.

As I wrestled all my rain gear and warm layers down to my knees and sat on the tiniest toilet in the tiniest bathroom in the world, I saw them reflected back in the mirror and I thought, *My God, if they could see me now, if they could see us now . . . what would they think? Would they have ever realized it would sometimes be like this?* I'm sure they assumed it would sometimes suck. So did we. But it's different, actually sitting there with your three pairs of pants down, leaning your weight against the direction of the sea and wind to keep the toilet seat from sliding off the bowl, looking at the smiling faces of your friends and family. You imagine where they are, too, and it seems so nice. You imagine them warm and dry—and level, for Chrissake—and you wonder what the hell you're doing. Then you go out into the cockpit and see Jimmie, the love of your life, and you remember.

⚓ ⚓ ⚓

So we sat in the cockpit, bracing ourselves until the sea and wind began, finally, to calm down a bit. Limbs aching with fatigue, wits at their end, we decided to give Jeeves a crack at the helm—and he agreed. For two hours, the last third of a miserable rehashing of water we'd already covered and wanted so badly to leave behind, Jeeves came out of retirement, substitute piloting in the name of our sanity. Thank God. So we just sat, watching as the multicolored boats of Port San Luis appeared in the distance, gradually growing to actual size like magic sponge animals emerging from thin plastic capsules in a giant bathtub.

It was still dark as we approached, and patchy cotton-ball fog stretched thin across the surface of the water, obscuring the scene.

Lights along the piers and shore reflected a blurry confusion of Vaseline sparkles on the dark water, and we could barely make out mooring balls and low-lying boats. It seemed too risky to anchor there (we couldn't see, and we weren't supposed to be there anyway), so we reconsidered and dropped our big fat claw anchor in a more exposed patch of water between two piers, one a research pier used by "Cal Poly" (California Polytechnic State University), the other a pleasure pier shooting perpendicularly from Avila Beach.

Once our anchor was set and the outboard raised out of its brackish realm and finally relieved of duty, Jimmie went on deck to sort out the main halyard's fucked-uppedness. I made hot chocolate and peanut butter sandwiches after reestablishing some order in the cabin, which was cluttered with wet sail bags, raingear, and a chaos of slid-off seat cushions.

When he came back down, we turned on the weather. Daylight-saving confusions aside, the arrival of the impending strong weather had been pushed back from 7:00 to 9:00 AM and changed from a gale watch to a small craft advisory. Dejected, cold, and totally exhausted, we put the mast light on—even though the sun was coming up—and went to bed.

"Mr. Rick's! What's Your Favorite Color?"

More than two weeks later, Jimmie and I could be found drunkenly karaokeing at Mr. Rick's, a cheese-dick SLO tourist bar. Shortly after our attendance there, we became a pair of crumpled bodies on the beach, one wearing glasses that became more and more warped the farther its face portion sunk into the sand. And, once awoken, the female counterpart to Mr. Bent Glasses could be found puking over the rails of Avila Pier and sobbing uncontrollably. I was scared.

At the time, what I claimed to be scared of was our rowing the dinghy back to the boat, something we'd done countless times by now. We had the dinghy tied up to a landing at the end of the pier, so we were far past the challenge of launching over the crashing surf, and the sea was in a pretty average, big-smooth-swell state. There wasn't much to be afraid of. But I had passed out drunk on the beach, as had Jimmie, and I was still rather inebriated and irrational upon waking. I was terrified that we were too drunk to be executing a return to *Cotton*, and dreadful images plagued my boozy consciousness.

I said this is what I was scared of. But I think perhaps I had been scared for a long time, scared of many things—of howling wind, of even small whitecaps, of the constant potential for oncoming weather to defeat us, either by quarantine in a bay like San Luis or, more literally, by consuming our flesh, devouring our mortal bodies, making us no more. Despite all the incomparable joy I'd experienced thus far, I had also been nervous for three months straight.

In my drunkenness, all this fear and nervousness was manifesting itself in one single dinghy trip: twenty yards, maybe, from pier to sailboat. So simple. Yet I saw us flipping and sputtering drunkenly about in the salty water. I saw tragedy. It took the form of another saline liquid and filled my eyes. I was blind to anything else.

Jimmie rowed us back safely, and we boarded our home and passed out in private as opposed to the likely-to-get-us-thrown-in-the-drunk-tank public beach. We were excessively sandy, and Jimmie's glasses were *super* crooked. He hoped, by applying gentle pressure, to bend them back into a usable form without snapping the plastic. He succeeded. Good thing, as he had no backup pair.

⚓ ⚓ ⚓

But how did this fiasco begin? you might be wondering. How did we end up passed out drunk on the beach? Why were we patronizing such an establishment as Mr. Rick's in the first place? There's an easy answer: we were drunk, and it was Karaoke Thursday.

Now, Mr. Rick's isn't exactly what you'd call our kind of bar. Portland is huge on karaoke, and it's become almost obnoxiously popular, to the point where you can't even get a song in without bribing the KJ in tips or finding some unknown establishment that hasn't yet been taken over by the Portland hipsterati. Nevertheless, the bars are usually pretty cool: dives, standard bar bars, or old Chinese restaurants looking to make an extra buck and bring in a fresh crowd.

Mr. Rick's, on the other hand, is the kind of place where spring breakers go to attempt getting laid, or at least shamelessly bump 'n' grind on the dance floor until hauled home by their frat or sorority siblings. It's the kind of place that offers huge, expensive, and hardly alcoholic novelty drinks garnished with plastic sharks and miniature palm trees. During the peak season, I can only imagine it's the type of place that's chock-full of tube tops and fake breasts and orange tans and lots and lots of hair product. It's the kind of place where the bartenders offer to let you do shots off their bodies and know how to tie the stems of cherries into knots with their tongues. It is a vacation bar, and it's not at all the kind of place we would normally find ourselves.

Yet, there we were, downing whiskey rocks (Jimmie) and whiskey sours (me), and singing our greasy-haired and grubbily dressed little asses off. We capped the evening with a stage-strutting rendition of our unofficial sailing trip theme song, Starship's "Nothing's Gonna Stop Us Now," and tacked on some obnoxious "We sailed here from Portland!" shout-outs before relinquishing the mics. We then paid our tab and promptly left the bar, which was closing and therefore kicking everyone out, at which point we sat down on the beach and immediately blacked out.

The rest has been told.

We did have one additional interaction with Mr. Rick's, however. The 2008 presidential election was approaching, and we were interested in going ashore to watch the ballots add up on live TV. I had been researching the area online and eventually resorted to calling Mr. Rick's to inquire as to whether or not they planned on showing any election coverage. We had yet to enter the place at that time, but we still had a pretty good idea what the scene was all about. The enthusiastic fellow who answered burst into what I assume was supposed to be a playful attempt at flirting with whatever bimbo he figured was on the other end of the line. "Mr. Rick's! What's your favorite color?" he asked with charisma-soaked sleaze. I didn't know what to say. I hadn't expected that. I sat, quiet for a moment, my mouth agape. Then, not knowing how to reply to such a greeting, I hung up.

"Dead Calm or We Won't Go!"

We ended up listening to the election coverage on the radio. And when Obama said in his acceptance speech, "To those who are huddled around radios in the forgotten corners of our world . . . ," we couldn't help but feel he was speaking to us, even though I'm sure we weren't exactly the folks he or his speechwriter envisioned. Regardless, a forgotten corner is exactly what we longed to make SLO. But devastating forecast after devastating forecast came crackling over the radio, and we refused to risk it. We did not set out to get ourselves killed. We set out to be together. And the former most certainly denies success of the latter.

So we waited. And waited. And waited—until finally we were dealt something we thought we could handle. But this time we'd take baby steps. Rather than sail straight from SLO to San Miguel, the closest of the Channel Islands, we decided to get a running start by sailing the twenty-two nautical miles to Point Sal, hospitably located in Vandenberg AFB Missile Testing Danger Zone #1. We'd stop there until midnight, then round Conception in the dead of night and tuck into Cojo.

The forecast we were so ready to throw ourselves into was, basically, for no wind at all. As such, we were fully prepared and looking forward to motoring the entire trip. (See how our goals and ambitions shifted? On the Columbia River, it was "Sail or nothing!" At the "Cape Horn of the Pacific," it was "Dead calm or we won't go!")

We were also almost out of water. Again. We measured this via a long, rigid piece of clear tubing we'd bought at a hardware store in Coos Bay; insert it through a small vent hole in our water tank, submerge it in whatever was down there, then put a finger on the end, like snatching a sip of milkshake in the tip of a straw. Four inches of water in a twenty-gallon tank lasted us about two weeks. We had less than an inch. We'd have to swing by Port San Luis before heading for Point Sal, something we weren't all that thrilled about.

Despite the fact that sea lions would surely be swarming the service docks like ants on an abandoned Cheeto, our plan was to tie up to one (a dock, not a sea lion), where I would fill the water while Jimmie rowed ashore for gas. This plan was thwarted when, approaching the intended service dock, we saw two masts, meaning the dock was at capacity, a boat on each side. Our Avila Beach anchorage was far enough away that we couldn't have possibly known that upon pulling up anchor, but now we had nowhere to go.

Jimmie threw Johnny Inflatable over the side and lowered himself in, gas cans in tow. I handed him a bright yellow walkie-talkie—a must-have item to our juvenile-adventurer minds—and he set off for the gas dock. Perhaps by the time he returned, one of the boats would be gone.

I was motoring aimlessly outside the mooring field, waiting for his call, when Jimmie's voice came over the line: "Mister Lingerie to Red Rooster; Red Rooster, come in." (We had already decided on "handles," mine an old nickname inspired by my reddish hair, Jimmie's a reference to the anime series *Macross*.)

"This is Red Rooster," I said. "Go ahead."

"Those two masts belong to a ketch. Come pick me up by the big blue troller."

A ketch! This whole time, I'd been aimlessly motoring around when the two masts were on the same boat! I scooped Jimmie up, and we headed over. What sea lions hadn't been driven off by the ketch scattered at our approach, but once we were almost close enough to swing in alongside the platform, we saw a small hard-bottom dinghy tied right where we intended to go. "Fuck it," Jimmie proclaimed. "Let's just go."

We'd had enough of San Luis Obispo Bay, of Port San Luis and Avila Beach, of neighboring towns Shell Beach and Pismo Beach and Arroyo Grande. We wanted OUT! We didn't care if we had no water; we didn't care if we didn't know the next place we could get water. We didn't CARE! San Luis Obispo had had its fishy central-Californian hands wrapped tightly around our necks for too long—TOO LONG! We'd come, left, gotten spat back by an alleged gale, re-anchored at least four times, spent Halloween, my twenty-ninth birthday, and Election Day there. We'd even attended the Pismo Beach Marching Band Review and Drumline Competition, for Chrissake. We were like residents. And we were at our wits' end!

So we left without water. Hard-bottom dinghy and two-masted ketch and sea lions and Point Conception, be damned! OK, not Point Conception, I take that back. *(Don't be angry, oh horror of the Pacific coast!)* But the rest of you, be damned! Our stay with you is over! Even if the next spot was Missile Testing Danger Zone #1, any place was better than here.

⚓⚓⚓

And so we were off, sailing in a light wind toward Point Sal, determined—yet again—to get our asses around Point Conception and through the door to fantastical *Southern* California. We'd been told two months ago that this was where the whole world changes, and dammit, we were ready to feel that change. Twenty-two-point-six nautical miles later, we were anchored at Point Sal, taking our planned break and waiting for complete calm, when we would finally set out on that long-awaited leg around Conception itself.

Point Sal didn't wind up being the most accommodating of anchorages. It was rolly and exposed, but it was only a waiting room. We prepped coffee and tuna sandwiches for our overnight voyage, and I made dinner: pasta with pesto sauce, a meal that would've been impossible without Jimmie's help on "roll control." I'd manage whatever was on the fire while he took charge of the tools and ingredients-in-waiting on the table. We were like a brilliant surgical team. In a kitchen that was repeatedly being picked up by an aquamarine forklift and dropped on its side with a clunk, we made pasta.

"Wooden spoon, please."

"Check."

I'd stir, add a touch of oil, shake in some oregano. "Mushrooms."

"De-lidded and drained," Jimmie proudly announced, handing 'em over.

An added challenge to making this particular dinner was our impending lack of water. As the trip went on, I became more and more adept at water conservation. Once we entered Mexico, information on the amenities available at ports was sparse, as were the stops themselves. In this case, we were probably going to be able to get water at Santa Barbara, the first stop after Cojo Anchorage, and according to the forecast we were counting on, we'd be able to sail on to Santa Barbara any upcoming day we chose. But, as we'd learned all too well, the weather can be fickle, so perhaps we'd be stuck at Cojo, as we were stuck in SLO, as we were stuck in Tillamook Bay, Coos Bay, and so on. So we learned to conserve.

That particular evening at Point Sal, our pasta was boiled mostly in reserved juice from canned vegetables, and our powdered sauce mix was liquefied by the same means. I caught the hot veggie juice-water under the colander when draining the pasta and whisked it right back into that packet of dried cream and basil. I probably depressed the foot pump that operated our galley's sink a total of four times that night. And we supplanted much drinking water, in general, with box wine, another crafty conservation technique. We did have a coffee habit, however, and we'd discovered much earlier that saltwater coffee is pretty disgusting (even though I drank almost a whole cup before admitting it).

We lay down at 6:30 PM and spent the next several hours trying to relax while simultaneously bracing ourselves against the constant undulation of the swell, the task for which the term "roll control" was actually coined. Roll control, for me, involved a specific splaying of arms and legs in a wide, almost swastika-like arrangement. The strategy is very similar to the design of catamarans: greater overall breadth discourages tipping and rolling. Together, we probably looked like some extra-limbed mutant frog airing out its crotch and pits.

At 1:30 AM, our zombie-selves crawled out of the V-berth, slit-eyed and bleary and half convinced they'd slept. Dead of night. Now was the time. So, after a quick Pop-Tart and a cup of coffee, we weighed anchor and left Missile Testing Danger Zone #1 in our peaceful wake.

⚓ ⚓ ⚓

As expected, the sea was slippery calm, the wind nil. I imagined a gigantic black garbage bag spread over this section of the earth, held in place by mysterious beings out of sight over the horizon, beings who ever so gently moved the edges up and down with a soft, buoyant motion that echoed out over that vast surface, reflecting white flashes of moonlight.

The unknown still attempted to balk our hopes, chattering at our heels, whispering softly down the hair-raised backs of our necks: "Pssst! Hey, you two. Yeah, you, you wannabe adventurers. Hey! What if the wind picks up? What if the sea *grows*? What if things . . . *change*? What if? What if? WHAT IF?!" But we ignored it. In fact, we drowned it. We put on music so loud it overtook the sound of the sea itself, and the sound of all its little taunting demons: the wind demons and wave demons and swooshing, mysterious sound demons, the foreboding gusts that sent shivers of worry all through my body. Drowned them out.

We put on the Killers' *Hot Fuss*—a pop-rock masterpiece full of emotive and, at times, uplifting lyrics (i.e., "Everything / Will be all right")—and we turned it UP. The music boomed out over the surface of the water, over that great stretch of shiny black plastic, past the missile testing grounds, past Point Sal and the sea lion–ravaged boats of San Luis Obispo, through the bumping concrete walls of Mr. Rick's and beyond. That night, when the unknown hissed, "What if?" we said, "Huh? What? Who's that? Oh, I'm sorry, I CAN'T HEAR YOU!"

⚓ ⚓ ⚓

So the night went on, with calm black waters rushing alongside our hull and music blaring over the surface, echoing to other parts of the world. Perhaps some afternoon beachcomber in Chōshi, Japan, fifteen hours into the future, heard Brandon Flowers crooning the words "Smile like you mean it" and followed his command. We did, too.

As the sun rose up over that dreaded corner of land, we smiled the most earnest smiles, our faces lit by gleaming yellow, the ocean around us turning to liquid silver, mimicking the amorphous chrome that formed and reformed Schwarzenegger's infuriating *Terminator 2* opponent, the evil T-1000. (This time of day was henceforth referred to as "the *T2* hour.")

Point Conception itself was a broad patch of green grass, like a high school football field tipped to a forty-five-degree angle facing the sea. At the bottom, the land turned flat right where a tiny white lighthouse stood before dropping in a kamikaze-sheer cliff to the sea. Brushy little hobby-train-set trees dotted the shore. All around, the paddle-like flippers of seals reached into the salt-mist air to wave hello to us. Hello, and welcome to Southern California.

"Copy *That*."

It isn't too often that someone comes knocking on your door when you live on a boat—especially an *en voyage* boat. The first time this happened to us, we were anchored in none other than Tillamook Bay. We'd been skulking around Crab Harbor for more than ten days, waiting out both a small craft advisory and a gale. Despite *needing* to stay until favorable conditions blew in (or breezed in, as it were), we weren't exactly sure if there was a limit on how long we were *allowed* to stay. So when the first port authority–type figure came a-knockin', we were sure we were either (a) doing something wrong or (b) overstaying our welcome.

Strangely, we had two visits in one day. The first was a friendly hello from a Garibaldi security guard. He simply asked us how long we intended to stay and how we liked the place. Then he putted away on his little motorboat. A few hours later, we heard a "Hello? Anyone aboard?" from outside the cabin and wondered if we were experiencing déjà vu. *Two visitors in one day?* We'd hardly interacted with anyone on land, let alone on the water, in weeks. At first we ignored the call, assuming it was a figment of our imaginations. "Hello? *Cotton*?" the voice asked again. Our heads popped out of the cabin like a couple of fuzzy Whac-A-Mole noggins. The Coast Guard officer who greeted us was more interested in technical information: who was aboard, when we'd arrived, if we were safe. Apparently a similar-sized blue sailing vessel had vanished off the coast during the previous days' storm.

"Not us," we said thankfully. "We've been in here waiting out the bad weather." The officer, a salt-and-pepper-haired man with thoughtful eyes, nodded. "OK, then. Well, take care."

The news of this man named Mark who'd been expected to bring his blue vessel into port but didn't, or hadn't yet, made it abundantly clear how easily we could perish, that people do, that he might have. We were at our first stop on the Pacific coast, with more than twenty-three hundred nautical miles to go—so many opportunities to fail, to become "Mark."

⚓⚓⚓

Our next notable run-in with port authorities occurred at San Luis Obispo. Notice a pattern here? If you hang around somewhere long enough, the harbor patrol thinks it's time to get to know you. Actually, we hadn't been in SLO too long before a harbor patrol dude came over to our anchorage and told us that, technically, we couldn't be where we were.

We were apparently located over an area notorious for rubbish dumping. Our anchor and line could be caught and tangled on any number of things, from old anchors and rudders to retired mooring hardware to a buried treasure, for all we knew. After returning from our ill-fated initial attempt at rounding Conception and anchoring over by the Avila Pier, in the "official" anchor area (where you are continually pummeled by incoming swell), we'd decided to return to our original spot near the Port San Luis mooring field and sea lion apocalypse. We'd moved far enough out so as to not interfere with any legitimately moored boats and tucked ourselves comfortably behind an outcropping of rock that was actually allowing us to remain fairly level and enjoy ourselves. Clearly, this would not do!

It was Halloween, our favorite day. Our orange and purple jack-o'-lantern pails sat on the table, brimming with Reese's and Almond Joys, and a steaming pot of mulled wine simmered on our Origo stove. On this day we were so looking forward to, Mr. Harbor Patrol informed us that we needed to move back to the proper anchor area near Avila Beach, where it sucked. Jimmie decided to plead our case.

"We were just over there," he explained, "but moved here because of the bad weather that's supposed to be coming in from the south" (true).

The harbor guy remained unreadable behind mustache and reflective sunglasses.

"We got here a few days ago," Jimmie continued, "and already tried taking off toward Point Conception, but had to turn back because the weather got too bad."

"Copy *that*," he acknowledged with a vibe of firm, boaterly fraternity.

"The waves don't have the room to build up here like they do over there," Jimmie offered. "That general anchorage seems like a bad place to be when the wind kicks up."

"Um-hmm," the man said, his position on the matter held hostage by silence.

"We're not in the way, are we?" Jimmie added innocently.

"No," the harbor patrol dude said, fingering his rough-looking chin. "No, you're not. But this is officially part of the mooring area. And it isn't very good holding ground. The bottom is covered with junk."

"We've been holding fine since we got here," Jimmie assured him. "We're willing to take our chances" (and we were). "It's just so much more protected here," he added.

"You know," said the mustachioed patrolman, whose name turned out to be Mike, "I don't care if you're here." He pursed his lips and huffed out his nose as if to add, "so there" to his statement. "If you feel safe here, just stay." He even noted that we could tell anyone else who might ask that Mike said it was cool. We were legit.

A few days later, a guy who suspiciously couldn't get hold of Mike came by and revoked our privileges, insisting that we belonged back in sucksville by the Avila Pier. But Halloween was over, and we were thankful we'd gotten to spend it in peace—our own kind of chocolate- and booze-laden, horror-movie-marathon peace. So we accepted our lot and moved. After all, we didn't have a choice.

"Yeah. We Don't Go There."

San Luis Obispo may not have been our favorite place, but the promised land of Southern California didn't exactly make a winning debut with Santa Barbara as its usher. We'd hoped, upon arriving after a short but pleasant stay at Cojo, to anchor near Stearns Wharf, the public pier that would make for easy land access. Now, I understand Santa Barbara is a beautiful, upscale California city; they do not want derelict boats and live-aboard scumbaggery swarming their pleasure pier and using it to come ashore each day. I get it. But we didn't expect it.

We couldn't anchor anywhere near Stearns Wharf, and the "general anchorage" was about as far from anything as possible while still remaining within the open scoop of coast one might consider the "harbor." This was the hierarchy: First, there's the actual marina, where a permanent slip for a boat our size currently goes for the relatively steep rate of $248.36 per month. Visitor slips are considerably more—$0.90 per linear foot per day (roughly $24 a night for us), a fee that doubles after fourteen days, meaning it would cost more than $1,000 for a boat like ours to stay four weeks. Next is the mooring field, where a vast quilt of inflatable balls and hulls bob at the rate of $300 per year, plus an additional $200 for access to "skiff row," a dinghy landing. (All together, that's not bad for an entire year.) And farthest down is the free general anchorage, where passers-through like us hooked a piece of sandy bottom and called it home for the night.

As Jimmie pointed out, at least there was a general anchorage, and at least it wasn't so rolly we couldn't stand being there (this thanks to the way-diminished size of SoCal swell). And besides, skipping Santa Barbara wasn't really an option; we had cookies to pick up.

My mother, thoughtful as she is (and unaware of the obstacles that often got in the way of our achieving any sort of planned business on land), had put together a care package for my twenty-ninth birthday and sent it general delivery to Santa Barbara. We only had to reach the post office.

Our first attempt failed. General delivery had been relocated, apparently, from the main post office to Victoria Court, a smaller branch with very restricted hours, so we'd have to try again. Enter obstacle #3 in the way of our seemingly easy care-package pick-up (#1 being our way-out anchorage, #2 being the difficult shore landing caused by our way-out anchorage). Because we were situated so ridiculously far from Stearns Wharf, we had given up all hope of actually rowing over to it. Our other option was a beach landing straight across from our anchorage, on a lonely stretch of sand below a few mansions and a cemetery. This would be followed by a long walk back toward Everything. The beach along Santa Barbara is so open to the ocean, however, that waves are free to crash at will against the shore. Still, the well-watered green of the oceanfront park and the palm trees lining paths along which joggers jogged and pedestrians pedded looked too appealing not to investigate. And we wanted cookies!

So ashore we went, with kicked-up wind waves piling themselves atop the meager SoCal swell and rushing toward the rocky hill speckled with tombstones and the tan sand below. Jimmie had become pretty skilled at timing our landings—eyeing up the swell, commanding us to row, and usually positioning us right atop a smooth, long wave we could keep up with and surf in on. Sometimes, however, the waves were just too big or fast, or the timing didn't work out, or a twist of current or wind spun us to our side and water rushed in. Such was our first landing at Santa Barbara. We didn't get dumped anywhere near as bad as at Capitola, but our pants were soaked, and it put a grumpy mood on the morning and sparked a lingering dread over our return trip.

But Santa Barbara was our first true Southern California town! We'd rung in our arrival with a small slice of brie, some Triscuits, and the second of our landmark bottles of Oregonian wine, this one a delicious port from Torii Mor Winery. I'd obtained the cheese and crackers from a small marina-side mini-mart while Jimmie had filled our gas and water at a courtesy dock the night before. He'd also run into a harbor patrol fellow, the messenger of the unfortunate news about the general anchorage. "No," he'd assured Jimmie, "you can't anchor any closer than that." We'd have to go "*way past*" the mooring field, "all the way out by East Beach."

Obstacle #4 turned out to be the fact that the birthday package wouldn't actually arrive in Santa Barbara until Friday, and it was Tuesday. (I obtained this information in an e-mail from my chronically late mother Wednesday morning.) So we had some time to kill.

That night of our first landing, we'd easily deemed the incoming waves too tall and fast to launch out over and found ourselves essentially stranded on the beach. Obstacle #5: big surf. We didn't know what else to do, so we picked Johnny up and hauled his ass all the way down the waterfront to Stearns Wharf, hoping for some way to put in. The walk is about two and a half miles, which isn't so long, and while an inflatable kayak isn't exactly heavy, it's damn awkward to carry—it's meant to float! And it's especially awkward when you're also hauling packs full of other random crap, er, supplies, in this case a mesh bag of small white onions, a jumbo canister of Tang, a box (or two?) of wine, and a new no-spill ceramic mug from West Marine. (Jimmie had accidentally broken my marlin mug in SLO; we replaced it with the same model, lighthouse design, which was more apropos of my skill set, anyway.)

Those two and half miles were also weighted with nervous stress and bickering thanks to yours truly, as the height of the surf we'd seen, coupled with darkness and the always-unnerving presence of thick fog, had filled me with trepidation. I didn't know what option we had other than launching from Stearns Wharf and rowing the two and a half miles back to the boat in the fog and waves, but I wanted another option, badly. I had seen some water taxis earlier in the day and sheepishly suggested that maybe we could catch one back. Mind you, it was after midnight. Obstacle #6: lateness of the hour.

When we finally reached the wharf, a security guy was hanging around, so we inquired about the availability of such fantastical craft. He said we'd have to wait until morning. We locked up the dinghy and looked for some sort of landing that would make the water accessible. If there was such a place, it evaded us completely. Obstacle #7: no landing.

Jimmie discovered a rusty iron ladder down the side of the pier and proceeded to work some Jimmie magic, carrying Johnny under one arm all the way down to the water, tying him to the ladder, then making several subsequent trips with seats, oars, and boots, hoping the motion of the waves wouldn't flip him in the meantime. All the while, I stood on the boards of the pier feeling nervous, watching Jimmie with admiration and faith.

When he made his final descent into the dinghy, I climbed over the railing and followed him down. We rowed thirty-five minutes into the night, in a general eastern direction, hoping to find our home amid the fog and field of masts. We rowed and rowed and rowed. Thankfully, the sky cleared as we went, and we were able to make straight for our boat, managing on-the-side swell the whole way. But it was fine. We arrived around 2:30 AM and went straight to bed, sore, crabby, and cookie-less.

⚓ ⚓ ⚓

Jimmie strove to find a way for us to go ashore once more without having it be an absolute fuck-all mess to do so. Thankfully, we were close enough to civilization to be ripping Internet off some poor Santa Barbaran with an unsecured network, so he put in a call to the local marina. The harbormaster told him that, yes, there was a courtesy dock (the one we'd briefly tied up at to fill our water and gas) but that staying at said dock for any longer than fifteen minutes involved overnight slip charges. Well, OK. Thanks for nothing, Santa Barbara!

Next on the horn were the water taxi fellas, who gave the same "You're screwed, Señor Vagabond Sailor, but I won't exactly say so because we're friendly and helpful here in tourist-happy Santa Barbara" line of crap we'd come to expect from anyone involved with this particular port. After a crazy-making back-and-forth regarding the "far anchorage," the water taxi guy finally said, "Yeah. We don't go there," and hung up. Obstacle #8: we were in the Twilight Zone of aqua-transportation. Our position did not exist as far as water taxis were concerned.

⚓ ⚓ ⚓

It was a calm morning when Friday arrived. We loaded some Pop-Tarts and pudding cups (we'd gleefully realized you don't have to refrigerate the latter) into a backpack, boarded the dinghy, and headed toward shore. But the waves were still too big, too fast, too violent on the beach. We lost our nerve and paddled—all the way over to Stearns Mothereffing Wharf.

In the vicinity of the wharf, the waves were far more subdued, so we took 'er in for a beach landing and locked up Johnny out of sight, our new bike lock threaded through a bailing hole and around one of the thick trunks of wood supporting Santa Barbara's elevated mall of seafood restaurants and souvenir shops. We headed to Victoria Court for my package. It was there! I popped open the Tupperware edges to find homemade snickerdoodles, an array of tiny Ghirardelli chocolates, Darjeeling tea, and upscale hot cocoa. I was so happy with my care package—and even happier to have achieved the goal of receiving the damn thing—that I gave a cookie to each of the post office employees and even handed one to a nearby dude begging for change on the corner.

What a successful mission! you must be thinking. *Obstacle #Zippo! Right?* Wrong.

When we reclaimed our dinghy, there was a WARNING OF VIOLATION stuck to it, compliments of the Santa Barbara Harbor Patrol. Of the fourteen possible preprinted rules we could have been violating, Officer Broumand couldn't actually find one that matched our crime. No matter. He simply *wrote one in.*

That's right, we weren't officially breaking any set rule, but they'd be damned if they were gonna let us leave our dinghy on their beach, tucked thoughtfully out of sight and recovered only a few hours later. Nope. That simply would not do. Above rule numero uno, in a clean, all-caps hand, our mustard yellow violation read: "PERMIT REQUIRED FOR BEACH STORAGE." He added in the comments section, "UNATTENDED ITEMS ON BEACH WILL BE IMPOUNDED/ REMOVED AS FOUND PROPERTY/ABANDONED PROPERTY." Santa Barbara strikes again!

This was the only place in 2,450 nautical miles of sailing, anchoring, going ashore, and locking our dinghy near the beach that we ever got in any degree of trouble for it. At least in the "Violations must be corrected by:" field Officer Broumand gave us until the next day. Generous.

"I'm Heading for the Ladder; Don't Respond."

One thing friends and family always ask us is what we *did* all the time. I mean, didn't we have *sooo* much time on our hands? Well, yes and no. We did have a lot of free time, both while sailing and definitely once we were anchored and just waiting for the next good forecast to come along, and during the latter of those scenarios, one thing we did was read, a lot.

A good portion of our time and effort also went into the simple act of eating. We prepared meals and consumed them and did dishes and repeated that three times a day. And we had only enough kitchenware— two bowls, two plates, one pot, and one pan—to make and eat one meal at a time, so dishes had to be done after *every* meal in order to prepare and eat the next one. Our only saviors were sandwiches, or the fact that we could alternate bowls and plates depending on the meal. By the time we were sailing down the northern coast of Baja, we'd sometimes just rub the debris off a bowl or plate, sans soap, and dunk it over the side while underway. The rushing saltwater was a decent enough pressure wash for us.

We also watched movies and TV series—taking in all of *Six Feet Under, Arrested Development, Super Dimension Fortress Macross, Neon Genesis Evangelion,* and the original *Star Trek* over the course of our travels—and played a number of video games through to their oft-anticlimactic finales. Jimmie practiced his trumpet (after we met, he'd begun playing again; I felt so touched by this that I splurged on a Bach Stradivarius for him, an extravagant birthday present he called his "dream trumpet"), and I played guitar. We ended up writing and recording an entire album of songs that year, christening ourselves Pony Canyon.

Jimmie tended to maintenance issues as they arose, while I handled more domestic tasks; there was always something to do. Besides all this, we prepared and drank plenty of tea and coffee. We sat outside and looked. We planned and speculated. We gave foot and leg rubs. We snuggled. We slept in. We made love.

These are all things we did aboard the boat; it was the things we tried to achieve *off* the boat that ended up becoming fiascos. We were living an incredibly *simple* life, but also an inconvenient one. I mean, a lot of the complications of modern living, the things you "have" to have (a phone, a car, an income) are also the things that make it easier. We had none of these.

So when Thanksgiving rolled around and we wanted to have some semblance of a traditional meal, challenges arose. While I've spent many an entire day (or longer) preparing a holiday feast, it was usually doing things like making pie dough from scratch and frying sausage, chopping apples and celery and onions, or shoveling butter into baking dishes and poultry orifices. We didn't want much, but simply going to the store to pick up a few things can turn into a real debacle when you're living on a boat that isn't anywhere near a dock 94 percent of the time (really, I did the math). This goes without mentioning that our "car" was an inflatable kayak, and despite our somewhat regular splurges, we were still getting by on very limited funds.

We already had a can of cranberries, a box of Stove Top, and some kernel corn—nonperishables were our forte, after all. Meat, on the other hand, was not. And what is Thanksgiving without poultry? Not Thanksgiving at all, I tell you.

Cooking any sort of turkey ourselves appeared to be out of the question. (We aren't *totally* unreasonable.) We only had a two-burner stove, one that ran on denatured alcohol and didn't get all that hot as it was. Though Jimmie had actually made biscuits and miniature pizzas earlier in the trip by turning a giant pot (which we eventually retired for practicality reasons) into a sort of oven, baking was just not in our repertoire. And baking a *turkey* of all things was definitely out.

Buying and preserving one was also out. (You know how meat juice gets when left out at room temp for a few hours? Let's just say we weren't interested in cold gelatinous poultry ooze for dinner.) We would have to retrieve some sort of bird in a time frame at least distantly related to the time frame in which we intended to consume said bird. Easier said than done, my friends.

We awoke Thanksgiving morn quite unusually (like I said, a 6 percent chance), at a marina. Because of our dwindling supplies and difficulty accomplishing anything in Santa Barbara, we'd decided our next stop would be a quick duck into Channel Islands Harbor, which, oddly, isn't *at* any one of the eight Channel Islands but across from them in Oxnard, California (a town we couldn't keep our juvenile selves from constantly referring to as "Oxnardz").

We ended up staying a couple days longer than we'd planned for financially, due to the imminent arrival, according to the NOAA, of "t-storms, lightning, funnel clouds, heavy rain and hail, and *waterspouts*." A waterspout (per Wikipedia) is "an intense columnar vortex that occurs over a body of water and is connected to a cumuliform cloud." The weather was the deciding factor behind our every move, and as fascinating as a waterspout appeared via Google images, we weren't that eager to witness the real deal.

Our stay at Channel Islands Harbor also introduced us to our very first dye tablet, a red disc about the size of a SweeTart that you're supposed to drop in the head so you'll be caught "red-turded," as it were, if you pumped out into the marina instead of into your (for us, unusable) holding tank. The harbor patrol folks usually, we'd read, put the tablet in for you, but the guy at CIH just handed one to Jimmie at check-in. We elected to not cast it in, as we'd been happily pumping directly out the entire trip, didn't have another choice, and were stoked to enjoy the sheer luxury of the location's full-service restrooms anyway. (I mean, endless pressurized water and full-sized mirrors and copious amounts of toilet paper? *Très chic!*)

As if perfectly timed for gratefulness, the weather Thanksgiving morning was spectacular: bright blue Californian skies, warm sun and crisp air, and a great sailing wind once the morning calm passed. We motored out past the entry jetties, and I steered while Jimmie played trumpet. The bright, brassy sound echoed out over the waves, and silver-gray fins began appearing in the distance and then alongside the hull. Soon I was enjoying the sight of dolphins racing and playing to the quick-noted drills in Jimmie's *Arban* book. It was T-shirt weather and we were sailing, my sleeves rolled up to my shoulders so I could feel the warmth on more skin. We couldn't have asked for much more. Then, I saw it: a huge blue-green mass under the water maybe fifty feet away.

Coincidentally, we were listening to the Decemberists album *Picaresque*, and "The Mariner's Revenge Song" had just finished. For those who aren't familiar, it's told from inside a giant whale; the narrator and his unknowing arch nemesis, both sailors whose vessel has been destroyed by said beast, are swallowed, and there play out the final act in a story of long-sought revenge.

It was honestly right after this track when an absolutely gigantic pale green *thing* under the surface blew a fountain of water into the air, drawing our attention suddenly to starboard. It was heading right for our beam and was clearly as long as our boat at minimum. We were panicked but also too awestruck to do anything. Both of us doubted a whale would run right into a boat, so we held our course.

It held its course too, and we soon realized there was another when two blowholes spouted water in unison and two immense whale backs broke the surface like a couple of giant stone wheels turning underwater. It was so surreal I might not have believed my own eyes if Jimmie hadn't been there to see it, too. We'd seen other whales from afar, but these two were right next to us—coming right *at* us—and HUGE! The fact that their bodies were larger than our current home was at once devastating and impressive. I felt tears in my eyes. It was not fear; it was pure awe. It felt like a balloon was inflating in my chest and reaching capacity. *But would they turn? Would these magnificent beasts veer off? Or would they run right into us?* We just stood and watched, waiting.

Our sails were full and carrying us along; we couldn't speed up to get out of the way, couldn't go any faster than we already were. We could alter our course, but which way? As their approach tightened, the first of the two slowly began heading aft. It was probably within a good twenty feet when it began its slight turn, but it felt like inches. Much later, in Baja, other sailors told us stories of boats being upturned by whales swimming right under or into them. Apparently, it *does* happen. Boats are taken down by these great creatures of the sea. But these particular creatures turned. Heading more and more to the west, they spared us. What a Thanksgiving, indeed—and we hadn't even eaten yet!

⚓ ⚓ ⚓

Our intended port near Malibu was a pretty *un*sheltered anchorage erroneously named Keller's Shelter. We arrived around 3:30 PM, and Jimmie quickly inflated the dinghy, broke out the walkie-talkies, and set off in search of a Ralphs (the Californian grocery chain made famous by *The Big Lebowski*). The modern-day turkey hunt was on.

I stayed on the boat to make sure our anchor was set because we'd just arrived. I can't tell you what, exactly, I would have done if we'd come loose, but there I was—alone, at anchor, for the first time.

After watching Jimmie dinghy off toward the pier, I broke out my logbook and caught up on the past few days. Then I sat in the cockpit and just looked. The sky was full of puffy gray clouds, like dollops of dirty whipped cream suspended among California's coastal mountains. The sun had disappeared among the westernmost puffs, and its remaining light was turning everything—the clouds, the fountainous palm trees, the metallic reflections of cars traveling along California 1—to a dusty mauve. I put some music on. A brilliant white egret landed on our solar panel, and I watched as it thrust its neck in and out, countering the weight of its delicate body in perfect response to the swell.

All the while, Jimmie was retrieving the perishable components of our Thanksgiving dinner: a whole rotisserie chicken, a Caesar salad kit, and a pumpkin pie. He also picked up a bottle of Yellow Tail. (You know it's a holiday when we splurge for non-box vino.) He'd walked a total of about four miles, and the goods were in hand. All he had to do now was get back to the boat. That's all.

The Malibu Pier, however, was now closed. This had never happened before in all our experience using piers to get ashore, which at this point was extensive. And it wasn't just "closed" by rule or shabby obstruction or posted hours; it was sealed off by a formidable twelve-foot gate flanked by wide concrete walls on either side. Access was completely shut off. There was still the beach, but you can't launch your dinghy from the beach when your dinghy is tied to a ladder at the end of the CLOSED MALIBU PIER! And you certainly can't swim, a daunting task at any rate, with a rotisserie chicken in tow.

Jimmie got on his walkie-talkie and hailed me. "I'm locked out," he said, before recounting the pier's imposing facade. "I'll figure something out. Hold tight."

"OK," I agreed. I then broke out the binoculars and tried to get a read on his situation, but it was growing dark and everything beyond the massive frontage, where Jimmie was surely prowling about with our chicken, was obscured. So I waited.

Being the resourceful chap he is, Jimmie found a few construction signs lying about, piled them loosely on top of each other, put the handles of the grocery bag in his mouth, and scrambled up to their precarious signal-yellow peak. From there, he hopped on an industrial power module, leapt from that onto the wall itself, and ultimately landed behind a restaurant on the other side. All the while, the fresh components of our Thanksgiving dinner had been hanging, literally, by the skin of his teeth.

He paused for an update: "Hey, it's Jimmie. I'm in." Then, quickly, with gravity, "*Don't respond.*" He'd noticed a couple of security guards milling about the restaurant's dumpster zone. One word from me and he'd surely be busted. I didn't know this important detail at the time, but I kept quiet.

From there, Jimmie sneaked through the shadows past the guards, who were thankfully engaged in a distracting conversation, and, farther down, deftly avoided a couple of janitorial folks sweeping and emptying garbage cans. In the faintest whisper, he checked in: "I'm heading for the ladder; don't respond." He moved from cover to cover—from hot dog stand to bench to giant potted tree—eventually arriving at the scrappy rectangular hole leading down to the ladder.

He paused again: "I'm at the ladder," followed by the emphatically hushed, "*Don't respond!*" He put the chicken bag back in his mouth, carefully aiming to keep the bird upright and sealed in its plastic case, then stuck a foot searchingly into the dark abyss until it hit flat metal, and took the rusty rungs one by one.

Upon reaching the dinghy, he found it bobbing upside-down. Flipping it over, he searched the damp, plasticky surface with one hand, his other hand gripping the ladder, his teeth still clinging to our dinner. Because of the large swell rolling through the pier supports, he'd anticipated this problem and brought two oars just in case, wedging them hard into the kayak's crevasses upon arrival. There was one! One had fallen out, but one remained.

He hailed me once more: "I'm on my way. Over and out."

I squinted into the sooty night as Jimmie coasted toward me, an oar alternately stroking the surface along either side of his tiny rubber vessel. Meanwhile, the lights of L.A. sparkled like the lonely factories of midwestern country roads—twinkling amber climbing up and over the hills and beyond. But not into the water. Away from the pier, the water was still and dark. Our world was the opposite of all those billboards and businesses, all the cars and lights and hectic clamor of the city. We were an island. Our own Thanksgiving island, floating, isolated, only thirty-seven miles from the second-biggest city in the country.

When it reached *Cotton*, that chicken, amazingly, was still warm. The next morning, we had our only leftovers underway: cold pumpkin pie slices, eaten in the cockpit with our bare hands.

"Snoochie Boochies! Do You Have an Anchor Permit?"

As much as it's unusual to have someone come a-knockin' when you're at anchor on a sailboat, it's even more unusual for it to happen in the middle of the night. But around 2:00 AM on our first night in L.A. Harbor ("America's Port," according to a huge L.A. Gear–ish mural), we were awakened to loud horn blasts and rays of white light beaming through the portholes. Jimmie sprang out of bed and quickly threw something on. I groggily followed as he popped his head through the companionway hatch to see what the fuss was about.

It was about us.

Though we read up on our intended anchorages as much as we could, we often arrived at a port with little knowledge besides where we thought transient boats were supposed to anchor and, hopefully, the shortest route to the cheapest grocery store. The fact that L.A. required a temporary anchor permit for boats just "passing through" had evaded us.

"You guys have a permit? You don't have one posted," stated a harbor patrolman with coarse dark hair and thick-lashed eyes.

"Ah, no," admitted Jimmie. "We didn't know we needed one."

"Yeah, you do," the officer answered, glancing over to a blond, younger HP guy who mostly observed and listened as if in training.

"What does that entail?" Jimmie asked innocently. I knew immediately his concern: money. We'd just gotten settled in here, we had a new autopilot to pick up at the San Pedro post office (we'd ordered a replacement for Jeeves off eBay), and, most of all, we were thoroughly enjoying the tranquility of our first snuggle harbor since Morro Bay, 233 nautical miles to the north. We didn't want to leave. But if a permit was even remotely expensive, we'd have to.

⚓ ⚓ ⚓

Also, Jimmie was tired. Very tired. He'd spent a good chunk of the morning pulling an unexpected stowaway up from the bottom of Keller's Shelter. Jimmie is far stronger than you'd imagine at six feet tall, roughly 175 pounds. He is very dense, possessing more concentrated power than his thin frame would suggest. But his opponent was one tough customer.

Normally, when anchoring, you let out a lot of what's called "scope," slack in the anchor line that lets you drift away at an angle. Typical scope is five to seven times the depth of water you're anchoring in (e.g., a depth of 25 feet would demand a scope of 125 to 175 feet). In rougher conditions, more scope is advisable. It simply gives you greater holding power.

When pulling up the anchor, one must first drag in all that scope, pulling the vessel from where it's been resting at the end of its line closer to straight up from the anchor, at which point a good jerk usually unsettles it enough to break you free. The amount of line out at that particular time shouldn't be much more than the depth of the water. Make sense? Sure it does.

So, we found it rather strange when, that crisp fall morning in Malibu—as a light breeze filled us with ambitions of sailing off our anchor and booking it to Los Angeles—our line was being pulled straight down with one hundred feet of scope still out. But we were anchored in only thirty feet of water. *How could this be?* And why was it so hard to budge with that much line out? We should have been able to draw in about seventy feet of slack.

It was a mystery. Plus, we were stuck—unless we gave in and cut our anchor line, losing valuable rope, chain, and our best anchor. So Jimmie pulled and pulled until his poor arms ached for relief, their cores burning. And still we sat, floating right above that mysterious line, one hundred feet of rope somehow pulled taut, perpendicular to the ocean floor, in thirty feet of water.

Later in the trip, he would have known to wind the slack around one of the winches, a helpful trick for increasing leverage, but we hadn't experienced enough of this particular brand of bullshit for that to be in our repertoire of tricks just yet. So Jimmie just tugged and tugged and—eventually—he began depositing rope, yank by little yank, on the deck. Progress! He heaved with his whole body. Pull! Heave! Pull! Ah!!!! Slowly his rival appeared, creeping up from the depths, exposing itself as the deep teal water became more and more transparent near the surface. What *was* it?

A rudder. A giant, old, iron rudder, encrusted with shimmering mineral deposits and the gray, cone-shaped homes of innumerable barnacles, their gross tongues flicking in and out. The whole thing was draped in slick kelp of deep purple and Jell-O green—streamers of the sea. It was tangled to hell in our anchor line. And *very* heavy.

I attempted poking it with the boat hook, urging it to spin in the direction that would unwind it. But it was going too slow.

"Stop!" Jimmie barked at me. He was at the end of his own rope. "I'll just do it."

He simultaneously held the giant metal beast in the air and jerked it around, freeing it bit by bit from our accidental lasso, giant strings of kelp dropping off like dismembered branches. I cowered a little at Jimmie's frustration, but I realize now it wasn't personal. Yeah, Jimmie was mad. Was he supposed to be happy about suspending a one-hundred-pound piece of boat trash in the air for as long as it took to douse the fiery love affair it was having with our anchor line? No.

He was mad, but not at me. Jimmie was always just trying to get things done.

And he did. The rudder eventually returned to its resting place on the sandy bottom of Keller's Shelter, covered over by "2 to 7 fathoms" (per the *Coast Pilot*) of salty Pacific. My funk drifted away as well, replaced by the excitement of our impending arrival in L.A. The morning breeze had faded, too, but the reliable afternoon gustiness carried us swiftly around Point Vicente and Rancho Palos Verdes, green hills covered in a beige armor of condos.

Then, just outside of L.A. Harbor, as we turned into the wind to drop the mainsail, a small pin connecting the boom to the mast snapped in two, and the boom itself fell into Jimmie's arms. You know, the *boom*—that thing the whole bottom edge of the mainsail attaches to? Yeah, pretty important metal bar. Another thing for Jimmie to carry. Another thing to fix.

⚓ ⚓ ⚓

So, when the harbor patrol woke us up at 2:00 AM, the last thing Jimmie felt like doing was raising the friggin' anchor to move. Or, worse yet, having to leave L.A. altogether and find some crappy oceanside anchorage that would put us nowhere near obtaining Jeeves's successor and would likely result in another log entry with the word "sleep" in quotations.

Ever hopeful, we waited for the patrolman's response. "We just need some information," he said. "I'll need to see your registration and ID, for starters."

Still assuming there was a fee in our near future, we complied. Jimmie handed over the documents, answered a few questions: It was a 1972 Newport. Twenty-seven feet long. We had fifty feet of chain before our rope and a twenty-two-pound Bruce-type anchor down. Fiberglass hull, nine-foot beam, five-foot draft. We planned to stay no longer than seven days. We were, indeed, "just passing through."

All the while, the blond patrolman, who bore an uncanny resemblance to Jay of Jay and Silent Bob, shifted his weight back and forth from foot to foot, directing the spotlight at our humble home but keeping it out of our faces. I stood silently in the cabin.

The cop in charge filled in the blanks, pressing a ballpoint pen to his carbon-copy pad of multicolored forms. Then he tore off the yellow page and handed it to Jimmie.

"That's it?" Jimmie asked.

"That's it. Just put that in your window and call the harbor patrol if you decide to stay longer."

A wave of relief spread through the dark space of our vessel. Jimmie handed the yellow slip down to me, and I set it on our homemade faux mahogany table.

"Where you two headed?" piped in wavy-blond Jay (whose voice was spot-on, too).

"Catalina," said Jimmie. As usual, not a word about Mexico.

"Italian Gardens is nice," said the lead patrolman, recommending an anchorage. "Might wanna avoid Avalon," he added, citing the most touristy port on the island.

"Thanks for the tip," said Jimmie. And, just like that, we retired to our bed and fell fast asleep in L.A.'s waveless snuggle harbor, the lights of the HP boat vanishing toward the city, a pale yellow paper Scotch-taped in our starboard porthole.

"Your Turn, Honey."

There were a lot of things we loved about L.A.: the great sparkling immenseness, the feral jetty cats, the San Pedro thrift stores, the "gigante" pizza special, the peaceful harbor and (what we used as a) dinghy dock. But the public transportation *sucked*. And there are NO public toilets.

The lack of places to easily pee in L.A. astounded us. You can't just go into a mall or a library in Los Angeles and empty your bladder. We realized that, as far as public restrooms were concerned, we fell into the same class as hobos and druggies, but that didn't make living with it any more pleasant. Our first day ashore, we retrieved our new autopilot—it was an older, analog version of Jeeves, which we named Rabo-Jeeves, loosely inspired by the few Rabobanks we'd come across in central California—and we also secured two additional water tanks, allowing us ten more gallons' capacity in prep for sparser facilities in Mexico.

Next, we headed toward RadioShack for some wiring tidbits Jimmie needed to incorporate Rabo-Jeeves into our electrical world. Paying customers would be able to use the bathroom there, right? Wrong. Nor at a gas station we patronized. Or a Rite Aid. No restrooms. That was the story. Everywhere. A general, sweeping, all-encompassing "No." Eventually we discovered a laundromat with a "pay bathroom." Jimmie put a quarter in a slot on the door and was admitted into a cramped closet featuring some semblance of a toilet and a paint-splattered sink.

But *baño* and transportation gripes aside, we made it to Grauman's Chinese Theatre and saw the Hollywood sign and—best of all—accidentally stumbled into the Westin Bonaventure.

From the outside, the Westin Bonaventure looks like the quintuplication of a giant mirror-covered AA battery, or the vertical chamber of a very elegant revolver. Shooting up through the roof of the lobby are four exposed elevators that project streams of color against the building's core, like primary-colored lightning bugs crawling up and down a slick, shining log.

We ended up inside after wandering across a sky bridge from the YMCA. The lobby was much like a fancy mall, with green-leafed plants adorning brick walkways and aqua-tinted pools accented with underwater lights. There were escalators everywhere and very formally dressed employees. We didn't talk to anyone. Hell, we didn't make eye contact with anyone.

We quickly got in an elevator—the blue one—and rode it all the way up to the thirty-third floor, marveling at the sea of lights below us. Jimmie held me in his arms, the scuz-napped threads of our hoodies communing over 367 feet of sky. Below us, somewhere in the dark, was Maguire Gardens, where, earlier that day, we'd superstitiously thrown bits of copper into the pool and made wishes we didn't share. I didn't write mine down either, but I remember: I wished for us to remain together and—more importantly—for us to stay alive. I also remember wondering if I was being greedy, asking for both.

⚓ ⚓ ⚓

Before leaving San Pedro, we went into our neighborhood Vons and bought the following: two cans of stewed tomatoes, two cans of spinach, a few instant miso soup cups, and a boxed pharmaceutical good called "Twin Pack Enema."

The Twin Pack Enema cost $1.99. It contained one little squeeze bottle of saline for each of us. I can't say why the over-the-counter disposable enema comes in twos, but it was convenient to our situation. That's how we operated: as a duo, even when it comes to enemas.

The reason for this particular partnership? We planned to fast during our stay at Catalina Island. We didn't have too much on the agenda and obviously both enjoy a challenge, so we figured why not detox? You can accelerate the cleansing properties of a fast by manually vacating your system. One way is to purge your stomach via the rapid-fire slamming of warm saltwater; another is to empty your bowels via a similar backdoor method. Or, for a full, complete expulsion of every trace of food currently in your system, you can do both. Being the happenstance extremists that we were, we went all out.

Clearly, Jimmie and I were close. We had lived aboard a twenty-seven-foot boat for four months thus far, and we were happy (happy!) about it. However, there is a place where one must draw the line. As close as we were, as much as we'd shared, neither of us wanted the other around for the course of our personal enemas.

In fact, we were each individually still grappling with the idea of a "personal enema" at all. We'd hoped to find some sort of laxative tea in the health foods section, but Vons's stock of natural medicinal elixirs was sorely lacking. The Twin Pack Enema was the next best thing we could come up with. And despite the cute "couple's" nature of the packaging, the "personal" aspect of their administration was essential if we were to go through with them.

But separation is not easily achieved aboard a tiny sloop. We'd have had to take turns dinghying to shore and back, in the cold dark, to really leave the other alone. The next best thing to actual solitude we could come up with was this: The person not in medias res would sit outside, in the cockpit, with the iPod. Music was to be listened to LOUDLY, with headphones, and said person was not to enter, or *even consider entering*, the cabin at all until he or she was approached by the indoor shipmate and given clearance.

So that's what we did.

You'd think with all the time we had on our hands we would have just fasted longer and skipped the acceleration process. But we were impatient, and we both liked the idea of getting to it. So we emptied our stomachs and intestines, one by one, soon after arriving at Catalina Island. I went first. After an indeterminate time alone in the cabin, I popped through the companionway doors, tapped Jimmie on the shoulder, and said, "Your turn, honey."

We drank only water for three days. A large part of our existence was removed: no washing dishes, no preparing meals, no consumption. We took a field trip ashore and walked the crumbly dirt roads. We saw hummingbirds vibrant as jewels, the skeletons of derelict vans, and the deep scarlet armor of departed lobsters scattered on the beach—Lee Press-On Nails for ogres. We walked from our side, Isthmus Cove, past the town of Two Harbors and over to Catalina Harbor, one of Southern California's two Coast Guard–designated "year-round safe harbors." We watched an orange cat climb a palm tree and discovered crazy, spiny plants that grow only on the Channel Islands.

We tried to pass the time and not talk about food. We felt weak. We played Yahtzee and watched movies, deciding on a Wes Anderson marathon. There is a scene in *The Life Aquatic* where Anjelica Huston's character makes a grilled cheese sandwich for Cate Blanchett. That about killed us.

⚓︎⚓︎⚓︎

We were the *only* sailboat in Isthmus Cove. Sure it was December, but it was Southern California. The sun was out, the sky blue, the average high around sixty-four degrees. Apparently, if you live there, that's cold.

It was almost Christmas, and at night the shore glimmered with multicolored lights strewn over trees and foliage, a garden of tiny illuminated gemstones. There is something surreal—to a northerner—about the sight of palm trees ringed in Christmas lights. But if I squinted my eyes a little, I could take those lights anywhere—to the Douglas fir in the living room of my dad's house, for instance, its myriad bulbs lighting up the dead end of Sherman Street through tan tweed curtains on a huge picture window. It almost felt like home.

It was upon that beach that we had a celebratory return-to-eating barbecue. We bought charcoal and buns and frozen burger patties at the Two Harbors General Store, open 365 days a year. We grilled them, completely alone on the beach, drinking Downtown Brown ale and sautéing onions for topping. This, of course, was after a slow ascension from the more tame stewed tomatoes and miso. Sitting at a picnic table with Jimmie, looking out over a dark, empty mooring field, the diamond of our anchor light floating off to the side some thirty feet in the air, with a dribble of oniony, beefy grease at the corner of my mouth, I was sure it was a dream. It was a dream I was living.

"This Is Fucked."

Apparently, gales can kick your ass no matter where you are—even if you're anchored in the richy richville that is Newport Beach, California. But being anchored there at all was notable. In a town where the average household income was estimated to be $151,967 in 2010 (according to the US Census Bureau's American Community Survey), and more than a quarter of the population makes $200,000-plus a year, we were downright flabbergasted there *was* a general anchorage. And it wasn't too horrible.

Stuck right at the southeast tip of Lido Isle—*inside* the breakwaters of the town's massive snuggle harbor—was a tiny triangle of water marked with cylindrical yellow buoys: the general anchorage. The bottom was nearly pure mud, not the most firm holding ground, but at least there was a place we could drop an anchor without our bank account instantly emptying.

To be fair, one can rent a transient mooring buoy for five dollars a night in Newport Beach, a surprisingly reasonable, *cheaper* than average fee. But no dollars are still better than five dollars. So, we settled ourselves in the general anchorage and gaped all around at the mansions decked out in Clark Griswold–level Christmas fanfare and their correspondingly epic mega-yachts. On the water itself, scores of electric party boats putted around the harbor, the sounds of drunkenness and bad music emanating from under their scalloped vinyl awnings.

The main drag in Newport Beach is lined with Lotus and Ferrari dealers, and the strip zooms with them, as well as Porsches and "Jag-U-ars" and every motorized wealth trophy you can think of—like a *Need for Speed* or *Cruis'n USA* course. I practically expected to see an 8-bit bikini babe holding a FINISH sign at the end.

We, on the other hand, were headed for the bulk-buying value of Smart & Final.

Smart & Final is a place we first discovered in Seaside, California, a suburb of Monterey. They sell discount restaurant-supply type items, including whole boxes of mayo and relish and mustard packets. Soon, our V-berth storage was so filled with backup condiments we thought we might seem like suspicious mayo smugglers upon attempting to cross the Mexican border. They also sold box wine.

After walking seven miles roundtrip to Costa Mesa's Smart & Final, we arrived at our dinghy, locked under a Pacific Coast Highway overpass, to discover that the tide had dropped dramatically. That morning, we'd easily rowed right up to the paved pedestrian path and disembarked. Now, between us and the water lay a long, sloping, bird-covered mudslide. It was the kind of mud on which you slip rather than sink. NO traction is possible; the top layer of slime just whisks right off at the hint of pressure. Also, it was extremely windy and only getting windier, and it was coming off the ocean, meaning we'd be rowing directly into it all the way back to the general anchorage.

Jimmie devised a plan. We would carry the dinghy as close to the water as possible using exposed rocks and chunks of pavement, then we'd get in and slide backward through the mud into the water. It worked! Paddling through the wind-tortured channel, on the other hand, didn't go so well.

We tried to hug the shore of the small channel, paddling among the moored boats and using them to cut the wind, but sooner or later we'd make it to the larger channel separating Lido Isle from the mainland, and the wind waves and gusts were sure to be sweeping through with exaggerated force there. Complicating matters was the fact that, in our confusion over how to get the dinghy past the low-tide mud slick, we'd left the bailing holes open. While fighting twenty-miles-per-hour gusts and wind chop at least as tall as the pointed tip of Johnny's bow, we were also sitting up to our flies in murky, icy water.

"I don't think we're gonna be able to cross that main channel!" I yelled through the wind. "Yeah, this sucks," said Jimmie. "Let's pull over!"

We were approaching the private dock of a massive white wedge of yacht with glossy black windows and a rotating module of high-tech equipment at its peak, some sort of radar contraption made of rods and balls. There were other boats tied up in the vicinity, but this one dwarfed them all. It blocked the wind. We rowed up along its starboard side and got out.

Standing there, in our mud-soaked jeans and sneakers, each wearing a backpack full of mayonnaise and cheap wine, we couldn't have been further from the sort of guests normally invited to mill about on these docks. We picked Johnny up and flipped him over. A mass of brown water hit the surface hard, pronouncing *SPLOPT!* as wisps and splashes got plucked up handily by the wind and carried horizontally toward the Pacific Coast Highway.

"This is fucked," declared Jimmie.

"Yeah, I'm freezing," I added.

We saw no other solution except to wait. But where? Not only did we have nowhere to go, we were standing on a private dock in a gated community in *Newport Beach* of all places, next to a tremendously expensive yacht with a gleaming white-and-black facade not unlike that of an Imperial Stormtrooper. What's more, its name was (you're not gonna believe this) *Mr. Terrible*. Yup. Mister Fucking Terrible.

One thing was for sure, we certainly couldn't leave Johnny Inflatable here, next to *Mr. Terrible*. And we weren't about to get back into the freezing, wind-whipped water and float back to the mudscipades that awaited us under the highway. So we picked Johnny up and carried him past *Mr. Terrible*, down the dock, and onto a loop called Bayshore Drive.

At Bayshore we took a right, knowing it would eventually connect with Highway 1. We weren't exactly sure what the rules of a gated community were—like, *Could we be arrested for being in here?*—but we were sure we weren't welcome, that we were guilty of some sort of trespassing, regardless of the severity. We were probably a thousand feet from the free, normal world.

It was a marvel, just being in such a place. Every home was tremendous, massive, ornate. Most of them weren't all that *cool*, but they sure looked expensive. And *exclusive*. Foyers with crystal chandeliers, evidence of multiple skylights and fireplaces, lots of brick, extensive landscaping featuring oodles of floodlighting, and front doors of solid oak. Palm trees and more palm trees. And behind most of the homes, private docks lined with extravagant sailboats and *Mr. Terrible*'s numerous offspring. *Keep your head down; look at the ground; walk, walk.*

The gates! A few incoming vehicles stopped, typed something into a keypad, waited for the gate to rise, and then drove on through. The exit lane, thankfully, was wide open. We walked casually on out, inflatable kayak in tow, our soggy sneakers leaving wet prints, and Johnny's butt trailing a stream of drips behind us.

⚓ ⚓ ⚓

We didn't get back to the boat that night until 11:00 PM. We killed five hours walking around Balboa Island and loitering as much as possible at a nearby Starbucks, sitting in our wet pants, our tired, cold feet transformed into swollen, flesh-colored prunes inside our soaked socks and shoes. Meanwhile, the wind kept blowing and our hopes of rowing home dwindled by the hour.

When we'd finally run out of distractions and all available patience, we walked back over to the ped path to assess the situation. The tide was back up, but the wind was still blowing straight across the bay, from exactly the direction we needed to go. One of our main concerns was now the very real possibility of being stranded ashore overnight without a single light on our boat. We always lit our anchor light overnight, and in a busy harbor with drunken party boats circling the islands, we weren't thrilled at the thought of our blue-hulled vessel sitting undercover along the edge of the general anchorage.

Also, it's not as though we had anywhere to go. In matters of lodging, we couldn't have been in a worse city for our financial situation; the cost of the cheapest room at the Newport Beach Hyatt Regency, for instance, could have bought us thirty-five Hot-N-Ready pizzas. Thirty-five! The only thing we could think of was to walk back to the Costa Mesa Vons, a twenty-four-hour grocery store, and wander the aisles all night. But we hoped it wouldn't come to that.

Standing, facing the dark wind, Jimmie had a thought: Perhaps, if we were lucky, we could put in on the north shore of Lido Isle and float downwind toward the public anchorage at its tip. If the wind gusted from the west, we'd be in the lee of the Isle, and northern surges would push us home. It was a sound theory; the only problem was, we were more than two miles from the north shore of Lido Isle, and the only way to get there was to walk—with the dinghy.

We each grabbed an end and started trudging down Highway 1. En route, we decided we might deserve a pizza if it seemed we'd actually be able to make it back home. Coincidentally, there was a joint called Laventina's Big Cheese Pizza on the way. We'd both made a note of it when researching the port; we were always apprised of our current pizza situation.

Blocks and blocks of sneakered steps and rubber-rubbed thighs later, we locked Johnny to an out-of-the-way fence and headed toward Laventina's. Taking in the conditions from this new vantage point, we became convinced that Jimmie's plan would work. In our optimistic minds, we had already earned that pizza. By the time we returned, a large sausage and pepperoni in tow, the wind had miraculously eased for the first time in nearly eight hours.

We boarded Johnny using a public-seeming dock in cahoots with a neighborhood park. I put the pizza across my lap, treating it as precious cargo, and Jimmie rowed us back with a new oar we'd acquired at Minney's, a famed Newport Beach yacht surplus store. A group of preteen girls cavorting on a dock cheered us on as we slipped past on the black mirror of water. The warm scent of Italian meats drifted up from that cardboard box, the savory aroma of fennel and salt hovering tantalizingly under my nose.

And wouldn't you know it? After we'd eaten our heavenly pizza and watched a few geographically appropriate episodes of *Arrested Development*, after we'd changed into pajamas and regained warmth and dryness in our limbs, I walked past our power module in the dark, on my way to bed, and unknowingly bumped the main switch. Our mast light, which we'd triumphantly turned on upon *finally* entering the cabin, was off all night.

"Protect Tender Vegetation and Vulnerable Animals."

We had gone to Minney's, shared a frozen banana (also geographically appropriate), and obtained essential supplies. We could have just left

Newport Beach, knocked out one more chunk of coast on the way to the ever-more-quickly-approaching border. But we were in a snuggle harbor, and the weather had been unfriendly.

In addition to a gale marooning us ashore and a subsequent bullet-shower rainstorm (that blew the seats right out of our dinghy, never to be seen again), it was COLD. And now our NOAA buddy was pronouncing a frost warning. "Protect tender vegetation and vulnerable animals," he said. The sky was clear and sun was actually beaming through our windows for the first time in several gloomy days, but it was that deceitfully bright sun of winter, the kind that shines even brighter, crisper on the coldest of days. In our home with no heat, we were the vulnerable animals.

Also, it was December 14, and there was something we had to see before leaving Newport Beach. We'd unintentionally arrived just in time for what is apparently "one of the most thrilling Christmas celebrations in the world!" OK. *I* said that. But the *New York Times* really and truly called the Newport Beach Christmas Boat Parade "one of the top ten holiday happenings in the nation." Not bad, eh? And its route was set to circle the general anchorage, right where we were, twice.

From the moment we arrived in Newport Beach, it was apparent this town takes yuletide seriously. The extravagant houses lining every waterfront street actually compete (in the "Ring of Lights" contest) for the title of best (or most garishly) decorated; boats, some of them as big as houses, do the same. According to the event's website, some boat owners have spent more than $50,000 on decorations. Fifty thousand dollars! I don't even want to know how many pizzas that would buy, Little Caesars or otherwise.

Even the less bourgeois beach regulars had the spirit; near a corn dog stand, we witnessed a scantily clad elder hippie performing "Hark the Herald Angels Sing" on a wooden flute, the airy notes drifting over the sand as wet-suited surfers watched the sets roll in, waiting for the perfect wave. Now it was time for the big event.

And, I failed to mention, it was the boat parade's one hundredth anniversary (it started in 1908), so people were going all out. Sitting aboard our humble craft, a mere anchor light adorning it, we witnessed what happens when people with little to no financial restrictions try to honor "100 Years of Holiday Cheer."

We saw Santa and his wife paddling an ornament-covered canoe, and a tiny kayak with an entire palm tree made of Christmas lights bursting upward from its rear seat. Sailboat owners had gone to the trouble of stringing lights up their masts and along every strand of rigging, creating an illuminated fleet of line-drawn vessels. Electric party boats puttered all around, blasting Christmas music and tinkling champagne flutes. Red and green running lights held new meaning.

And then there were the mega-yachts. The mega-yachts were *insane*. One was completely transformed into a tropical island; giant glowing palm trees lined its pilothouse, and the deck took on the guise of a sandy beach with waves of blue lights flowing over it.

Another featured the number 100 in giant red digits and an animated bottle of bubbly repeatedly popping its cork as a scaffold reaching fifteen feet off its bow boosted neon green dolphins into the air. A fire-breathing dragon wearing a Santa hat stretched the length of one deck, jetting flames of light repeatedly into the black night air. Everywhere, neon Santas and reindeer bounded from atop the highest decks.

Music blared from every direction, mimicked by sound-sensing lights and dancing silhouettes. Out of all the boats, though, there was one you could see no matter where it was in the harbor—a blinding giant of pure neon. This particular boat depicted an icy wonderland featuring jutting triangular Christmas trees on every level, the safety lines all around encrusted with tiny blue lights like snow drifts. Giant packages with bows were clustered around the largest tree, and a huge banner read 100 YEARS OF CHRISTMAS CHEER! It was as if the holiday display at New York's famous Macy's had slid right down Thirty-Fourth Street onto its decks.

Blasting Mannheim Steamroller and Trans-Siberian Orchestra turned up to eleven, its light show morphed from one icy color scheme to the next, casting a glowing sweep of violet or hot pink or periwinkle across the water. It was mesmerizing and pretty darn '80s, not unlike one of those fiber optic balls at Spencer Gifts—except that it was a multimillion-dollar yacht.

Around and around they went. People danced. People cheered. People got very drunk. It was freezing-ass cold, but everyone was outside being festive as hell, including us. We'd armed ourselves with cider and rum, a two-tone cheese log, and half a gallon of eggnog. We even set our propane burner in the cockpit as a sort of "campfire" to warm our hands by. Smooshing hard, cold cheese across a Wheat Thin and trying not to break it, I glanced across the harbor and noticed that even *Mr. Terrible* flashed a strobe light now and again.

"It's *Never* Like This Here."

San Diego was big. San Diego was important. It was our last stop in the United States, and we had official business there. Foremost, we had to go to the office of Conapesca, Mexico's National Aquaculture and Fishing Commission, and get our Mexican fishing licenses. Aquaculture, we learned, is "the large-scale cultivation of aquatic organisms under controlled conditions, for use as food or for other economic purposes."

San Diego also demanded efficiency. Being one of the country's "10 Best Weather Cities" (per *Farmers' Almanac*), it is not a place that looks kindly upon transient-sailor types. The most convenient anchorage we could find was Mariners Basin in the larger Mission Bay. A passing-through type of vessel such as ours could be there for seventy-two hours. The pressure was on.

Mariners Basin was about ten miles from the Conapesca office in downtown San Diego. We arrived on a Sunday, giving ourselves, very intentionally, the maximum number of business days before Christmas to get things done. We hoped to accomplish everything on Monday, December 22, but you know how things go. We might need (non-nautical) leeway.

Our anchorage was right across from an amusement park featuring an old-fashioned wooden roller coaster called the Giant Dipper. It was built in 1925. The Giant Dipper, along with most everything else at Belmont Park, had since been updated, but a white roller coaster on a beach-strip park felt very old-time California to us. Each time we went ashore, we got to walk past a mirrored carousel of ornate rabbits and horses, smell cotton candy and popcorn, and hear children screaming all the way down the Dipper's seventy-three-foot drop.

According to the NOAA, San Diego receives an average of 10.33 inches of precipitation a year. Those 10.33 inches typically come down over forty-one days. In 2008, San Diego got all 10 inches in one day, December 22—or at least that's how it felt.

That Monday, we put on our raincoats and boots and paddled through the drizzle to Mission Point Park. We took a string of three buses (the #8, the #88, and the #120) and spent about an hour and a half making our way downtown. When we finally reached the Conapesca office, the gentleman working there handed us a roll of paper towels. We were that wet. He then broke the news that we couldn't pay cash for our licenses; we'd have to get a money order.

So we reentered the downpour. Through eyelashes jeweled with rain, we saw the towering green trees of Balboa Park glistening to our left, every palm blade an expressway for speeding droplets. Walking down Fifth Avenue, one block from the famous zoo we couldn't afford admission to (forty-two dollars per adult!), the parking lanes became veritable waterslides—sheets of pure, moving agua. We were beyond soaked. Rain seeped from our faces down the necks of our raincoats and into our sweatshirts underneath. It filled up our boots. The downpour was consistent, a straight day-into-night deluge. And every person we talked to in San Diego that day said the same thing: "It's *never* like this here."

⚓ ⚓ ⚓

In L.A., we'd noticed that every single money-holding establishment you can think of has an epic tower downtown—a steel megalith covered with impeccably Windexed glass. We, the two broke-ass sailors, ironically had an account at the bank with the tallest tower, U.S. Bank (also the tallest building on the West Coast). It, in some weird, abstract way, was the keeper of our funds, electronically linked to a piece of plastic in Jimmie's wallet that surrendered virtual dollars at our command. It was our citadel of macaroni and cheese, our bastion of box wine.

We'd consolidated our funds before leaving and chosen U.S. Bank not for its impressive seventy-three floors and three-hundred-plus feet of white scalloped windows, its glass crown and rooftop helipad, but because it boasted more ATMs along the coast than my Key Bank. Our choice paid off. In San Diego it was only a mile and a half to a U.S. Bank, but it was one of those swanky downtown branches where everyone's in a suit and the employees greet you at the door as if you're about to make important investments. We were not. And we were saturated to our very bones.

We got in line between the navy blue belts stretched from stanchion to stanchion. A highly cosmeticized brunette, all blow-dried and put together, called, "Next!"

We walked up.

"Hi," said Jimmie. "We need to get a money order." I nodded in agreement.

Our bubbly brunette was just too curious. She couldn't resist asking us what we were up to, why we were out on foot in such weather. We responded in our typically conservative way, only saying we were sailing after a series of follow-up questions.

"So you two are *sailors*?" Her mascaraed eyes widened. "That's so *interesting*."

"Well, not exactly," Jimmie explained. (We were always reluctant to call ourselves "sailors.") "We just wanted to hang out and not work for a while, so we sort of figured out how to sail."

"Oh my *GOD!* That's the most adorable thing I've ever heard!" she exclaimed through mauve-lined lips. "Cindy, listen to this . . ." she trailed off, ducking her head into a nearby cubicle.

"I'm sorry," she blushed, "that's just *too* cute. Do you have a website or anything?!"

We did. Sort of. We had a collection of photos she could check out if she wanted.

Oh, yes. She wanted. So we wrote down the address to our Photobucket page.

Cindy peeked around the wall of her cube and smiled at us. Our polished brunette happily directed us to a nearby Travelex (for pesos) and then waived U.S. Bank's customary five-dollar money order fee. *She insisted.* Cindy silently approved.

Back at Conapesca, the gentleman took our money order and offered us more paper towels. He had a mustache and kind eyes. He made sure Jimmie didn't mean to put "James" on his paperwork (he didn't; his full name is Jimmie) and, with a knowing, paternal demeanor, he assured us that we needn't stress about checking in at Ensenada. "We say 'Welcome, do as you please,'" he explained.

Another rain-soaked, three-bus, hour-and-a-half trip back to Mission Point Park and we were home. We had Mexican fishing licenses; there were five thousand pesos in our absurdly low-security cash box, a black-and-silver receptacle stamped with the word VAULTZ; and we'd even managed to make one bubbly brunette bank teller's day.

"We Wanna Wish You a Merry Christmas."

I have always had a hankering to run away. Who hasn't? When I initially moved from Chicago to Oregon, some little part of me thought I might not ever talk to anyone I knew again. Of course, that didn't happen—and I have no reason to write off friends and family—but there is an appeal to the thought of it. Just to be left alone. And how much closer to running away, as a bona fide adult, can one get than

to board a sailboat bound for Mexico with one's true love? Not much.
And most people don't make it anywhere near that.

That said, we did occasionally feel distant—even lonely. We were
isolated, and that can wear on you. After leaving our calm little haven
in the shadow of the Giant Dipper, we rounded Point Loma—the kelp-
plagued, tongue-shaped flick of land forming the western side of San
Diego's entrance channel—and went to our next short-stay anchorage,
Glorietta Bay.

We motored in past gigantic aircraft carriers flanking San Diego
Bay, past the skyline and under the San Diego–Coronado Bridge.
Glorietta Bay was nestled right up to a golf course (we could have easily
been hit by a rogue ball) and opposite the famed Hotel del Coronado,
which lights up like an electric gingerbread house at night. Our spot
was beautiful and secluded. It had a seventy-two-hour limit.

Fine. We needed only a few days. Some wintery weather had been
forecast, and we wanted to wait it out before making a run for the
border. Also, it was Christmas Eve, and it sounded nicer just to sit and
wait and be together than to brave a whole new country.

Thankfully, we'd thought to prepare during our rainy day on the
town, loading up with sweet treats and canned Chinese food for
Christmas dinner. I cut letters out of notebook paper and pinned
them to my big red Goat Feet socks, creating "sockings" as decor. I
accidentally did Jimmie's "J" backward, but the end result, once hung
from the cabin-top railing, was festive. Maybe not as festive as a
Newport Beach Boat Parade yacht, but not too shabby for us.

Fuzzy with midday cocktails and alive with the holiday spirit, a
feeling of bonhomie swelled within us. We wanted to send a gift! But
what?

Jimmie had it: a song! We would record a song.

As scattered thunderstorms raged outside the boat, casting a blue-
green light over the anchorage that intermittently gave way to bright
bursts of sun, we hunkered down and crafted a sweet jam we thought
worthy of sharing with our loved ones. Several hours and vodka-and-
Tangs later, we had digitally put down our own rendition of "Feliz

Navidad," featuring Jimmie on trumpet and me on vocals and acoustic guitar.

The next day, we sent an MP3 to everyone on a pretty long e-mail list—old coworkers and acquaintances, musicians I had interviewed and whose music I respected, and of course family and friends. It was true: we did want to wish them a Merry Christmas, from the bottom of our hearts. It was the best sentiment a couple of sequestered sailors could come up with. And it was pretty good. Better than a necktie or a tin of peanut brittle anyway.

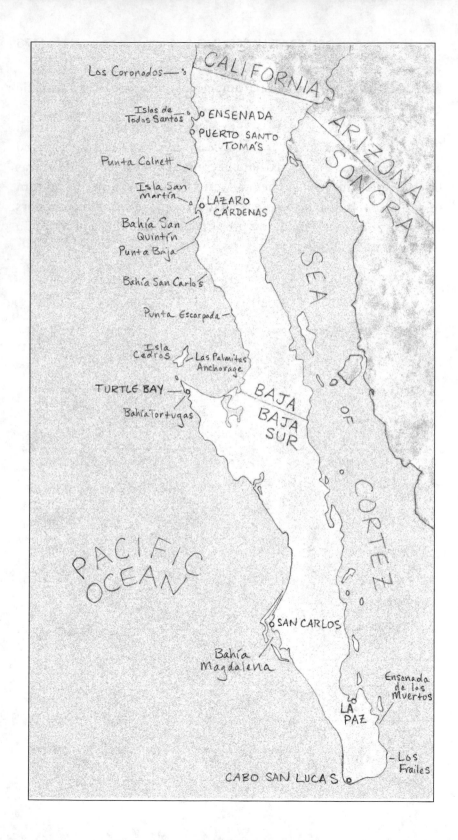

III

BAJA

HUNG OUT TO DRY

"This Kind of Stuff Happens Every Day Around Here."

We ate strange things on our trip—things we came up with out of sheer boredom with the usual—like stuffing sandwiches, which, if you think about it, are actually bread sandwiches. Bread between bread. Jimmie came up with that one, and you would have thought it was the doggone theory of relativity. "Stuffing sandwiches!" he exclaimed. "Doesn't that sound good to you?!"

It kind of did. But the reality of it being chopped-up, seasoned bread between slices of *other* bread hadn't escaped me as it had him. He simply viewed it as a tasty thing we hadn't yet eaten. So I grilled them like Reubens or patty melts—except, you know, instead of delicious corned beef and Thousand Island dressing or hamburger, grilled onions, and melted cheese between the slices, they were filled with . . . bread. Yum.

Actually, they weren't bad. And we were excited just to have something different. Now, we were about to enter a whole world of different—cruising Mexico—but we had to get there first. Our stop *primero*? Los Coronados, a stepping-stone on the way to Ensenada.

Los (or Islas) Coronados are a group of islands just over twenty nautical miles south-southwest of San Diego. (It was more like seventy straight to Ensenada.) We would jump from there to Islas de Todos Santos and, finally, to La Ciudad de Ensenada, where we would get legit.

The sail to Los Coronados did nothing to dissuade us from this plan. The sun sparkled silver sequins over the surface of the water, and we were sailing toward islands, something Catalina had taught us was *awesome*. Also, there were dolphins! About halfway there a pod of playful dolphins began swimming right alongside our bow. They flipped onto their sides and backs, displaying light-colored tummies and looking up at us with one eye at a time, their curved mouths grinning. This seemed to bode well for our border crossing.

Our digital camera was capable of recording video. And though we hadn't thought to use it for that purpose yet, silvery striped dolphins inspired new ideas. Pointing at our playful marine escorts, the dusky islands in the distance, or me, kneeling in a bright blue windbreaker on the bow, Jimmie narrated. "This kind of stuff happens every day around here," he kidded. But it wasn't far off.

⚓ ⚓ ⚓

Los Coronados means "the crowned ones," and the islands, big sloping hunks of rock dusted in kelly green vegetation, seemed to hint at a royal underwater assemblage whose headpieces were the only things to break the surface.

It was a little anticlimactic, crossing a border that can only be seen on maps and arriving at a nondescript lump of land in the ocean. But there we were: Mexico!

We anchored just off the eastern shore of the southernmost, largest island. The wind was light for the moment, and we bobbed gently in our lone spot, with only a few birds and outlying fishing boats as witness to our having arrived. I got out a pair of huge binoculars and tried to identify the feathered creatures on the shore.

It wasn't until the sun went down that things got bad. Real bad. The wind, which we'd expected to be from the northwest, was blowing hard straight down the ocean at us, from the north-northeast. The eastern coast of South Coronado runs pretty much straight north and south, meaning our spot on the lower east side would have put us comfortably in the lee of a northwestern wind, but we weren't shielded, in any way, from the strong and growing stronger nor'easter. If the birds ashore had felt inclined to classify *us*, they would have been correct to identify a couple of sitting ducks.

We tried to go to bed. But the wind waves built and built until we were being thrashed so violently on our line we thought things would start ripping apart if we didn't release ourselves. I heard a great *THUNK!* in the cockpit. Jimmie got up. I followed.

One of our brand-new five-gallon water tanks had been thrown from the cockpit bench to the floor. It landed on a bolt that was part of the tiller housing, and the impact burst a bolt-shaped hole right through it. Precious drinking water poured all over the cockpit floor.

I placed the other portable water bag on the floor to prevent a repeat offense. Jimmie opened the cockpit storage to find gas tanks rocking with fervor to and fro. The rigging banged overhead, the bow leapt up and slammed down with each watery hunk of wind chop that passed. "We've gotta get out of here," he said. I was tired, but I knew he was right.

We started de-bagging the sails and reluctantly putting outdoor clothes on, transforming the space from home back to boat with a quicker turnaround than we preferred. Jimmie switched the power from mast light to running lights, but instead of overhead white being replaced by red and green on the nose and a white-glowing stern, everything went black.

Something was wrong with the running lights. *Pitch, plop, pitch, plop; rattle, rattle, crash*. The sounds of destruction serenaded us like a Car-X commercial. We needed to go. But we weren't about to set off on our first leg of Mexico, an overnight leg, with no running lights.

Jimmie put a flashlight in his mouth, grabbed his multimeter, and wedged his shoulders and chest into the anchor locker in the hammering bow. The multimeter had somehow gotten turned on in storage, and its nine-volt battery, the only one we had, had run out. Add the fact that our fuse box was wired in a completely nonsensical, getting-wackier-since-1972 fashion and you've got yourself a tricky task even on dry land. I just sat there, listening to the chaos around us, not wanting to stay, but not wanting to go either.

Working some electrical magic, Jimmie got our running lights burning again. He could take the flashlight out of his mouth and return to a somewhat upright position, at least for now.

Little did he know he'd find himself engaged in a plethora of other troubleshooting tasks—including siphoning gas from a fuel filter— soon enough. By the end of this particular leg, the following items all broke and/or required maintenance: the depth meter, our handheld GPS, James Brown, Rabo-Jeeves, and the bimini (a retractable cockpit shade). The tiller bolts even loosened up and needed a quick tightening.

Most of these issues turned out to be minor misunderstandings between man and machine. But Jimmie was right: this kind of stuff happens every day around here.

"Where the Hell *Are* We?"

The second definition of "at sea" in the *Collins English Dictionary* reads: "in a state of confusion." The first is, simply, "on the ocean." This particular night, we were *so* both.

Upon arriving at Islas Coronados, we'd noticed a few perplexing structures in the distance. They looked sort of like low barges, their decks circled in chain-link fencing. But, like I said, they were far off in the distance, and we didn't concern ourselves too much with them.

We just needed to get going, and we did. Fast.

Though at anchor the effect of the brisk northeast wind was agitation and destruction, it was excellent for sailing—much more pleasant to move *with* than be pummeled *by*. We sailed off our anchor and had to skirt a few nearby fishing boats, but then we were home free. We would rather have been asleep, but at least our boat wasn't getting the crap beat out of it. It was moving. For now.

As we headed southeast from our anchorage, we found ourselves approaching some of the strange fenced obstacles we'd noticed earlier. They weren't barges at all. They were huge—as in forty-to-fifty-foot-diameter huge—floating rings filled with webbing and cordoned off by rope fencing around their perimeters, like giant kiddie pools made of PVC and fishnet. Right in the middle of otherwise clear coastal waters, right in the middle of our route.

They were lit with tiny white bulbs, so we simply steered clear. We didn't know what they were, and we didn't need to find out. We just needed to get past them and out, onto free water. Only—surprise, surprise!—one of them *didn't* have a light. As such, I didn't see it—*at all*—until we were less than a boat-length away.

"COME ABOUT!" I hollered to Jimmie. He threw Rabo-Jeeves's metal hand off the tiller and grabbed it, swinging us to port so as not to jibe in high wind (which can be dangerous). We avoided the collision and the jibing. Just in the nick of time.

Jimmie sailed us back a little way, close-hauled with the wind sweeping over our starboard bow, so we could reassess.

OK. We turned around again. There it was in the distance, the ring we'd almost collided with, floating ominously in the dark, waiting to snag us into its web and hold us prisoner or break a hole in our hull or serve us up as a tiny meal to some horrible sea monster waiting in its confines! To its right was another, with a light on it. They seemed to be the only ones in our close vicinity.

"Do you think we can go between them?" Jimmie asked.

"Yeah, I bet we can," I said, assessing the distance between the rings. We'd just thread the needle and be out, past all this aquaculture bullshit.

He adjusted our heading and went for it. Looking good. Closer, closer. We were between them, sliding over the black water toward their closest points. Shit. They were tied together.

Now that we were in there, up close, we could see the pair of rings was connected by two thick-ass lines just under the surface of the water. We passed over the first.

Our rudder caught on the second. Fuck.

So we sat there, held by one measly rope only feet under the water. Stopped. On the Mexican ocean. Nowhere to go. No idea what to do. Wind pushing the snag farther and farther into place underneath us.

⚓ ⚓ ⚓

On a trip like ours, it becomes commonplace to find yourself thinking, *Where* are *we?* or *How the hell did we end up* here? Albion, Hunters Cove, Catalina. Paradisiacal, magical retreats. Hidden corners of the world. This was one of those "Where are we?" moments—but not for the same reasons.

We tried lowering the mainsail to decrease forward motion. We jiggled the tiller, then threw the outboard on high and tried to reverse. Then we repeated all these attempts while Jimmie leaned out of the cockpit with our boat hook and pressed down, as hard as he could, on that line.

It wasn't a "measly" rope, I must admit. It was some braided Voltron of heavy-gauge rope, the whole monstrosity about as thick as your average telephone pole. You know, those underwater telephone poles made of sea-slimed rope? Yeah. One of those.

Jimmie got off the boat. Yup. He got *off* the fucking boat. In the middle of the ocean. He was clinging to the safety line on our starboard side, standing on the hard plastic aquaculture ring, and pushing down on our leash with the boat hook, hoping this approach would give him more leverage.

I was horrified. Even if he freed us, what then? Would I float off, leaving him standing on some aquaculture ring in the middle of nowhere, unable to get back?

He pushed and he pushed. He shoved that rope down and wiggled it and told me to move the tiller this way and that, run the outboard, try raising the sail a little, etc.

Nothing. Nothing worked! We were stuck. Not only were we not getting anywhere, we could only imagine our predicament would be frowned upon by authorities. We were surely guilty of trespassing, vandalism, something. We half wanted the fishing boats back by the Crowned Islands to see us, come help us, but we were also worried that they'd catch us at it, whatever *it* was.

One last, multifaceted effort: With the mainsail lowered, we would back up hard with the outboard. Jimmie would simultaneously push down—HARD—with the boat hook. The moment we were (hopefully) released, he'd jump on board and kill the motor while I raised the mainsail and moved us forward. All in one fell swoop. We gave it a shot. It didn't work.

We were at a complete loss.

There, standing in the cockpit, looking at Jimmie, his soaked sneakers bobbing up and down on some crazy-ass ring miles from real land, his hand grasping our safety line—the only thing connecting him to our boat—I had the most "Where the hell *are* we?" moment of our whole trip. We'd been in Mexico less than twelve hours and we were totally lost. Not geographically, so much, but spiritually. I mean, what the hell had we gotten ourselves into? A bind that we couldn't get out of? A one-way ticket to prison? Where *were* we, indeed? What the hell were we doing? *What the fuck was going on?*

⚓ ⚓ ⚓

I suggested we cut the line. I didn't see any other way.

"Hand me the hacksaw," Jimmie said plainly. I did.

He then painstakingly sawed through thick hunk of line after thick hunk of line, each one twisting around and braiding through the others, until the whole mass broke, our boat bumping against the main float the whole time, Jimmie standing on that same absurd hoop, hanging on with one hand as it rose and fell with the swell. His ankles were completely submerged at times.

Our hacksaw was not great, but Jimmie severed that evil corded mass, one thread at a time, and once we were free, he walked along that hard plastic ring just like he was leading us off a gas dock, jumping aboard at the last moment. We were *off*.

"With Viagra, Everything Is Possible."

By the time we reached Ensenada, we were fairly certain we'd be arrested for international ecoterrorism. There was sure to be blue paint from our hull on the shorn ropes of their aquaculture contraption, and the Mexican navy would have no trouble identifying us as the offending jackasses once our turquoise vessel sailed into port.

It sounds funny in retrospect, but we were scared. Reviewing the e-mail to our family and friends in which we told the story of the dreaded aquaculture ring, we didn't say we sawed through the line. We just said we got off. We must have truly considered the possibility that information regarding this would get out, reach the Mexican government one way or another, and get us in trouble. So we withheld that information, even from our loved ones.

That's how a lot of things—docking, the weather, the sails themselves, that damned aquaculture ring, the daunting *aduana* (customs) office we were soon to encounter—made us feel in the moment: wary, insecure, even stupid. Admittedly, we also felt smarter than everyone a lot of the time. We were onto something so simple, so doable, so exciting. The rest of the world must be fools to stay ashore! And we were proud too—of coming up with such a plan and actually doing it. Especially *after* our trip, we felt overwhelmingly proud. But you don't get that—you don't get to feel that—until you've actually done it. All the way.

Now, however, we were in the epicenter of insecurity, our first stop in a foreign country. We had to check in, get visas, import our boat, and, though we didn't know it yet, obtain insurance. Lucky for us, it was Sunday, meaning everything official was closed. For now, we just had to arrive, and that was complicated enough.

⚓ ⚓ ⚓

Before leaving the States, we'd acquired a book called *Charlie's Charts*. It is a well-respected resource meant to "assist boaters in identification of approaches to anchorages and marina facilities and provide information regarding navigation, entry procedures, routes, weather and travel to prime cruising areas." The edition we had was for the "Western Coast of Mexico, including Baja and the Sea of Cortez." Perfect.

While *Charlie's Charts* did turn out to be immensely helpful in its descriptions of many Baja anchorages, it was completely unhelpful the first time we tried to use it, for anchoring at Islas de Todos Santos. We wanted Ensenada to be an in-and-out affair, and we planned to stop at the Islands of All Saints to rest, regroup, and then launch toward our first Mexican city for official business.

There were a number of complications upon approaching Islas de Todos Santos, discrepancies between what we expected, thanks to Charlie, and what we found. We motored all around the islands looking for anything even close to the *Charlie's Charts* description, or any appropriate anchorage at all. There was only one little spot, which already had a fishing boat in it. Oh, and did I mention there were aquaculture rings everywhere? Well, there were.

Another book we'd acquired, a gift from my mother and stepfather, was the Moon travel guide to Baja. Since we were finally *in* Baja, I whipped it out. Hmmm. *What does it say about Todos Santos?* Oh, it's a world-renowned surf spot where waves can exceed sixty feet high? You don't say!

But it *did* say exactly that. Apparently, just off the northwest tip of the northernmost island is a spot nicknamed "Killers," which most surfing resources (including *Moon Baja*) warn is "not for the uninitiated." South of Killers, near the channel between the two islas, are two other surf spots: "Chickens," where you go when you can't hack Killers, and "Thor's Hammer." And when do people travel here just to surf these monster waves? Winter. It was late December.

That. Was. IT! We'd had it! We were heading straight for Ensenada. None of these wack-ass island stop-offs. The sun was baking down on us, and we'd sailed all night after meaning to take only a little twenty-nautical-mile jaunt from San Diego; we were ready to be somewhere already.

So we headed toward Ensenada, population 466,814, where *Charlie's Charts* said we could anchor. For free.

We entered Ensenada Harbor, a massive green, red, and white Mexican flag waving overhead, and circled the area that Charlie said was open for general anchoring. There were no markers, no indication of an anchorage at all. We were stumped. Was it just unmarked? Should we go ahead and just drop the damn thing?

We might have . . . except for this dude, this Mexican-edition-Roy-Scheider-lookin' dude (long thin face, flat nose, dark furrowed skin), standing on the docks and whistling at us with great ardor, waving his arms energetically through the still, warm air.

We looked in his direction. He beckoned. Hard.

We acquiesced. We desperately wanted to anchor, but we motored over there reluctantly. We didn't know what else to do. He guided us into a spot and said, in pretty darn good English, "No more anchoring in the harbor. Port Captain's rule." We didn't know if we could believe him—maybe he was just trying to get a couple of dupes to pay for a slip they didn't need—but we didn't know a thing besides what Charlie had told us, and that wasn't panning out.

So we nestled ourselves into a small slip, which we were told cost one dollar per foot per night. We'd need to be there for two nights: take care of business the next day, stay the night, leave the following morning. We followed him up a wooden ramp to a deserted office. He wrote us a receipt for fifty-four dollars, even though we hadn't given him any money. Perhaps it was a bill? It sure looked like a receipt.

We were beyond tired, but we were too excited to rest. Our boat was stopped not on a floating ring off Los Coronados but in Ensenada, a.k.a. the "Cinderella of the Pacific," straight-translated as "Cove." Ashore we went! To explore! To EAT!

⚓ ⚓ ⚓

Ensenada's streets were lively and loud. They were filled with vendors and taco stands, the latter boasting huge glass goblets filled with salsas in a variety of colors. There were many, many pharmacies; our favorite had a bright yellow awning sporting a little "Superviagra" man on the side. He was blue and diamond-shaped with arms and legs—and a red speedo. His speedo looked . . . full. He was grinning and possessed the thick black eyebrows of a ladies' man. Next to him in white and red script were the words MUCHO CALIENTE. Above him it said, WITH VIAGRA, EVERYTHING IS POSSIBLE.

Down every street, vendors shouted, "*¿Tacos de pescados, amigos?*" Yes, we wanted fish tacos. But we wanted *tortas* more. And we got two of them for sixty pesos (about $4.50 at the time). The guy at the stand spilt open a couple of *bolillos*, threw them on a griddle, then proceeded to hack a bunch of carne asada into tiny, tender morsels with a cleaver. He piled them on the bread with cilantro, onions, salsa verde, and avocado. They looked awesome. "*Muchas gracias*," I said, a brown paper bag descending into my hands. I was proud of myself for ordering in Spanish.

By the time we finally turned in, we'd been awake for thirty-six hours.

"¡No Tenemos Seguros!"

Upon arriving in Mexico, our Spanish was not impressive. Jimmie spoke none, never had, and although I'd taken a few years in high school and a review course (mostly as a blow-off) in college, the latter had happened ten years prior. I hadn't practiced or studied at all on our way down the Oregon and California coasts. That said, I remembered a surprising amount of basic vocab and still understood how to construct simple sentences and conjugate verbs in the present tense. Plus, I was armed with one of those Random House pocket dictionaries with the plastic cover (from 1983). I thought I'd figure it out as needed.

I was about to get a crash course.

Things went smoothly at first. The man at the immigration counter spoke English. He gave us a few forms to fill out, we paid the Banjercito teller, and—voilà!—we had visas. Next, we had to submit forms to the port captain's desk. This did not go as well.

The couple in front of us were the absolute worst type of Americans you can imagine: stocky dude with blond crew cut and aviator shades yelling at the Mexican receptionist under the misguided impression that volume allows people to miraculously understand languages they don't speak, his pudgy blonde wife standing meekly by his side, looking unnecessarily frightened.

Crew cut man, though obviously a guest in another country, acted like he owned the place, conducting himself with a general air of entitlement and superiority and engaging in a lot of scoffing. They were just so put out. The lady at the counter clearly hated them—and had every right to. We understood that. But they were not the duo we wanted warming things up for us. *Two fucking A-hole gringos.* "Next?" *Oh, two more.*

This woman (as exemplified by the ignorant A-hole's yelling) did not speak English. I attempted some broken Spanish. We were barely grasping a few fragile filaments of language that could snap at any moment. I asked her to slow down—"*más despacio, por favor*" (a phrase I would say often)—and gathered that we needed two things: proof of insurance and a receipt for our slip in Ensenada.

For the slip, we had the receipt the Mexican Roy Scheider had given us the day before. We hadn't paid anyone any money yet, but we still had a piece of paper with an official-looking stamp on it. We hoped it would do.

"Where is it from?" she asked (*en Español*).

I tried to read the blurred ink of the stamp, made out the words "Royal Pacífico." So that's what I said, over and over: "Royal Pacífico." She shook her head. We didn't understand.

"*¿Tienen seguros?*" she asked, moving to the next subject. No, we didn't have insurance. We had done a fair amount of research on the topic of Mexican boat insurance and had come to the conclusion that we didn't need it. We did not plan on staying at a single marina in Baja. That, as we understood things, was the only time one needed insurance: to stay at a marina. I tried to explain this, saying, "*Sólo ancle, sólo ancle*"—"only anchor"—meaning we were exempt from needing insurance. Right?

No. Not according to her. We assumed she just didn't understand our uniquely ghetto approach to cruising, that she'd never encountered gringo sailors so dedicated to thriftiness that they would *always* anchor out. I realize, only now, that we were incongruously docked at a marina amid this debate.

"*Necesitan ustedes seguros,*" she said. ("You need insurance.")

"*No necesitamos seguros. Nosotros sólo ancle,*" I responded. This went on for a while, ending in a showdown:

"*Necesitan ustedes seguros.*"

"*Pero, no tenemos seguros.*"

"*¡Necesitan ustedes seguros!*" she insisted.

"*¡No tenemos seguros!*" I assured her.

That was it. She looked at me blankly, her deep brown eyes devoid of emotion. Her patience was shot. She completely ignored us and helped the next customer.

For probably a good ten minutes we stood there, foolishly, not sure if she was doing anything in relation to us or not. She'd picked up the phone at one point, and we considered the possibility that she was calling the Royal Pacífico Marina to verify our stay.

Turns out, the Royal Pacífico isn't a marina, it's a boat—a charter boat for sport fishing. It was docked, as we were, at the Marina Baja Fiesta, but that was completely unclear to us at the time.

A friendly looking, well-dressed, English-speaking fellow who'd been hanging out on the sidelines, watching and waiting, approached us. He was a paper-handling hustler of sorts. We asked him if he knew of a nearby insurance office. Yes, he did. He gave us directions and reassured us that—despite our *ancle*-only style, we did need insurance to import our boat. This was unhappy news, but at least it was delivered with confidence, and in a language we could understand. At least now we knew it really was necessary.

He offered to handle our affairs, take care of everything for us, but we declined. We were far too headstrong and independent (and cheap!) to consider paid, professional help. Yet.

⚓ ⚓ ⚓

We went in search of *seguros*, a search that, initially, proved fruitless. We couldn't find the office the man described. We did know, however, where the office for our "marina" was, so we went there. We were secretly hoping that we might get away with not having to pay at all, that whoever was working might accept our piece of thin, receipt-pad paper with its blurred blue stamp as proof of payment.

She did not. After some confused conversation, we handed over payment for two nights in our slip, and the receptionist kindly gave us a letter of receipt with a good clean stamp. She even handed over an aqua-colored business card with Marina Baja Fiesta printed on it.

Jimmie went to the boat to do some Internet research regarding the whereabouts of *seguros* offices. I tried to do the same verbally with the marina receptionist. Jimmie was more successful.

When it came to my early attempts at speaking Spanish in Baja, I often found, and then stuck to, a phrase that I knew could get across some essential part of our message (as with "*sólo ancle*"). That phrase in our dealings with the Ensenada insurance agents was "*más barato*" ("most cheap"). We were terrified of the cost of boat insurance, and though we try not to be cynical, we could only imagine that an insurance agent might want to take advantage of our seeming idiocy.

The first office we tried had a huge poster in its window depicting people having loads of fun aboard a recreational fishing boat. The text below their smiling faces read Barcos in large letters. Upon entering, we were informed that, despite the poster, this office did not sell boat insurance.

We referenced our *Moon Baja*, attempted asking around, walked a lot, and accomplished little. Once we'd eventually found a place that did sell *seguros para barcos*, we were stuck getting it there, whatever the cost. It might have been the only place in town, and we didn't have all day. In fact, we had only until all government offices—*aduana*, *inmigración, la administración portuaria*—closed. Time was running out.

After another tedious back-and-forth—"*Queremos* (we want) *seguros más barato.*" "*Este es el seguro más barato.*" "*¿Es verdad?*" "*Es verdad.*"—we forked over thirty-four hundred pesos (around $260). We sure didn't want to, but we didn't seem to have a choice. Then, at last, back to Official Business-ville we went, insurance papers in hand. *The clerk lady will be so proud*, I thought. We did, indeed, have *seguros*.

⚓ ⚓ ⚓

It had been a long day. It was hot and dusty, and we'd walked a ton, eaten little, drank not enough. Sound like I'm making excuses? I am. When we reentered the *aduana* office, our hustler dude was standing there, wearing his dark tie and shiny gray-striped dress shirt, looking very cool and together. Within moments of being back in the world of customs, we gave in and solicited his help. It was so worth it.

He told us what to fill out, translated for us at the counters, even ran somewhere nearby to make photocopies of our passports (which we apparently needed). Seemingly simultaneously, he processed our boat importation documents and checked us in and out of Ensenada with the port captain. He was amazing. He charged us twenty-five bucks. They were the last of Jimmie's *dólares Americanos*. After an entire day of forking over money and being confused, we surrendered them gladly. Muchas, *muchas* gracias, paperwork-hustling amigo, wherever you are.

⚓ ⚓ ⚓

Shortly thereafter, we found ourselves enjoying a couple of soft-serve vanilla ice cream cones and sampling mescal in a high-end liquor shop. We were feeling euphoric and accomplished—we hadn't even been arrested for aquaculture tampering! We bought a bottle.

It came complete with the traditional *gusano* (worm) suspended in olive-gold liquor like a gross little embryo in amniotic fluid. (I might have eaten it if Jimmie hadn't been so disgusted by the idea.) Joining the bottle on the dinette, spread across a hot pink folder we'd purchased at a San Diego Rite-Aid, was the evidence of our legitimacy: a stamped *importación* document with a faded outline of Baja on it, our brand-new visas, a receipt from the Banjercito, our Oregon title and registration, and black-and-white duplicates of our passports, pale next to the navy blue leather and gilded lettering of their originals.

Not a single person ever looked at those papers the entire time we were in Mexico. Not once.

"This Guy's *Asking* for It."

It was only after we had crossed the US-Mexico border that the incredible length of Baja itself occurred to us. Clearing customs in Ensenada had seemed accomplishment enough—we were there! Then we looked at our charts. We were so not there.

What remained of our journey—a hard reality for us to face—was a distance that almost matched the length of California. Even if it were all smooth sailing from here, it'd be about eight hundred nautical miles of smooth sailing (from Ensenada to Cabo San Lucas). Eight hundred nautical miles until we could finally get off the Pacific Ocean.

Now that we were in another country, there were also some key differences to consider—notably water and the Web, two pretty major resources in our world. Marinas and gas docks with drinkable water would become fewer and farther between. Using the Internet would require going ashore and finding (and paying to use) an Internet café, as Wi-Fi was nonexistent along the desolate coast of Northern Baja.

But the one absolutely huge difference was that, suddenly, we had no weather.

So far, the NOAA (and our ability to wait out any badness it might portend) had been our main safety net. It was something we'd grown to rely on very heavily. Now, it no longer existed. We had anticipated this and did have a backup plan: We didn't intend to sail farther south *without* weather advisories. We expected to replace our means of getting them.

Jimmie had purchased a shortwave radio before we left. Sailors are hypothetically able to use shortwaves to pick up "nets," which are set up and run by former and/or fellow cruisers and feature regular broadcasts of weather, relevant news, and sometimes friendly correspondence (i.e., "Amy and Jimmie on *Cotton* say hello to Rob on *Summer Wind*"). Nets were our only potential source of weather information, and we were having a hell of a hard time getting them in.

Not getting them in meant going out in God knows what. Which is why, at Puerto Santo Tomás, I started to get very nervous.

⚓ ⚓ ⚓

It had been a weird trip into the anchorage. Just as we rounded Punta Banda, the sky took on the look of a custom-airbrushed T-shirt or carnival prize. Pixelated streaks of purple and pink swept across the horizon, the sky a perfect gradient of navy to baby blue, and a tiny sliver of bright white moon, like some deity's clipped toenail, hung in the upper corner. It could have only been more bitchin' if it had said, "Amy hearts Jimmie" across the top in loopy black script.

Then, as quickly as this diaphanous wash of pastels had appeared, it vanished—or, rather, we vanished, into an alley of pure white fog. We rode through a maze of such alleys, hallways of cloud, all the way to our intended anchorage, unable to see a single concrete, directional thing but that word on our GPS: "destination." We heard a troublesome thunking against the hull upon entering the cove and knew what we were dealing with: kelp. We were probably farther from shore than we needed to be, but too blind to explore more thoroughly, we dropped anchor.

Our first full day anchored behind Punta Santo Tomás, the point that makes the *puerto*, as it were, was New Year's Eve, 2008. We considered ringing in the new year at Greenwich Mean Time (midnight would have been at 4:00 PM our time) so we could sleep through the local celebration in order to get up super early (like 4:00 AM) and head for our next stop. But we felt ill prepared to celebrate as 4:00 PM approached, and any excuse to postpone our new sailing-with-zero-information lifestyle sounded fine to me.

So we partied, somewhat more traditionally, in the early evening—at least as much as two people can party on a twenty-seven-foot sailboat in the middle of nowhere, which is pretty hard, apparently. We had filled our water tank with whatever had been available at the dock in Ensenada. It must have been potable, because we didn't get sick, but it was definitely weird. It had a sort of thickness to it, a viscosity you don't expect from water. No matter. We mixed it with Wild Berry Tang, mixed that with vodka, and rang in the New Year.

When that concoction was gone we broke out the André Cold Duck, which is basically sparkling alcoholic grape juice; it costs about $2.99 a bottle, so we'd bought one in anticipation of needing something like champagne.

I threw up (from booze, not Ensenada water) and we both passed out well before midnight, only to wake up around 2:00 AM and wonder what the hell happened. I was fully clothed. Jimmie was naked. We rose and ate macaroni and cheese. We also drank a lot of water—from our remaining, unslippery stash.

⚓ ⚓ ⚓

We would soon meet a sailor named Jays, pronounced "Jace" and presumably short for Jason. (Since the spelling J-A-Y-S suggests a collection of blue birds or a bag of potato chips and makes no sense, he will heretofore be referred to phonetically.) Anyway, Jace told us story after story of how fucked up his "damn boat" got at the hands of awful storms. At Cojo his anchor plating got ripped right off his deck by high winds. He'd seen sails torn apart in transit and standing rigging pop out of its hardware. He'd seen it all.

Then he mentioned how he'd just gone out one day, even though the forecast was terrible, and crossed the notoriously dangerous Columbia River Bar on the *ebb* tide—exactly when you're not supposed to do it. He subsequently got stuck out at sea, unable to cross back due to rough weather and poor timing. As we listened to him, we couldn't help but think, *This guy's* asking *for it.*

Some sailors do. But most of the seasoned sailors we talked to agreed on this point: going out when you know you shouldn't is what gets you in trouble. Some people just can't wait—they're on vacation for a certain length of time, or they need to be somewhere on a certain date—and that's exactly why we'd given ourselves a year, so we wouldn't have to rush, so we'd never *have* to go out.

Unlike Jace, bad weather didn't tempt us at all. We didn't crave some dramatic face-off with the gods of the sea, didn't picture ourselves atop the mast yelling at the heavens like Lieutenant Dan in *Forrest Gump.* No thanks. We'll take ten to fifteen knots, sun, and flat seas, thank you very much. That attitude had gotten us this far, along with the blessed NOAA, good decision making (for the most part), and patience. It is impossible, however, to make good decisions without information.

⚓ ⚓ ⚓

We stayed one more day at Santo Tomás and nursed our hangovers. It was January 1, 2009. We'd had no more luck with the nets, still no idea what to expect upon leaving.

I'm not sure if Jimmie ever truly considered quitting, but at this point, I did. We talked about other options, such as trying to sell the boat in Ensenada or San Diego. From there we could perhaps buy a motorcycle, or even trade for one, and travel Baja via the transpeninsular highway instead. Jimmie may have been humoring me by even discussing it; we may have been humoring ourselves, or merely coping. But I actually quite warmed up to the idea, going ahead on two wheels instead of one hull. I am not good at giving up. I must have been really freaked out.

But we kept going. We had just gotten there, and we couldn't give up on the nets so quickly. Perhaps we were in a bad place for reception. We had looked at a regular land forecast in Ensenada, and nothing crazy was in the works then. We would use our best judgment, take the shortest legs possible, and keep trying to get the cruisers' nets as we went along.

In the meantime, we employed a combination of old-fashioned methods: taking barometric readings, watching the clouds (there was a chapter on this in our *Chapman Piloting*, a classic tome on seamanship I'd gotten as a going-away gift from my boss at *Willamette Week*), and relying on instinct. We were sub-amateur meteorologists, but we were trying.

The next leg was fifty nautical miles; there was no way around it. I cleaned my raspberry-colored puke off the port side before we took off.

"Let's Just Say He Was a Fighter."

Despite all our trepidation, we reached our destination, Bahía Colnett, with minimal tumult. Day number one of zero-forecast sailing in the bag! A much-needed boost to our confidence. We anchored behind Punta Colnett, a giant Twix bar thrust westward into the Pacific, its rocky mass striped horizontally in thick bands of chocolate and cookie, and we slept.

⚓ ⚓ ⚓

Everyone always asks us if we fished all the time. No, we didn't. When you're sailing—especially as people who don't really know how to sail—it just sounds so much easier to break out a can opener and have another meal of chicken noodle soup and Saltines than it does to capture an animal. Or at least that's how we came to feel about it after just one successful trolling experience.

En route to Isla San Martín, a quick stop-off between Bahía Colnett and Bahía San Quintín, we were sailing well. It was windy enough to be moving along nicely but not so windy as to cause any alarm. The sun was shining brightly and we were warm for a change, two things that make everything seem less daunting. We still had no weather information, but we were feeling good. And we had recently become legal fishermen as far as Mexico was concerned. So I threw out a trolling line.

Back before we left Portland, we had imagined a menu rife with seafood: clams, scallops, abundant fish. But, thus far, we had only harvested a bucketful of purple varnish clams and a few crabs (Dungeness, we think) back in Tillamook Bay. The latter was done via the unignorable lure of Vienna sausages, an off-the-cuff bait concept executed by Jimmie. I got the clams in a more standard fashion, using a clam gun and trudging around the cold, wet sand looking for air holes. Almost every air hole yielded a clam (and usually a number of ghostly mud shrimp as well). Turns out, sticking your arm down a dank tunnel of sand and feeling around for the hard shell of a clam is super fun.

But fishing was not a strong suit for either of us. I had done a fair amount of trout fishing with spinners in Colorado at my mother and stepfather's behest, and Jimmie had done some bobber fishing in Oregon mountain lakes, but both of these approaches are fairly different from trolling for huge ocean fish. Nevertheless, I was given the pre-trip title of "Fishmaster McCullough" during our early make-believe sessions, and I felt it was my duty to be in charge of reaping our sea harvest. As such, I read up on the art of sailboat trolling, bought the appropriate gear, and spent a couple of days early in the trip tying lure setups with heavy-duty fishing line and swivel-snap connectors, enabling us to trail a variety of fluorescent squid-type things and metallic fish behind our vessel with ease.

The idea is to have a long rope attached to your stern cleat with a small portion of stretchy material worked in so the fish's initial strike doesn't snap your line. At the other end of said rope is some actual fishing line that terminates in an attachment loop for a variety of lures. This may not sound that complex, but it took some doing. Eventually, we had a little tackle box with all the tools we thought necessary to beckon some fresh fish onto our dinner plates.

Five months after departing, our fishing exploits thus far could be summed up as follows: making a few casts into Yaquina Bay to no avail, having "probly a tuna" on before nearly crashing into the Florence jetty and being pulled over by the Coast Guard, trying a few more fruitless casts at Hunters Cove, and then not being able to legally fish along all of California. But, here we were, sailing on a beautiful day off the coast of Northern Baja, scooting along so well that we were just kicking back. Why not go for it?

I tied a bell to the stretchy part of our line so we'd be notified of a strike if we were otherwise distracted, and then I threw the whole mess astern. In the time it took for me to toss out a few fish-preparation ideas—teriyaki steaks, breaded and fried for tacos, stir fry, sandwiches— we heard a distinctive *ding-a-ling!* Holy shit! A flash of silver sparked the water, fins smacked spray into the air, and something gunmetal and blue raced in our wake. A big, beautiful bonito was on our line. *Now what?*

Jimmie told Rabo-Jeeves to take five, grabbed the tiller, and steered by hand so I could get fish-acquisition gear out of the cockpit storage. Armed with a gaff, a bucket, and a small, bright orange fish whacker, we waited about five minutes (hoping to tire the thing out a little) and then pulled 'er in. Alongside the boat, our silver catch did seem docile and tired. Jimmie gaffed it and held it out of the water for a bit before thunking it on the head with the orange mallet. It wriggled in defiance. We planned to eat the thing, but we still felt kind of bad about killing it. It was so huge and majestic—and so stubborn.

A good couple of cracks on the head didn't seem to achieve much, so Jimmie resorted to using our winch handle, a trick some other sailor had mentioned once. He spun the hardware end around on its swivel handle, getting some momentum behind the impact. Blood poured down from the gaff, squirted through the air. Still, the fish squirmed and bent, flicked this way and that. *Hmmm.*

We'd heard people say you can spray liquor on a fish's gills to knock it out, but this seemed like a waste of booze. Jimmie tried punching it with the winch handle a few more times, and it appeared to be stunned. Perhaps we could just set it in our giant white plastic bucket and wait until it suffocated. *Gently, gently.*

Blood was everywhere: sprayed onto the jib, trailing tiny red streams through the cockpit, spotting our hands and clothes. We were a mess. Our boat was a mess. The fish was a mess, lying in a pool of saltwater-thinned blood. It seemed dead now. Jimmie gaffed it again. *We might as well hold it over the side and rinse it off,* he thought. Good idea.

He hefted the thing, which was striped in deep blue and violet lines along its green-silver back, and held it over the side. Coming in at an estimated thirty inches long and weighing about twenty pounds, it wasn't the easiest beast to just toss back and forth (it was roughly the length of my torso), but Jimmie was holding it at arm's length and being sure to lower it carefully while keeping the hook firmly planted in its lower jaw.

Transparent red mixed with crystal blue as its relatively miniscule amount of blood met the massive bath of the Pacific. Then—like we'd jolted the thing with a little thalassic defibrillator—it sprang back to life, twisting and turning on its gaff as if it hadn't just received countless blows to the head and a lengthy oxygen-less nap. *What the fuck?!?*

It began all over again: Jimmie spinning the hard metal end of the winch handle around and walloping our poor bonito in the noggin with it, his timidity waning in an effort to put the damn thing out of its misery. More blood splattering the cockpit, and the two of us waiting, peering into the flat, black poker-chip eyes of our dinner. And waiting. And waiting.

Finally, it seemed our fish had undoubtedly expired. We reluctantly, sheepishly lowered it over the side again, rinsing away the deep red murder evidence. This time, it stayed dead. Jimmie held it there while I filled bucket after bucket with saltwater and splash-rinsed the cockpit, pinkish fluid rushing out the open transom. The fish now awaited its gutting and cleaning—a task that fell into my realm. Jimmie went back to sail maintenance and, eventually, a switch to motoring when the wind shifted to its common place, directly in front of us.

Meanwhile, I attempted to fillet my first fish. My stepfather had given me a crash course in filleting before we left, but this training seemed suddenly useless in the face of our giant catch and my tiny fillet knife. After some tedious weaving of my paltry shiv through all manner of fish flesh, I broke out the hacksaw—the same saw, incidentally, that had broken us free from the clutches of our Islas Coronados aquaculture ring.

The hacksaw seemed the only thing capable of beheading the fish and cutting through its spine, both things I apparently thought necessary. Even without its head, with all meat cut free of skin and scale and bone, there was still so much fish. Too much fish, definitely, for two people. We didn't have a refrigerator and could only eat so much. Guilt set in—guilt for killing an impressive beast of which we would have to waste a fair portion.

The best thing we could come up with was to share with the sea. Surely if we dumped our surplus meat and scraps over the edge some hungry little community of creatures would be overjoyed to scavenge the crumbs.

⚓ ⚓ ⚓

So, after all that work—hauling in and relentlessly beating a poor creature of the sea, reviving it and killing it again, beheading and dicing it into kabob-size hunks, sharing the offal with its brethren, and eventually breading and frying the remains—we had fish tacos. I served them with rice, corn tortillas, and a trashy attempt at chipotle cream (Tapatío plus mayo packets).

They were pretty tasty, but a bit more demanding, prep-wise, than even my most elaborate dinners thus far. So that was it. We didn't fish again. We can-opened and dry-mixed our culinary butts off and were happy to have mac and cheese and relish for our tuna.

Now, whenever anyone's stunned at our meager angling spoils, dropping their jaw and repeating, incredulously, "*One* fish?" we simply shrug and reply, "Let's just say he was a fighter."

"Unless You Feel Adventurous, *Do Not* Attempt an Entrance."

Bahía Santa María is a large bay along the coast; Bahía San Quintín, on the other hand, is a long lagoon-like bay *inside* the coastline. *Charlie's Charts* includes Santa María as a potential anchorage, but venturing farther in is cautioned sternly against. "Unless your vessel is shallow draft and you feel adventurous," Charlie warns, "*do not* attempt an entrance." Apparently, the entry is narrow, shallow, and constantly shifting. "Entrance and exit from this spot can *only be done at high water*," says Charlie, again employing a few emphatic words. Nevertheless, we wanted in.

We did have a shallow draft (four feet three inches, though we always thought of it as five for good measure), and we *were* on an adventure. If we got in, we'd be closer to getting gas, supplies, and maybe some drinking water. We had to try. And we knew the inner bay would be *so* nice. It would be a like a big, warm, placid lake. Not a moldy, gray, you're-trapped-by-a-wintry-gale lake (I'm looking at you, Tillamook Bay), but a pleasant, sunny Mexican lake. We wanted that. After a string of bad anchorages and wakeful, rolly nights' sleep, we needed it.

⚓ ⚓ ⚓

One state you don't want to be in when aboard a boat is stopped. Anchored, yes, fine. But even at anchor you move around plenty. Even tied securely to a dock, the hull lightly bobs with passing wakes or swings gently on its dock lines. I'm talking straight stopped. That means something has gone awry.

Over the next week, we would find ourselves stopped three (yes, three) times. The first was, not surprisingly, on our way through the often "shoal and impassable" entrance to Bahía San Quintín. Had we trusted technology more than our instincts, we would most likely have cleared the entry without issue. But when faced with what looks like a route leading directly onto the beach, one is left little choice but to go with one's gut—even when one's gut is mistaken.

We had planned a route with our Nobletec, as usual, and this was a tight one. We had to be far enough into Bahía Santa María to skirt the roiling flows coming around the *cabo* but also far enough *out* to avoid another surfing-on-breakers incident à la Florence, Oregon.

Jimmie carefully hand-steered us while I went up on the bow and looked out at the murky, wave-curdled water and—directly ahead—at

Punta Azufre, a buff-colored knob on the eastern side of Bahía San Quintín's tiny entry. If we stayed on our current course, it appeared we could go ahead and plan on running right into it.

But that's exactly what our GPS track had in store, heading straight. We considered the fact that our perspective might be deceiving us, but as we got closer and closer to Azufre's tan, sandy spit, we veered to port—directly into the sandy bottom.

Within moments, we'd slid well into the shoal roping off most of the inner bay. Stopped. Our keel nestled in ocean-soaked mud. Our home was a bright turquoise mass stuck between Mount Mazo, a dusky volcano rising above Cabo San Quintín, and the low beige mound of Punta Azufre. Had these three forms been in a "One of These Things Is Not Like the Other" segment of *Sesame Street,* the "other" would have come easily to even the densest of kids.

One of these things just doesn't belong. Maybe that's what the three *panga* fisherman who swooped around the corner thought upon finding us, two gringos in a stationary blue behemoth, tiny shoal-level breakers pummeling its hull every six to eight seconds.

They sped up to us in their whitewashed slab of boat, a hefty outboard hung off the back and built-in lockers full of ice and the day's catch circling the interior.

"*¿Necesitan ayuda?*" they asked.

"*¡Sí!*" we responded.

I was able, however haphazardly, to portray the essential (though I'm sure it was obvious): "*Necesitamos aguas más profundas, por favor.*" They took two of our dock lines, tied them into a V, and puuuulled us in zig-zagging motions to deeper water. We were in!

Jimmie gave the *pescadores* 140 pesos for their trouble. (They wanted thirty US dollars, about twice that, but we were out of American moolah and, grateful as we were, still had our budget to mind.) I happened to have a copy of Dr. Seuss's *Huevos Verdes con Jamón* and threw it in after getting a few nods in response to the question, "*¿Tienen ustedes niños?*" I thought it was a clever tip at the time, but I think they would have preferred another two hundred pesos.

"Hold Tight."

Our next grounding we can at least blame on someone else.

The breadth of San Quintín's inner bay, we were soon to learn, is an illusion. The wide-spread banks flush with opaque water give the impression of a "full" bay, but much of it is only inches deep. We'd stayed one night near a settlement of empty-looking buildings called Pedregal, but we knew the farther up we anchored the smaller the distance we'd have to row and/or walk to get supplies. With all this in mind, Jimmie crafted two more routes: "Deeper Lagoon" and the even more ambitious "Crazy Deep Lagoon."

Deeper Lagoon went pretty well, with average depths of ten to twelve feet and only occasional scares in the six-to-seven-foot range. There was even an anchor-friendly area in the twelve-foot realm. *But what the hell*, we thought. *Let's push it.* We went for Crazy Deep . . . but found ourselves instantly discouraged. Depths were dropping rapidly. We threw JB in reverse and headed back.

Then, just as we were about to settle for Deeper Lagoon, a sky blue *panga* sped up. The two fellows aboard announced that if we followed them they could lead us via the channel up to an anchorage right next to the Old Mill, a small business complex with a landing. The clear leader of the duo was a middle-aged Mexican man with a strong brow, leathery skin, and uncharacteristic sapphire eyes. He seemed trustworthy, but I was suspicious of an unmentioned fee.

"It's deep enough to anchor right here, though," offered Jimmie, not one to jump on another man's bandwagon (or landing, as it were).

"Sure it is," said the leader in perfect English, "but it's the only rocky area in the whole bay. Follow us and you'll be all set: nice anchorage, land access. I own a restaurant and bar up there. Whatever you need."

"Yeah, it's real nice!" shouted the white man with him in something like an Australian accent. He was nodding enthusiastically and grinning. They seemed like a novel pair.

Jimmie and I glanced at each other, shrugged with our eyes.

"Lead the way!" shouted Jimmie.

The Mexican man was on a cell phone, navigating the area with an easy confidence; this was his home and he knew it well. His passenger occasionally glanced back at us, nodding encouragingly or brushing the hair from his eyes.

Scooting along behind them, we watched as the depth meter's readings dropped . . . and dropped. *They know what they're doing, right?* Despite the pilot's apparent familiarity with the bay, he led us—six feet, five feet, four feet—right into a silt bank. And we stopped. Again.

Once our "guides" realized they'd left us motionless behind them, they spun around and half-assedly attempted to pull us off with the biggest rope we had between us. Nothing doing. We were very stuck. And the tide was going out.

Carlos and Dylan, as we came to know them, said they'd go get a bigger rope and return. We were left with nothing to do but sit and wait—hung out to dry.

About forty-five minutes later, just Dylan—a guy who'd given Jimmie a "weird feeling" right from the start—came back. He had no bigger rope and no bigger boat and no good news. "Carlos had to run," he told us. And Dylan himself was on his way out to lead a few friends up from the outer bay.

"The tide will be up in a few hours," he offered as consolation. "Hold tight."

Not too long after, Carlos returned, all apologies and with thicker rope. He broke us free and led us far up the bay, into Crazy Deepness we'd never imagined. We anchored near the Old Mill and then secured a stern line—with Carlos's help—to his high, pier-like dock. Strangely, tied just to the north of us was a decrepit green sailboat with the name FLORENCIA painted in white letters next to its home port, FLORENCE, OREGON, where we'd almost duffed it on the jetty rocks.

It was a very stable arrangement there by the Old Mill, with a view of volcanic cinder cones to the west and vast, dry spaces to the east. We still had to get in the dinghy and paddle over to the boat ramp to get ashore, but the trip took about ten strokes each way. Not bad.

Meanwhile, Dylan had gotten his friends stuck in the mud.

⚓ ⚓ ⚓

Carlos, we learned, was an ex–business exec who'd lived and worked in San Diego for years. He gave it all up to come home to Baja and open a restaurant in the middle of nowhere, on Bahía San Quintín. We liked him.

His place was a transient home to a strange collection of people (although to be fair, any collection of people was strange to us after 120 nautical miles of absolute nothingness in Northern Baja). There were the Belgian sailors: a white-headed man and his graying wife, both with thick, furrowed skin and thicker accents. There was *Phoenix*, which housed the aforementioned glutton-for-punishment Jace, as well as his yellow-haired wife, Brenna, and a grade-school-aged daughter. (For some reason, the *Phoenix* crew had a hard time grasping the name of our boat; every time we reiterated "*Cotton*," they seemed puzzled, and I would think, *You know, like the fabric—the "FABRIC OF OUR LIVES!"*)

And then there was Dylan.

Dylan, described (drunkenly) by Jace as a "dweeb," had ear-length, straight, gold hair and was always wearing khaki shorts and either a wrinkled plaid shirt or an oversized crew neck sweater. There was something pretty '90s and subtly wealthy about his look—like a knock-off William McNamara or movie adaptation of a Bret Easton Ellis character.

A South African political refugee (the accent was Afrikaner not Australian), Dylan was there with his wife and father, the latter being some sort of ex-politico who Carlos told us was "not welcome back" in the Rainbow Nation. The three of them would motor out of Bahía San Quintín once every twenty-eight days and call in their coordinates in order to reestablish the motif that Dylan Sr. did not belong to any country. According to Carlos, they had to go at least twelve nautical miles (about fourteen land miles) into the Pacific—far enough to be in international waters. And if they ever had the gall to take their white asses back to South Africa, rumor was they would be executed.

Their vessel/dwelling was interesting in its own right. An off hybrid of fishing troller and sailboat, it was big and bulky and looked like it would have been lucky to catch either breeze or bonito. It mostly just puttered about by inboard diesel or remained anchored while its inhabitants drove the dirt road to Lázaro Cárdenas and back or sat drinking Tecates at Carlos's bar.

It's strange, too, that a family of live-aboard refugees had a vehicle at all, but Dylan drove a Bronco-esque contraption, frequently toting Belgians and Americans and Mexicans to town for gas and supplies. One serendipitous day he even chauffeured our gas cans back to the waterfront for us.

"Hello, Good-bye."

Though Lázaro Cárdenas has about seven times the population of Seneca, Illinois, in many ways it was not unlike my small midwestern hometown. There was a main drag, a grocery, a few shops, and a park, and like Seneca, the main attraction appeared to be the ubiquity of gas stations. If you were a kid there, the most exciting things to do were ride a bike, go to the *panadería* for a sweet roll, or goof around in the park. That's pretty much what we did.

We stopped at a roadside *lonchería* (snack bar) for a Fanta and a *limonada*. This particular operation, like many in Baja, was essentially a food cart with a local mom making ham-and-cheese sandwiches inside. But rather than being designed for easy mobility and small-space efficiency, it was exactly like a regular kitchen, with full-size fridge, oven, and range; a counter and shelves; even a sink of dirty dishes, all of it crammed into a trailer, like one compartment of a dollhouse separated from its frame and set on the side of Mex 1.

We also attempted to get Internet. Wi-Fi in Lázaro Cárdenas seemed like a long shot, but you never know. We found a shady spot in the town park and broke out the laptop. Something unexpected happened next. No, we didn't connect to a network, we became unsuspecting celebrities. Seriously. Forget Fanta or *pasteles* or the "Leo Mania" VHS box set we saw in the gift shop down the street (DiCaprio's allure knows no borders); *we* were the hot, now thing. Within moments of unfolding our cordless computer and attaching its extreme-reception antenna, we were surrounded by children, their eyes peering at us in wonder. We smiled friendly, close-mouthed smiles at them and went about our business. They stayed. They stared.

"*Hola*," I offered. Nothing. Then a tiny girl in faded orchid-colored shorts took a few steps forward and gave me a sweet little hug. Her wispy brown hair was tied with a ribbon at the top of her head. I patted her on the back. She retreated into the group again.

"No available networks," said the little globe in the corner of the screen. *Fine*, we thought, *this is getting kind of weird, anyway.*

We slid our relatively cheap Compaq notebook into our backpack and got up. "*Adiós*," I said, and we waved gently at their stunned little faces. They merely blinked. A few dogs scuffled in the dust. A bird squawked. We walked away, a team of grave faces staring at our backs.

"That's Stupid."

The next day, Jace, a tall, sinewy guy with messy brown hair who was ever clad in cargo shorts, informed us of a birthday party. Some of the locals were throwing down at the *panga*-rental place later on, he said, and he'd been told to "invite the neighbors."

We were on the fence about what to do. A Mexican birthday party sounded intriguing and potentially fun, but we were also skeptical of our invitation. Did they really want a bunch of cracker-ass sailors crashing their party? Or had Jace invited himself, and us as well? We didn't want to impose—or to mooch. We decided to hoof it down to the closest mini-super (short for mini-*supermercado*) to buy a few snacks and play the night by ear.

The sun was nearly down by the time we turned back toward Carlos's place, and as we approached the *panga* complex we heard an amplified guitar and a guy singing "Sweet Caroline" in Spanish. The smell of hot coals was in the air, and a murmur of voices filled gaps in the music. It seemed the party had started. All the gringos were there: Jace and Brenna, the Belgians, Dylan and Co., and they seemed welcome. We figured we would be, too.

A few hours later, Jimmie was chatting it up with the Belgian guy, holding a plastic tumbler of scotch in one hand and a slab of beef on bread in the other. The grill we'd smelled was an epic collage of meats and fire—a stone rectangle the size of a hopscotch court right in the center of the party, its crimson-black embers glowing under crusty oyster shells and huge sides of beef. A table littered with thick slices of white bread, condiments, towers of clear plastic cups, and a seemingly endless array of liquors was nestled against the rental office.

Everything was very help-yourself—except for the sea urchin. Some guy whom I remember only as a dark figure with a Tupperware bin made several loops around the party crowd offering tastes of raw sea urchin. It looked kind of like pink grapefruit. Jimmie and I each took one. It had a strangely creamy texture and briny-mineral taste similar to oyster. Jimmie liked it so much he had another—then suddenly felt he might be sick. (It was a false alarm.)

We got trapped for a bit by Jace, who was delivering a lengthy monologue on the merits of homemade tortillas and the longevity of cabbage. In the midst of this, he reached into a small leather sheath on his belt, brandished his oyster knife and demoed it, slicing along the seam of several fire-roasted shells and offering up the salty wet meat inside.

"Mmmm," we purred.

When Jimmie complimented his specialized tool, Jace proclaimed, flabbergasted, "You don't have an oyster knife?!" Well, we'd have to get one, he continued. Dammit-all-to-hell, if he had an extra, he'd have handed it right over!

Our mooching reservations behind us, we heartily accepted all that was thrown our way: beer, tequila, steak-wiches, scotch, grilled oysters, sea urchin, more beer. We eventually made our way over to the birthday boy, a linebacker-sized man wearing a black-and-gray potato sack pullover, the kind that was so popular in the early '90s. His face was almost as wide as his body, and it was the kind of deep brownish red that only happens when a naturally dark person gets very sunburned and/or drunk.

When presented to him, we both shouted "*¡Feliz Cumpleaños!*" He smiled and chuckled and shook our hands. Everyone looked back and forth at one another smiling and nodding. Then the language barrier and the fact that we were strangers took over and we went silent. Someone thought to raise a drink. "*¡Salud!*" we chimed in.

We socialized more effectively with the gringo sailors. The Belgian woman was singing "Love Me Tender" with the Mexican guitarist, so I talked to Brenna, who was very drunk. She explained, in detail, the trials of cruising with children. I could imagine, I told her, though I couldn't really. We saw many sailors with dogs or children or both. It seemed overwhelming enough to be just me and Jimmie. Her drunken monologue made me thankful for the simplicity of our situation. Before long, she was carted off to dance wobbly with one of the locals.

Mr. Belgian, weathered and white as any stereotypical salty seaman you can think of, told Jimmie all sorts of things: the detailed history of his vessel; about boating, during some previous era, down the Amazon or some such crazy-big, famous river. They got to talking about anchors. Jimmie told him of the rudder he'd pulled up in Santa Monica and how he'd almost cut the line.

"That's stupid," said the Belgian, in commiseration more than judgment. "You should never cut away your anchor no matter how stuck it is, because that's just lost money you could have used to buy a nice dinner." True that.

⚓⚓⚓

Carlos was a man of his word; the Old Mill did provide us with many conveniences. We were able to tie up to a dock *for free* and stay, as we were often reminded, as long as we wanted; we were treated, on the night of our arrival, to a couple of on-the-house margaritas at Carlos's restaurant; and one morning, as we were in the midst of retrieving complimentary water from the restaurant sink (nearly thirty gallons' worth), Carlos offered us a surprise breakfast of crab claws in paprika, served fresh off the stove in the Old Mill's professional stainless-steel-everything kitchen.

Carlos was not only honest, he was gregarious, generous, and an excellent taker of tequila shots. Jimmie and I respected him, which made us all the more wary of taking advantage of his hospitality. So we took our water and ate paprika'd crab claws on his insistence and tipped his bartender who'd lived briefly in Oregon as well or better than we would have in real life, and we stayed for only three nights. Then Jimmie and I said *adiós*, gave him hard handshakes and hugs, respectively, and moved on—back toward the outer bay, back toward the ocean.

We were happy to be on our own again, eager to get anchored and relish in the calm of the inner bay all on our own, with no neighbors. Then we grounded. For the third time.

We'd been successfully motoring through the reverse of our Crazy Deep Lagoon and Deeper Lagoon routes, respectively, with no major depth scares. (We even stopped briefly near our earlier Pedregal anchorage and purloined some Wi-Fi in order to download SeaTTY, a weather-faxing program. Many boats at sea, especially commercial vessels, get their weather info via weather fax, and although we didn't have a fax machine, apparently you can download a "fax" right onto your laptop in this day and age with the help of a shortwave radio. The radio receives an audio signal containing weather data, and through the magic of sound cards and computing wizardry, that signal is translated into a visible weather report. It was a new ray of hope on our lack-of-forecast situation.)

Things were going well, but we were back in the visually deceptive sheet of water that covered everything from the makeshift channel to the rocky shore below Mount Ceniza, where there's no telling what's ten feet deep and what's two. As it happened, we went from one to the other too quickly to stop it.

Once we'd accepted our grounded fate (a feeling that was becoming awfully familiar), Jimmie rowed our anchor out in the dinghy and dropped it in deeper water so we could gradually tug ourselves toward it when the tide returned. Currently, it was on the ebb.

By the time the tide had gone all the way out, we were completely balanced on our keel, with absolutely no water anywhere around us. Even the dinghy, tied from the back by a now-slack dock line, was grounded. Mud the color of wet cement, sprinkled with a lime green confetti of seaweed, surrounded our turquoise hull, a deep gouge behind us where our keel had slid into place. After several hours (enough time to include lunch and some significant lounging) and with each little spit of the ocean back in our direction, we finally began to float again.

It'd be silly to say grounding three times—in the same area!—didn't bruise our egos a little. In fact, I cried about it. This last one had been my fault. But the boat was fine, and at the end of the day we had everything we wanted: anchorage in twenty to thirty feet, a dinner of warm tomato soup and tostadas from Lázaro Cárdenas, and each other for company. Just each other.

At night, whales came in on the high tide and swam around our boat, blowing fishy spray into the air and arching their backs through the glassy surface. I wondered if they had trouble navigating the entrance to the inner bay. They were locals, though. They probably knew the way.

"Everything OK?"

Our next few Northern Baja stops—Punta Baja, Bahía San Carlos, Punta Escarpada—were merely steps toward Isla Cedros. At 87.1 nautical miles, the distance out to Cedros exceeded our "terror trip" around Cape Mendocino by 2.6 nautical miles. And it wasn't just a long way, it was a long way *out*, with the great big Sebastián Vizcaíno Bay placing sixty-two standard miles between the island and the coast. And we'd still only managed to download half a weather fax.

The natural world had thrown some crazy stuff our way—like the time we'd seen a small offshore island, San Geronimo, turn upside-down on itself in a mind-boggling, heat-induced mirage, appearing as an hourglass of land growing out of the sea and into the sky—but we were still plugging along. So why not sail to an offshore island three times as far from Baja as Catalina is from L.A.? No biggie. It was far more efficient than skipping along the inside of the bay. And beyond Isla Cedros was Turtle Bay, a sheltered sailors' haven we expected to be full of *torta* stands and *bancos* and perhaps even a liquor store. For once, we put eagerness before fear.

The thing we inadvertently discovered in doing so was the particular bliss of solitary night sailing.

⚓ ⚓ ⚓

Amazingly, we could see Isla Cedros, a dusky bump on the horizon, before it was even dark. We were still astoundingly far from it, a good sixty nautical miles, but we were pointed straight at it, and there was no other land at this direct heading into the Pacific. It had to be Cedros. And, wouldn't you know, that distant rocky bump grew a little larger with each passing ripple.

As the sun went down, we spent some time on deck lounging on our "comfort module," otherwise known as a backrest pillow with arms. We were sailing along just fine, but our post-dinner coffee buzz was wearing off. We could push through, stay up all night, but—in a move that separated our unified sailing dyad for the first time in five months—we resolved to try taking turns in short shifts, three hours each. Jimmie would start.

I went below decks (I say this as if we had more than one) and lay on the converted "snuggle dinette," which we'd prepared as a nearby bed for the person who wasn't piloting. Sleep in this situation was sort of a one-eye-open kind of half sleep, but it was still restful. I could hear things happening on deck—the slide of the traveler across the hatch, the loosening and tightening of sheets, the rush of water under the hull, and the *ree, ree* of Rabo-Jeeves moving our tiller back and forth, making subtle adjustments to keep us on course—but these noises were commonplace, much like the ceiling fan in your bedroom or the drip of a faucet. They were almost comforting. So I napped, lightly, until 2:30 AM.

When I took over for Jimmie, he did the same: slept with one eye and ear open, calling up an "Everything OK?" if a noise struck him as strange or the wind seemed to pick up. But there I was, sailing alone, in the dark. Everything seemed to stretch infinitely—sky, air, water, stars.

It's strange how much the human body responds to the sways of nature when living so exclusively with it. Sun goes down and you are tired. Sun comes up and you go. And on those rare occasions when sailing overnight, you become a tiny witness to the earth's motion within its solar system. The Big Dipper and Orion and the Milky Way, and all the stars and planets you can see, appear from beneath the horizon and make their way across the sky, traveling in a long, graceful arc, as hours pass. You see the sun and moon both rise and set.

The only scare I had was from dolphins occasionally bursting—like torpedoes and completely unannounced—through the surface of the water, shooting as high into the dark air as our safety lines. The first one startled the hell out of me. But when your demon in the night turns out to be a playful dolphin, that's a pretty freakin' good place to be.

I hung what we called the "rock module," a small portable speaker unit for the iPod, on a doorway hinge and listened, ecstatically, to whatever I wanted. Jimmie and I have very agreeable musical taste, but there's something liberating about not having to consider the other—

at all—when making a selection. That might have been the best part: rocking out. By myself.

When my three hours were up, I didn't even rush to wake Jimmie. I let him sleep until he woke on his own, which wasn't much later. We both had a weird, instinctual sense about our shifts. He came up and together we found our way to the second of two possible anchorages, Las Palmitas. *Charlie's Charts*' cryptic anchorage descriptions weren't much help in the dark, but that isn't why we'd passed the northernmost option. We'd passed it because were enjoying ourselves. We wanted to keep sailing.

⚓⚓⚓

The next leg of our trip took us past Puerto Morro Redondo, where salt from Guerrero Negro's huge evaporation ponds across the bay—like, six million tons of it per year—is loaded onto ships for export. Near the industrial dock was a vast field of white, as if a freak snowstorm had hit Isla Cedros in one square spot and was stubbornly refusing to melt, despite the heat.

Compared to the epic (for us) journey out to Cedros, it wasn't far at all to the next stop, Bahía Tortugas, roughly thirty-eight nautical miles. And it's a mere twelve standard miles if you draw a straight line from the Island of Cedars to the tip of the Vizcaíno Peninsula, that massive spur on the west side of Baja. That twelve-mile distance encompasses a lot, though. It officially separates Baja Norte and Baja Sur, changes the time zone from Pacific to mountain, and switches the unofficial state beer from Tecate to Pacífico.

Passing Punta Eugenia (Vizcaíno's tippity tip) meant we had crossed into the last state of our trip, Baja California Sur. There weren't any more land borders to cross from here on out—only that final, imaginary line between the Pacific Ocean and the Sea of Cortez.

"Enrique, Dieciséis."

Turtle Bay was full of sailboats, as is often the case. It's one of two stops on the "Baja Ha-Ha," a two-week rally from San Diego to Cabo San Lucas that takes place every October, and it's graciously tucked behind a lot of protective land to the north. In fact, it's perfectly ensconced in in a good three hundred degrees of land, leaving only the southwestern entry available to oncoming weather. Pretty inviting.

We were later than the Ha-Ha folks, an event which, ironically, is open only to boats *over* twenty-seven feet and specifically those "designed, built and . . . maintained for open ocean sailing." But there were still plenty of gringos lurking about, and we ended up meeting a few of them, to greater and lesser degrees of chagrin.

Our least favorite, to be sure, was a fellow we now refer to as "the Baja Bandidos guy." He claimed to be some kind of writer, though I'll admit I didn't take his scribelihood all that seriously. I would have, however, if he hadn't seemed like such a douche. His main fault was a snide attitude toward the locals, particularly the boss man of the public dock, Enrique. Now, we weren't huge fans of Enrique's operation ourselves, but only because we're incredibly cheap and stubbornly self-sufficient. Our "writer" friend had issue with Enrique ripping people off, which he may or may not have done, but based on our experience, he seemed like an entrepreneur you could choose to deal with or simply ignore. And I can't say I blame the guy for trying to make a buck off the constant influx of sailors taking advantage of the port.

That said, our experience with Enrique's crew was infuriating, awkward, and confusing. We would rather have skipped it. But it still wasn't all that pricey, even by our standards.

⚓⚓⚓

We got to Turtle Bay around 2:30 PM *mountain* time and couldn't resist heading ashore. We were pleased to see a floating dock extending from the beach, just west of a long cinder-block wall reading Bienvenidos a Bahia Tortugas (sans accents) in big, black block letters. This town of

2,671 people welcomed us. It had a Pemex (Mexico's state-owned—and only—brand of gas station) and mini-supers and Internet and, according to our slightly outdated guidebook, a bank. A thriving metropolis with dirt roads—and we wouldn't even have to make a beach landing!

Within seconds of tying up to the floating dock, we were instantly greeted by a young Mexican boy in tan shorts and a white T-shirt. He was eager to help in any way he could: reaching out to take oars or a dock line, steadying our boat as we disembarked. We shook our heads in the negative manner, and I said, "*Estamos bien*" a few times, but we couldn't shake him. His helpfulness was ebullient.

By the time we'd reached the shore end of the dock, we'd been assigned a more grown-up helper, a big, heavyset teenager named Pedro. He asked if we needed to know where a *mercado* was, and our natural response was, "Sure." We thought he'd just point us in the right direction. Oh *no*. Pedro was now our tour guide. We naively didn't realize we were hiring the guy.

We found Pedro to be a little thick because the guy couldn't take a hint. Once we realized what was going on, I repeatedly told him, "*No necesitamos ayuda. Estamos bien. ¡Adiós!*" But he wouldn't budge. He'd just say, "*Enrique, dieciséis.*" I realize I probably have a horrible midwestern American accent when I speak Spanish, but I do understand Spanish pronunciation, and I was making pretty basic statements: "We don't need help. We are fine. Good-bye!" But Pedro was not getting it. All he said—over and *over*—was "*Enrique, dieciséis.*" Enrique, sixteen.

We knew *why* he was saying it. It was a basic advertisement for his employer, Enrique. Just dial up channel sixteen and Enrique will deliver to your cockpit whatever you might desire: water, gas, groceries, directions. "*Enrique, dieciséis.*" All they needed was a jingle so he could sing it to us instead of stolidly repeating it—you know, *really* get it stuck in our heads.

At the *mercado,* we awkwardly browsed while Pedro stood in the doorway, waiting, we figured, either for some sort of payment or to show us to our next destination. I went over and told him again that WE WERE GOOD, using the best Spanish I could muster. But he wasn't about to leave without a tip. Jimmie eventually forked over twenty pesos (a little under two dollars at the time), and Pedro finally turned and left, dragging himself back toward the dock, kicking up dust as he went.

Just under two dollars probably sounds pretty weak. But it was money we were shelling out for something we didn't want. It was also twenty of our quickly dwindling supply of any pesos at all—money we'd have to get further on than we ever expected.

⚓ ⚓ ⚓

Our sailing-scribe anchorage-mate told us he planned to "out" all the "Baja Bandidos" along the peninsula in his upcoming opus . . . or post . . . or whatever. Give other cruisers a heads-up as to whom to do business with and whom to avoid. Perhaps he felt hustled by Enrique and his crew. And I guess we felt that way after our first landing, too. We were new to the bay, and they bamboozled us. I sure wouldn't call the guys "bandidos," though. Capitalists, sure. But crooks, not so much.

Plenty of sailors, I'm sure, didn't mind forking over some cash for directions, help carrying supplies, someone to watch over their dinghy. We didn't care for the help or the expenditure, so we didn't land at the floating dock again. We simply paddled to a nearby beach and locked our dinghy to a drainage pipe near the tide pools. The bay was so calm, so well sheltered, that coming in and launching over the surf was no issue. The surf was nonexistent.

From where we first beach-landed, we had to walk through a Mexican naval base to get to town. It consisted of a few buildings surrounding a gravel lot full of military vehicles with big knobby tires. Here and there, imposing men in dark-colored uniforms and aviator shades hung around, huge guns on their backs. The scene was a little intimidating. One of the men came over. I was carrying a trash bag.

"*¿Basura?*" he asked.

"*¡Sí!*" I responded.

He approached, grabbed the bag, and swung it into a nearby dumpster.

We smiled and said, "*¡Gracias!*"

"*No problema*," was his response. We decided we liked the Mexican navy.

Before cutting ourselves off entirely from Enrique's posse, we used them to get gas. Some dudes from the dock were motoring around the anchorage, and Jimmie flagged them down manually, forgoing the "*dieciséis*" part. For a fee of two hundred pesos (around fifteen bucks), Enrique's men would take our empty gas can ashore for us, fill it with gas, and return it. That was too sweet a deal for even us to resist.

We were hoping they might also have potable water at the rickety dock, something we would have happily hauled our six-thousand-pound ass over there for. So we swung by (on foot) to ask. Guess who met us at the end of the pier? Yup. Pedro. I asked him in Spanish if there was "*agua bebible*" or "*agua potable*," just to cover my bases. His response was, simply, "*Enrique.*"

"Snuggle Hard or Go Home."

It turned out the dock water, which was advertised as "purified" under a list of services on the pier, was only pure in that it wasn't *salt*water. You could use it for cleaning and laundry, but not to drink. This is exactly why we'd bought portable tanks back in L.A., both for added volume and in the event that we couldn't just pull up to a dock and stick a hose in our boat, as we were accustomed to doing in the States. We suspected it wouldn't be that easy across the border.

We had no idea, however, how hard it would actually be. We had two five-gallon portable tanks and a twenty-gallon tank on board. It would take roughly four tanks (two trips) to fill everything up (counting what we already had), which meant hauling ten gallons of water from whatever mini-super we filled up at, rowing them by dinghy back over to the boat, hauling them aboard, dumping them in, and then repeating the whole affair.

Naturally, we chose the closest mini-super with drinking water for sale. They had what was essentially a serious-ass office-style watercooler, and you could purchase *garrafones* there or bring your own containers. Once we had our two tanks filled up (one of which had a delicately patched hole after being busted in our Los Coronados wind-wave beating), Jimmie attempted something that was perhaps silly but definitely awesome.

He'd brought our boat hook along, thinking he could hang a tank over each end, hoist the bar over his shoulders, and carry them much like Mel Gibson carries cans of gasoline in *Mad Max 2: The Road Warrior* (a Jimmie fave). I say it was awesome because I love that Jimmie not only appreciates his heroes, he emulates them, whether superficially (dying his hair black during an Elvis phase) or physically (striving to play screamin'-high trumpet notes like Maynard Ferguson or hauling water à la Max Rockatansky). Unfortunately, our boat hook, a hollow aluminum pole, bent right in half under the weight of the full tanks.

I offered to take one, share in the load, but Jimmie refused, taking one tank in each hand and walking, a stern look on his face and with as brisk a step as possible, to the beach.

One gallon of water is said to weigh approximately 8.34 pounds. This means Jimmie carried 41.7 pounds on each side of his body, both arms extended straight down his sides, each hand grasping a dinky red plastic handle. That's 83.4 pounds overall, carried for a distance of maybe half a mile. That's also 83.4 pounds (65 percent of my personal weight) that I was now about to lift up and over the gunwales of our boat. Because I offered. I wanted to help.

Once we were at the beach, I said, "Why don't you let me paddle these back?" One of us had to do it (we didn't think Johnny had the wherewithal for both of us plus all that H_2O). Jimmie was skeptical, but with some convincing and his help launching off, the hefty load nestled between Johnny's orange flanks, I was afloat, carrying 83.4 pounds of water for us to blend powdered milk and spaghetti sauce packets into, brush our teeth with, and drink as coffee, Tang, or just plain water. I was the pipeline bringing that most essential fluid home. I had to succeed.

I tied the dinghy to our stern cleat and climbed aboard, looking back at Jimmie's silhouette on the beach. Leaning over the side of the boat, I grabbed the handle of one of the jugs and heaved with all my might. Nothing. I heaved harder, heaved again. I tried changing my position, adjusting the angle of my arms. Nothing. I hadn't lost hope, but I didn't know what, exactly, to do. I needed another method. I looked over at Jimmie's dark figure again, sitting on a log. I couldn't let him down. Not after all this way.

I opened a cockpit storage area and looked aimlessly around. My gaze landed on a small white rope. I leaned back down into Johnny and tied the rope to one of the red plastic handles. This gave me a little leverage, and—suddenly—I had one of the tanks elevated! I leaned it against the hull for support and dragged it upward, along the curved turquoise fiberglass.

Almost . . . there . . . sliding . . . ascending . . . until BAM! It stopped, the tank's soft side jammed up against a rounded bump of molding where the hull meets the deck. The bump stood off the boat maybe half an inch, but I could not seem to lift those 41.7 pounds far enough away to clear it. Fuck.

My arms were shaking, tense with fatigue. I took a short break, tried to build my strength—physical and mental. I could beat this. I could lift these two heavy-ass tanks into this cockpit. I knew I could. With all the fortitude I could muster, I reached down again. I grabbed my rope and swiftly elevated the first tank, drawing it up the side and—*UHN*—over that fucking rib, up over the side and IN! The first tank was in.

Before I lost my ambition, I transferred my rope setup and went straight for the second one, repeating the motions as swiftly as possible. Done! The second tank was in, too.

I stuck the two metal prongs of our water tank's key into a silver disc with matching depressions, turned it, and accessed the cavity where we usually just stuck a hose and waited. I tipped the first clear plastic cube over, its spout settling into the fitting, and went into the cabin for a glass of water, depressing the foot pump and completing the cycle of mini–super–to–mouth.

Once the second tank had drained, I put the two empties back in Johnny, lowered myself in, and paddled back to shore. Then we did it—the whole damn thing—again.

⚓⚓⚓

The morning of January 24, we were thinking of leaving Bahía Tortugas. We'd been there for almost a week, our barometer readings had been steady for the past few days, and one of our neighbors who appeared to be pretty on top of his game had just taken off. We were debating checking the weather at the local Internet café when we realized we weren't going anywhere.

Our bilge pump came on. *Cotton* was taking a monster leak. But where the hell was it coming from? Were we suddenly, inexplicably sinking?! Jimmie investigated pronto, initially suspecting the water filter junction, where a hose from the main tank connects to a purifying cylinder just aft of the galley. No problems there. He poked around some more, little fountains squirting out of our rear every minute or so.

After checking all the places where tubes and hoses connect and bend, Jimmie finally inspected the tank itself. There it was: a cracked seam. Water was seeping right out of the tank, trickling through big, butter-colored bulges of insulating foam and into the bilge. The crack ran about halfway down the tank, meaning close to half the water we had so painstakingly hauled from town only three days before had just gotten spat right into the bay. Useless. Gone. Wasted.

Now, rather than leaving we'd have to figure out some way to (hopefully) fix the tank and then refill the damn thing—at least the upper half of it. *Ugh.* We went to town.

We'd seen an auto parts place on one of our previous trips ashore (in fact, we'd seen a four-wheeler speed directly into it, as if the driver planned to shop *while* driving), and we hoped they might have a clamp and/or sealant. The man there was incredibly friendly. He drew us a map, labeling two nearby *ferreterías*, and spoke in simple, slow Spanish. He also highly recommended and sold us a package of J-B Kwik, a fast-curing sealant he said would work on *plástico*. After failing to find either of the hardware stores (despite the map), Jimmie decided he'd try doing the job with just J-B Kwik.

Back aboard, he had a pretty successful time patching the dry parts of the seam, but a tiny trickle along the bottom of the crack persisted. We attempted layering Kwik Seal (a caulk-type substance we used for just about everything) and even candle wax over the remaining seepage, but all we got was watered-down Kwik Seal and candle wax and J-B Kwik. (Apparently sealant companies are fond of the letter *K*.) It took us until the next day to admit it, but we would have to drain the tank further if we really wanted to fix it. So we did.

We emptied almost all of the water we had gathered, our hearts breaking a little as we heard it drain into the bay. Jimmie thoroughly dried the seam and then J-B–welded the hell out of it. Because it was the "kwik" version, it would take only four to six hours to completely cure. We passed the time scraping sea lettuce from our waterline and barnacles off the stern. Sitting sideways in the dinghy, we took turns holding onto the side and wielding an ice scraper, forcing chunks of marine life—ivy green ribbons and crusty gray cones—off into the beryl-colored water.

⚓ ⚓ ⚓

Six hours later, we timidly approached the cracked tank, crossing our fingers and hoping for the sake of our trip that the damn thing was sealed. The J-B Kwik appeared to have set, its mercurial surface more dark metal than wet cement. Jimmie dumped any auxiliary water we had into the tank, and we went ashore with our empty five-gallon jugs. Both of them. Again.

Because we felt unsure about aggressively filling our Franken-tank right away, we only bought one jug's worth, placing it in a large canvas bag and carrying it back together, each of us taking a strap.

Adding to the frustration of this situation was the fact that we were going broke. Or, rather, we had money in a bank account but absolutely no access to it. The Banamex we'd hoped to patronize was closed, an empty shell on a ghost-town strip. There were no ATMs, and the Telecomm location a couple of guys suggested was both dauntingly foreign and appeared only to wire money. I'd learned the correct phrase from our *Moon Baja*: "*cajeros automáticos.*" Using this knowledge, I asked at several mini-supers where we could find such a machine, an "automatic cashier," as it were, and no one had any idea.

We didn't need much, but we did need water. We would continue to consume water as long as we were anywhere, and we'd need pesos to get it. Now, we realized, we'd need to be somewhere else if we ever hoped to get more pesos.

We devoted the next day to correspondence and what had become the main focus of our lives: water. We needed to check the weather, top off our water supply—the repair on the tank had held!—and get the hell going. We were feeling slightly better about our money situation because, in order to use the Internet café, Jimmie had thought to round up all of our American coinage. The proprietor there told us she'd take US *dolares*.

We set up a free trial membership for Buoyweather.com, a resource that provides wind and wave information for any coordinate you choose, and we sent a few "don't worry" e-mails. We were quick and efficient about it. We went up to the counter to pay and discovered that the woman had meant *dolares* quite literally: *bills*, not coins. Our quarters, nickels, and dimes were useless. So we surrendered even more of our pesos.

But there was also good news. The day before, we had taken a different route to the beach and discovered a mini-super very close to the anchorage. They had a water tank. The price for ten gallons was thirteen pesos, only one peso more than at the farther-away stores. It seemed worth it.

When we arrived at this new, superconvenient convenience store to actually *get* water, the cashier told me it'd be twenty pesos to fill both jugs. "*Pero*," I said, "yesterday I was told only thirteen." She agreed to stick to her coworker's quote. Thank God! It would be twenty-six pesos to fill four jugs' worth. We counted our money. We had twenty-five pesos and seventy centavos. Thirty freaking centavos short! If only the Internet café had taken our American change! But it hadn't.

It was what it was. We filled two jugs. I rowed them out, hoisted them up, poured them into the onboard tank.

For a moment, the bilge pump fired up again, and I was terrified that the seam had cracked. A sick feeling filled my stomach. My heart hardened, descended like a rock into my bowels. I tried to be calm, observe the situation. The second jug, I realized, was more than was needed to reach capacity; I had simply overfilled the tank, and the spillover had set the bilge to work. I righted the second jug. The bilge spat its last few spats and stopped. *Phew.*

I rowed back to shore. It was terribly windy; the tide was high and the waves were up. Jimmie stood on the beach and guided me in, telling me with hand motions when to wait and when to go for it. He was the master of dinghy landings. I'd brought both tanks back with me, one with about a gallon left in it. I thought we might be able to get by on our remaining cash since we wouldn't be purchasing two *full* tanks—you know, show the clerk our little surplus and get a prorated fee. Jimmie made the executive decision that it wasn't worth it and told me to use the remaining change on whatever I wanted. What a guy.

I paid for our third and final tank, added a package of Oreos, and we were broke. Completely out of pesos. Based on Buoyweather.com, we planned to leave Wednesday, and it was only Monday evening. We shared the cookies-and-cream sandwiches, converted the dinette, and lay down on it, heavy with fatigue. Jimmie turned to me and said, "Snuggle hard or go home." He then promptly fell asleep. It was 7:45 PM.

"¡Ándale, Arriba!"

Our stay in Turtle Bay wasn't all hard knocks, though.

Free from Pedro's shopping guidance, we found Mercado Patrón, a cache of comestible delights: a cheddar-cheese variety of Instant Lunch we called "queso cups" (thank you, Maruchan!); Nido, a powdered milk substance we suspected was for babies but which we really enjoyed (it was much creamier than typical powdered milk—and enriched with so many vitamins!); and a new ramen with dehydrated *champiñones* (mushrooms) in its sodium powder.

We also came across something after our very own hearts: Mezcalito.

Mezcalito, though technically a *licor*, is the Mexican equivalent of box wine. It's incredibly cheap, it's available in large quantities (1.75-liter jugs are sold in a connected six-pack, like soda), it tastes good enough, and it does the job of making you a happy bit o' fuzzy drunk. When mixed with Zuko (like Kool-Aid in more exotic flavors: *guayaba*, *tamarindo*, *piña*, *jamaica*), a pretty OK cocktail is achieved. We preferred it with lime-flavored Zuko. Mix the two (don't worry about ice), put a lime wedge on the edge of your glass, and you've got what we deemed a "Turtle Dog," named after all the lazy, dusty dogs populating the shady storefronts and cement steps of Bahía Tortugas.

And, finally, we discovered *huevos*. Yes, eggs.

In the United States, eggs are pasteurized to reduce the chance of salmonella contamination, but this also weakens the eggs' natural defenses against other contamination. Thus, refrigeration is needed. This is not the case in Mexico. Farm eggs that have not been pasteurized can just sit on the shelf—in the market, in your kitchen, or, in our case, on a boat.

Yes, the cashier (who spoke a little English) confirmed, you could keep eggs out of the fridge. They'd be good, she thought, for about a month if kept in a relatively cool, dark place. We would've been excited for *anything* different (see: mushroom ramen, tuna salad sandwiches), but this was special, not only because eggs are so versatile but because Jimmie and I both *love* them.

When we got back with our first flat (three dozen!), we cleared a special area for them on top of our bureau. They would be shaded, cool, nestled into a bath towel for added security. Not that they would last long. Our egg feasting began that night with a meal of fried rice generously studded with rich, savory scrambled eggs. We had fried-egg sandwiches the next morning; then over-easy eggs atop *pan tostado*, a Mexican bread product like huge Melba toast; egg salad sandwiches for lunch; and potato salad featuring chunks of hard-boiled egg (with a dressing fashioned from mayo and mustard packets) soon after. We were *focused*.

⚓ ⚓ ⚓

We were also focused, as always, on *tortas*. We scoured Turtle Bay for *loncherías*, food carts, anything. We went by plenty of storefronts claiming to serve tacos, pizza, "mixtos" (?), hot dogs, even Chinese food (featuring "*chun kun*," something we later discovered to be an unusual egg roll). But none of these places were open. There were *panaderías* aplenty, but no *tortas*.

(The Baja Banditos guy and the crews of the other fourteen or so sailboats in the anchorage spent an awful lot of time at a particular restaurant on the beach, owned by a gringo; we'd been invited and might have found *tortas* there, but we didn't like the idea of segregating ourselves into Whitey-Whitesville, so we passed.)

Then there was Lonchería de Ensenada, a small diner. Its door was open when we passed by, a woman visible inside. But when I popped my head hopefully through the door and asked, "*¿Abierto?*" the lady scowled at me, made a shooing motion with her broom, and said, "*¡Ándale!*"

If you go with the Speedy Gonzales mentality, "*¡Ándale, arriba!*" sort of evokes teamwork, considering he's cheering his cheese factory compadres to safety in his film debut. But "*ándale*" is a form of *andar*, which means "to walk" or, loosely, "go on." In this particular case, it was definitely being used to say, "Scram!" And we got the message.

Believe it or not, this exact same sequence of events happened *twice*. She could have just said she was closed . . .

There was also a roadside cart we'd seen many times that read TORTAS Y TACOS, BIRRIA DE RES along the front. It was always closed up—until one fateful day, when we saw a woman and a little girl standing in its vicinity, the scent of cumin and peppers wafting out over the sunbaked streets and a bit of steam escaping from under the cart's metal flaps.

We walked up and inquired about *tortas*. Nope. Despite the sign, they did not have *tortas*, but they did have tacos, *birria de res* tacos. We didn't know what that meant. We ordered three each. The little girl packed them in a bag with cabbage slaw, a cilantro-and-onion relish, some salsa verde, and a pouch of radishes.

We were on our way back to the waterfront when the girl ran up to us with a Styrofoam cup; she gestured that it was to go with our meal. "*¡Gracias!*" we said and took it. It had a plastic lid with vents, like the coffee cups of oil-change places or hotel lobbies. It had broth in it. It turns out that *birria de res* (a spicy beef stew, we were to later interpret) is eaten by filling a tortilla with beef or what have you and then dipping the whole shebang in broth. The French Dip of tacos.

We enjoyed them while drinking midday Turtle Dogs, carefully dragging the meal out by alternating bites of tacos with slaw and radishes and sips of lime-cloaked cheap-ass mescal. It was close enough to everything we had hoped for when dreaming of Bahía Tortugas.

But what the Lonchería de Ensenada lady said was right: it was time for us to go on.

"A Big One, for Reals."

Stagnation breeds ambition, apparently. After what ended up being two weeks of apprehensive weather monitoring and sitting on our hands in Turtle Bay, we went ahead and became real-ass sailors. The next few days weren't filled with stops and starts, anchor-up and anchor-down, with *Cotton* sitting in a harbor, waiting for a comfy invitation to leave. No, for the next few days we emulated our idols; our life at sea passed like a series of snapshots, flickering images along the reel of Southern Baja. We existed only as boat, water, sailors, movement. We simply *went*.

FRIDAY, 8:07 AM: We forsook our Zucaritas (Mexican Frosted Flakes) in favor of leaving with a surprisingly full morning breeze.

8:32 AM: Jimmie asked me if I was tired of sailing. I didn't say yes; I didn't say no. I simply said that I was beginning to want to just be where we were going already. He agreed.

9:15 AM: Not long out of Turtle Bay, the wind picked up astoundingly, blowing hot and dry off the dark hills south of Cabo Tortola, the sickle-shaped headland that forms Bahía Tortugas' lower edge. It was certainly the "passes and canyons" effect we'd heard the NOAA guy warn about back in the United States. Damn near every arroyo we passed sent a chute of warm air our way. I'd gotten into trying to rate the wind we encountered by the Beaufort wind force scale, and I deemed this to be a "fresh breeze," seventeen to twenty knots.

5:17 PM: After crossing the twenty-seventh parallel, we did something unprecedented: we passed up a perfectly good anchorage—Bahía Ascunción—in broad daylight. We willingly signed on for the fifty-some nautical miles beyond. All along, we'd talked about doing longer stretches, really going for it. From Trinidad Head, we thought we might zoom around Mendocino, right past Shelter Cove and on to Albion; little did we know we'd be thanking our lucky stars we were alive by the time we finally saw Shelter Cove.

Back in Oregon, we had considered a long haul from Newport to Coos Bay but had ducked into our poorly chosen "escape route," the Siuslaw River, instead. One tiller down.

We could have sailed from Dana Point straight to San Diego, but we stopped—at a marina, even—in Oceanside, cutting yet another leg into more manageable pieces. But now we decided we would sail on, *overnight*, to Punta Abreojos, a gumptious one hundred nautical miles from Turtle Bay.

5:37 PM: We drew dry spaghetti straws for shifts. I got 6:00 to 9:00 PM and midnight to 3:00 AM. Jimmie got 9:00 PM to midnight and 3:00 to 6:00 AM. I was to go first. In about twenty minutes.

6:00 PM–9:00 PM: Turns out, the six to nine gets the sunset—not a thing to be sneezed at when you are at sea, in Baja, with absolutely nothing between you and the horizon.

2:33 AM: Second shift. The wind was fierce. I needed to reef the main. It was something I'd never done myself, and I wasn't about to try it. I didn't want to wake Jimmie up, so I decided I was just gonna (stupidly) ride out the higher winds with way-loosened sails luffing perpendicular to the boat. But stupidity makes a lot of noise, and my avoidance tactic woke Jimmie up anyway. He helped me reef the main and put the jib back on. I managed the lines and steering.

4:38 AM: Jimmie began to see flickers of light in the water to port. In the gauzy dark, the shapes of dolphins zoomed through the black water, sending firework sprays of phosphorescence in twinkling yellow-green paths behind them. One popped out of the water, breaking the neon stream, then reentered, barely breaking the surface, fireworks back on.

SATURDAY, 6:15 AM (we're calling 6:00 AM the beginning of a new day here, not midnight; just roll with it, OK?): We were both up again, approaching Abreojos. We'd beaten our longest sail (eighty-seven nautical miles to Isla Cedros) just by coming this far, and we were already talking ourselves into more. We'd planned two more legs between Abreojos and the next major port, Bahía Magdalena: a seventy-nautical-mile stint to San Juanico, followed by a ninety-nautical-mile leg to finish it off. But we were so jazzed about the idea of a multiday sail—now that we were actually doing it—we couldn't stop! Bahía Abreojos sat there, very visible and close and inviting. We veered off and left it, never to be known by the likes of us.

6:47 AM: Jimmie made coffee and gave our first crate of eggs a proper send-off, frying the last of them for breakfast sandwiches underway. What more could a *compañera* ask for?

9:21 AM: Jimmie played trumpet to a blank landscape, crisp sound slicing through thin air.

11:55 AM: I made lunch—bean and rice tacos. We covered them in hot sauce, eating while sitting in the glaring sun, beads of sweat clinging to our greasy hair. Jimmie joked that we might as well have made some hot coffee to go with. Little did we know we'd later develop a penchant for hot coffee on hot days—ordering café sans *hielo* often in one-hundred-degree weather.

6:53 PM: All the air above the western horizon turned bright coral and glowed. Crazy frost-tipped clouds seemed illuminated from within, their silky puffs smudged across the fiery coral like a still-wet Bob Ross painting. Every bit of color and light bloomed with effulgence. God had gotten stoned that night and shined a black light over the scene. Amazing. Breathtaking. Words don't work.

SUNDAY, 6:32 AM: Jimmie let me sleep in. When I emerged, the sight of land and sound of surf startled me. The last time I'd been outside, there was nothing but dark and stars. Now he was tacking toward San Juanico, an anchorage 103 nautical miles from Bahía Tortugas, an anchorage beckoning us to come in, to drop the weight of our anchor and our bodies and stay a while.

6:45 AM: Jimmie wanted to move on, to give San Juanico the same flippant "see ya later" we'd given Ascunción and Abreojos. He was on a roll that refused to be stopped. I liked the idea, too, but was very tired. We were going on very little collectively. Also, we were concerned about thick, low clouds to the south, in the direction we'd be heading, if we kept heading.

6:52 AM: Jimmie tried for the "Amigo Net," a shortwave network known to cater specifically to Pacific Mexico. He hadn't had any luck the day before, and he didn't now. We'd still been diligently checking the barometer, and it had been pretty steady . . .

7:03 AM: We say fuck it. How could we stop now?

7:04 AM: One minute and roughly ninety degrees later, we'd completely changed course—from heading toward the pleasant, available anchorage at San Juanico to heading south-southeast, into the big open space between La Península Vizcaíno and Baja's dog ankle, if you will. It was as if some switch—a fuck-all, we're-so-ready-to-be-someplace-really-*nice*, somewhere-that's-*not*-the-Pacific-fucking-Ocean switch—had been flipped. Ominous clouds or not, it was Mag Bay or bust!

8:13 AM: Crossed the twenty-sixth parallel.

3:16 PM: Booby attack! A brown booby suddenly descended upon our starboard spreader, biting at it in hopes of what, we did not know. Its webbed feet were splayed out, yellow and plasticky in front of us, and then, just as abruptly, it dismounted and landed in the water nearby. WTF?

4:00 PM: The wind picked up, afternoon-style, but more than was typical—more than any afternoon thus far. We switched to a reefed main and jib. The sea was more riled up than even the strong wind would suggest, and for the first time in quite a while, we had the dreaded what-ifs.

We sat together on the windward side of the cockpit, something we never really did, despite it being a very typical thing to do on a sailboat. We talked and held hands and tried to take our minds off the large, unsettling wind waves building all around us and bumping us hard to starboard. I had planned to make us spaghetti for dinner, but the boat was too rockin'. We went with PB&Js.

My first shift was drawing near, and I was feeling nervous. Although I got the sunset period, the onset of night also raised the general scariness factor exponentially. Also, we were as far offshore as we'd ever been, close to twenty nautical miles due to the curve of the coast.

After we ate, I rubbed Bag Balm, a salve I'd bought on our last day in Portland, from a tiny green tin into Jimmie's dry fingertips. He mentioned pulling an all-nighter together, thinking it might be fun to go balls out on the last leg (and knowing it would comfort me), but we agreed we'd need whatever meager energy we had left if things got any heavier. So Jimmie sat with me until 6:15 PM and then I sent him to bed.

8:59 PM: Jimmie, ever punctual, emerged just in time for some smooth sailing, literally. In fact, all three remaining shifts were easy and enjoyable after having our hair on end all afternoon. And as the lonesome overnight hours pushed into morning, the dark shadow of Isla Magdalena began to appear from a shroud of morning mist, a mysterious woman dropping silk to reveal herself. It was a comforting sight, as had been the appearance of the island's signal light, winking at us hours before.

MONDAY, 6:25 AM: We passed the twenty-fifth parallel, meaning we'd traveled twenty whole latitudinal degrees south—more, actually. Portland sits at 45 degrees and 31 minutes north, and that additional 31 minutes means 31 nautical miles. See, there are 60 nautical miles (also known as minutes) in a degree. That means 60 minutes (or nautical miles) times 20 degrees plus 31 extra minutes equals 1,231 nautical miles straight south. The geographic coordinate system makes a lot of sense!

6:33 AM: Jimmie had rounded Cabo San Lázaro, a western point surrounded by "wrecks" on the map, by the time I was conscious and back in the cockpit. We were approaching Bahía Santa María, a small alcove on the outside of Bahía Magdalena, a cup in the eponymous island that makes the western edge of the bay. It was a popular, easily accessed anchorage, but it was blanketed in fog. And it was only forty nautical miles more to San Carlos, the town we planned to anchor near way up *in* Mag Bay, the town one of Carlos's buddies said could provide "everything you need."

6:48 AM: Our wind totally died. We were going half a knot, thanks to the current alone, our sails hanging limp like dew-soaked sheets on a line. We couldn't stop now, tired as we were and tempting as Bahía Santa María was, even under its veil of mist. We had to go on. But we'd also have to motor.

7:22 AM: It was behind us, the last possible anchorage we could have taken, the last option for shortening what Jimmie eventually named "a big one, for reals," when tallying up our route with the Nobeltec. It was very one step at a time, but it *was* a big one—bigger than we'd ever entertained. Even if it had flitted through the back of one of our minds earlier in the route, no one ever said, "Let's sail straight to Mag

Bay!" Or, "How 'bout we take on 292 nautical miles in one shot, cut more than half of southern Baja off in one fell swoop?" But that's what we did.

9:31 AM: Mexican shrimping boats—baby blue and white with long trolling arms and huge nets poised to drop and trap their prey—passed us, heading north in search of little Caridean creatures, all legs and feelers and sweet meat in an armor-crust.

11:37 AM: After days now of south, south, south, we turned east, past Punta Entrada and into Mag Bay. There were chutes of water spraying up in every direction, as if we'd stumbled upon some grand saltwater fountain, the natural Bellagio of Baja Sur. But it wasn't a manmade miracle of hydro-design. It was whales. Gray whales. It was breeding season, and they were everywhere.

Tour boats from San Carlos were plentiful, too, taking tourists right up to whales, letting them lean over and touch the behemoth natives, get their photos with them, even kiss them.

Then, far off in the distance, one breeched. Jimmie and I peered into the silver-gray morning, across the sweeping bay, at the head and upper body of a giant whale, its mug all crusty with barnacles and who knows what else. It shot upward, baring its chest and arching backward, then crashed down, splattering a great smack of white foam into the air, the silky blue enveloping it.

And there was *Cotton*, in the middle of it all, a sole sailboat carrying two humans groggy with sleep deprivation. Surreal.

2:47 PM: Three hours later, we were finally just shoreside of San Carlos, where a red-and-white-checkered pier extends into the bay like a huge Purina ad adorned with fishing boats. We had motored the entire way up, through a channel that was more interpretive than "marked" and where every buoy was absolutely crawling with either sea lions or cormorants. The whole "big one," I later estimated, included about thirteen hours of motoring, four or five of which were racked up approaching and entering Mag Bay. That's only one-sixth of our entire four-day sail spent motoring. Not bad!

Even after four days, this particular stretch seemed longer than all the others. Maybe it was the boredom of motoring or the apex of our fatigue. Or both.

⚓ ⚓ ⚓

We had sailed for almost four days straight, in shifts, without stopping. We passed six perfectly good anchorages: Thurloe and Asunción, Hipólito and San Juanico, Abreojos and, finally, Santa María. We could have taken them all; we could have taken a week, seven sails, to do what we did in one. Seventy-nine hours after leaving Turtle Bay, we finally beheld an anchorage we intended to use.

"There Is Not a Crewman Aboard Who's Not in Need of Rest."

I'm sure Jimmie is the only other person who understands the particular emotion—the exact, crushing feeling—that came when, after four days, three nights, and 292 nautical miles of drifting over the liquid face of the Earth, we were grounded. Again.

The anchorage we were so excited to reach appeared to be a little out in the middle of things, exposed and near the channel. So we went in a little farther than planned and dropped our anchor in eleven feet— after which we quickly drifted into the vast shoal north of the checkered dock. We couldn't fucking believe it. After all that success—all the encouraging real-ass sailing, all the changing of sails and toughing out the hairy parts—we were stuck. "Dismay" is perhaps most apt.

We didn't seem *too* stuck, as the bay bottom was soft and felt forgiving when we slid into it, but it was one hour, roughly, past high tide, so we wouldn't be getting any help there. Jimmie raised the anchor while I fired up the motor, hoping to push us off by the sheer power of James Brown.

No luck.

It had become quite windy, so Jimmie raised the genoa (our larger jib). Nothing again. We remained stationary, our big white sail full of wind a futile decoration, a paper cocktail umbrella. Amid the chaos of being suddenly grounded, we'd forgotten the comfort module was leaning against the mast, and when the genoa's sheet rushed across the foredeck, pulled briskly by the filling sail, it was swept right off the deck. Just like that, the overstuffed pillow-with-arms that we'd grown to love for its back support and versatility was gone.

Maybe it was the exhaustion, or despair at the knowledge that the next high tide wasn't until 2:30 AM, but I almost cried. Watching it drift downwind toward the wharf as our un-grounding effort unsuccessfully continued, I felt my heart break a little for a pillow.

After getting about eight hours each of real sleep over the entire four-day trip, we were not too stoked about the idea of staying up for eleven more hours just to get properly anchored. We didn't see any other option but a do-over of our San Quintín technique: Jimmie inflated the dinghy and rowed the anchor out to deeper water while I deployed the rode (anchor line), which was covered with gross fish slime and very odiferous thanks to *Buzos y Pescadores*, a fishing boat we had been anchored next to in Turtle Bay. Ever since pulling up anchor on Friday, we'd noticed a fishy stench coming from the anchor locker.

Now, as Jimmie rowed into the wind for deeper water, I led the slimy line out through a small hole in the deck, past the bow pulpit and trailing into the bay behind him. Once he was back aboard, he used one of our halyard winches to help crank in the line while I ran the motor and aimed us toward the deeper water. We rotated some, but it was clear we weren't coming loose.

Jimmie then re-boarded the dinghy, re-rowed out into the wind—high (from a kayak's perspective) wind waves splashing over the bow and onto his lap—and made another attempt. But first he'd have to pull the anchor *up*. Pulling an anchor up from the high, hard deck of a regular boat is not easy, and pulling an anchor up from a soft inflatable dinghy only a dozen feet above the actual anchor is nearly impossible. But Jimmie did it. Aside from the fact that his head would have been six feet underwater, it probably would have been easier for him to have gotten out and done the job while standing on the bay floor. Fucking ridiculous.

When Jimmie came back to start winch-tightening attempt number two, we made a horrifying discovery. I'd somehow looped the rode around one of the pulpit's metal supports. Cranking on the line, in this state, could tear the bow pulpit right off the deck. Jimmie would have to row out a third time, pull the anchor up from the dinghy a second time, row back so we could untangle my bungle, row out once more, re-set the anchor, and then return to try winching us into flotation again.

Jimmie had the bright idea to whip out the laptop and map an ideal anchor location with the Nobletec. I stood in the cockpit, smelling like a Cannery Row employee, watching the tan bump of our comfort module bob in the distance. My eyes burned.

This was it: Jimmie would row out, lift the anchor from the dinghy, and drop it in a more educated location. I deployed the line as he went, calling out each rubbery place marker so he'd know how far he'd gone. He dropped it and rowed back, soaking wet, then alternately tightened the line and peered at the computer's lime green boat icon, making sure it moved, that something was happening.

Meanwhile, I held the line, keeping it from slipping. I felt so horrible about the bow pulpit screwup; so sad for the pillow-with-arms; so overwhelmed by the coating of fish slime on our hands, pants, deck, cockpit; so sorry for Jimmie for being the stronger of the two of us, that the hot saline in my eyes spilled over, tracing clear lines in the dried salt on my cheeks. I tried to find a non-fishy area of my hoodie sleeve to wipe them away. I didn't want Jimmie to see I'd broken.

⚓ ⚓ ⚓

We were pretty sure at this point that we'd be waiting and winching until 2:30 AM. It was easy to see through the water, and it was not deep. The bottom appeared to be only a couple of feet below the surface, so close I could make out minuscule spiral shells in the sand. But Jimmie kept at it, his teeth clenched; his arms working to the point of burning, trembling; the exhaustion of repeated anchor lifts tearing his muscles apart. He kept thinking, *Just a few more pulls.*

He'd shed his black hoodie and was wearing just a T-shirt, despite the chill brought on by wind and dampness. Then, more gradually than suddenly, he felt that we were floating. The front part of the boat had lightened, received a boost from the buoyant water. Crank, crank, crank; fish slime on rope around silver metal spool; inches, inches, inches. Then, finally, water engulfed the hull, held it in a brackish embrace, lifted it up away from the sand and tiny shells on the floor of Mag Bay.

The depth meter read eleven feet. I fired up the motor and pushed us toward our anchor, where Jimmie raised it one last time, thankful to be doing it from the deck, however mucilaginous. We motored into thirty feet and dropped it, the true punctuation mark on our epic sail. We were anchored and floating, the white warehouses and gray smoke stacks of San Carlos conspicuous ashore, roughly eighty-two hours after leaving Turtle Bay.

We sat in the cockpit, aching with fatigue. The sun was descending, leaving a flamingo-colored afterglow behind the black peaks of Mount Isabel and Isla Magdalena. Jimmie poured each of us a shot of Mezcalito, which we took in the cockpit. Once something that could narrowly be described as energy returned to us, we made nachos: half a bag of *totopos* we'd saved since Bahía Tortugas topped with beans, pickled jalapeños, canned cheese, and onions—like stadium nachos but much bigger.

We ate them while watching our next episode of *Star Trek* ("Shore Leave"), in which Spock says to Captain James T. Kirk, "There is not a crewman aboard who's not in need of rest. Myself excepted, of course."

"Dinero en Minutos."

Well, we weren't Vulcans, and even the long, hard sleep we got once we finally crashed didn't top us up to normal functioning awareness. But we were up, and we were ready for some "shore leave" ourselves. The tide in the morning was very low, revealing the flat expanse of shoal that had made our arrival so miserable. Now we saw how far from the shore one really had to be to avoid grounding: probably a good forty to fifty yards. At the moment, half of this distance was still covered in a thin sheet of water, just enough to float a dinghy over.

The rowing was lovely. A light morning breeze occasionally riled the crystal water into delicate ripples, but mostly it was calm. Tiny silver fish flitted past like an infantry of sequins. Below us, speckled like powdered sugar over a sheet of lemon bars, were countless more of those spiral-cone shells, each no bigger than a canine tooth.

Eventually, the water was too shallow to support the dinghy under our combined weight, so I volunteered to tow Jimmie the rest of the way to the beach. I was wearing flip-flops, he sneakers. Plus, I wanted to do something nice for him after the multi-anchor fiasco the day before. He lay flat on his stomach to even the weight distribution and happily took a ride.

We locked Johnny to a mangrove stump and, after exploring a tall stone wall and discovering a gate (and a guard), we moved the other way along the beach, marveling at cockleshells in tangerine and plum, looking for a path through the swampy thicket of exposed roots. We found a narrow opening near a building that said Mo Bi Dick on its side and emerged near the intersection of the primary highway into town and Calle Puerto La Paz, a.k.a. Main Street.

I soon found myself having what I felt was my most successful *en Español* conversation yet. It was with a woman at a hotel lobby desk. She told us she did not have an ATM but that we could, indeed, get money with a credit card at the Telecomm office in the plaza.

Hallelujah! We would have money. We stopped near a giant whale skeleton and took photos, giddy as tourists. San Carlos was full of bleached white buildings with festive murals depicting agaves, farmers, and tequila bottles in canary yellow, grass green, and cobalt. We spotted several *antojito* stands, a large *mercado*, and a hardware store. There was even a Pemex near the waterfront. It appeared the guy at Carlos's was right: this *puerto* did have everything we needed.

⚓ ⚓ ⚓

When we got to the Telecomm, there was a huge line, lots of parents with kids, men in construction-type hats, and absolutely no shade. The sign outside read Dinero en Minutos. We stood in the glaring sun and waited, the only gringos there. I tried to think of what I would say, in Spanish, to ensure the clear communication of our goal.

That, it turned out, was not the problem. The clerk understood what we wanted—to use Jimmie's Visa debit card to get money—and I even explained how the hotel matron had told us that this was essentially the town's *cajero automatico*. "No," said the clerk. A word that's the same in so many languages: "No." We would not be getting any money here. That was not how Telecomm worked.

I asked where the closest ATM was. Perhaps we would walk there, even if it was beyond reason. It was in Ciudad Constitución, she said, thirty-four miles away. That was too far even for us. Hell, Cabo San Lucas was only about five times as far. With the wind, at least we'd have a ride.

We were screwed. We'd traveled all the way up into the northeast corner of Mag Bay, which stretches over thirty standard miles from end to end, to reach San Carlos, a port that might as well have not existed. All the groceries and gas and tasty treats held within were inaccessible to us.

The gas and water and groceries we had—the same stores we'd been using since we left Turtle Bay—were *all* we had, and they would be all we had until we reached Cabo, a for-real urban metropolis of more than sixty-eight thousand people. There was no other choice but to leave. More than that, we had to make a run for it.

"No Tenemos *Nada*, Hombre."

Somewhere along Baja, our can opener broke and a menacing famine threatened to take hold of our twenty-seven-foot universe . . . at least until I remembered a very tiny, rather strange backup can opener I'd packed just in case, a gift from an eccentrically generous uncle of mine. It was about the size of a razor blade, and it unfolded to reveal a cutting edge and enough of a handle for sawing along the rim of most metal cylinders. It worked, and we were beyond grateful to have it, but we were hoping to replace it every time we shopped, which, lately, was never.

Now, a different threat was upon us: the threat of running out of just about everything.

I had measured the water just as we entered Mag Bay and recorded eleven inches in the tank, plus a little in one of the backup jugs. According to earlier calculations, that could actually last up to five weeks. But that was already three days ago, and the complete lack of refill options was discomforting.

Information was another void. We'd been able to connect briefly to an unsecured network while anchored off San Carlos, but we were only ever granted "local" access, which means no Internet. Our only other hope was catching "Don Anderson's Summer Passage," a forecast on the Amigo Net named after the broadcaster and his boat. We'd had no luck with our weather-faxing system, and our experience receiving the nets had been less than inspiring.

We'd sailed to Punta Belcher, twenty miles back toward Punta Entrada, on a Wednesday. The following morning, Jimmie tried as hard as he could to hear what Mr. Anderson had to say about the Ensenada–to–Sea of Cortez zone. For whatever reason, we just didn't get him. So we spent one day at Punta Belcher, that Thursday, recording barometer readings, observing clouds and things like halos around the moon, and trying get our courage up to leave Mag Bay and make for Cabo, to sail 160 nautical miles, with no bailout options and no hint of a forecast.

As far as food went, by the time we left Mag Bay, we had three ramen packets each, some canned vegetables and soup, a little pasta, and a few potatoes. We had no eggs, rice, refried beans, tortillas, cereal, or onions, and we predicted that we would run out of bread, stuffing, Pop-Tarts, granola bars, and oatmeal by the end of our next leg. One hundred sixty nautical miles, we figured, would take roughly forty-eight hours to cover, considering our usually pretty slow speed. That would give us plenty of time to consume most of whatever we had left.

Ironically, we'd been approached by food salesmen en route to Punta Belcher. A *panga* sped up to our side, a man aboard yelling "*¡Langosta! ¡Langosta!*" We heard "*costa*," which means "coast," and assumed we were doing something wrong. Perhaps we were too close to the coast? Or there was some news of the coast that we should be aware of? We looked helplessly at the *pescadores*, confusion on our faces. The man who'd been addressing us turned quickly around, accessed a bin under one of the *panga* seats, and held up a dark red lobster, its legs and antennae fanning out around its thick body.

"*¿Langosta?*" he asked again. *Ah*, we got it. *Lobster*. "*Langostas demasiado pequeñas para vender*," he said, and suddenly I understood. These were the rejects, too small for the market. "*No. No, gracias*," we responded, explaining, "*No tenemos dinero*." And we didn't. We didn't have any money. In fact, *no tenemos* nada, *hombre*.

⚓⚓⚓

Among other things we (rather suddenly) didn't have was power. Friday morning, the screen that monitored our solar-power intake and indicated how full our batteries were was illuminating its red light, rather than the green we'd been getting used to seeing in Mexico (or the less alarming yellow). Jimmie suspected something fishy in the fuse box but had no way to check what amount of juice was flowing through which wires since we'd never replaced the nine-volt in his multimeter.

Red means low, however, not empty, and we expected some sun throughout the day. The only things we'd have to turn on, really, were the depth meter on the way out of the bay and the running lights after sundown. We'd probably manage. But it didn't do much for the dire-straits feeling we already had about damn near everything.

In other bad news, the Amigo Net doesn't include weather in its Friday broadcasts for some reason. We knew this, but it was a low blow to remember that we couldn't even try for a forecast. I wonder now if they don't bother because of the superstition that sailors should never leave on a Friday. Well, we left Portland on a Friday, and we were leaving on a Friday now.

"Sailing Is Just Like Vietnam; It's Totally Boring Until You're About to Die."

It had been very windy overnight, and we hadn't gotten a whole lot of sleep. Still, we arose early and got our acts together. Whether we liked it or not, it was time to go.

We sailed off our anchor and out of Mag Bay on a good, north-ish wind. On our way, sailing between Islas Magdalena and Santa Margarita, the two puzzle pieces of land that form the outer bay wall, we were again surrounded by gray whales. Magdalena Bay is one of the only places in the world where gray whales come to calve. They swim thousands of miles from all over the world just to end up there every January through March. We happened to be there in February.

Now, we were back on the Pacific for our last leg, our au revoir to a body of water, the biggest in the world, that we ended up on only by geographical circumstance; we lived in Portland, so the Pacific was unavoidable. With a good stiff boost behind us, we flew our wings out to either side, their great white surfaces impersonating the appendages of so many snowy egrets. We were hauling ass, going over five knots so consistently, and for so long, that our estimated time of arrival became noon on Saturday. Arriving at any time on Saturday hadn't really seemed a possibility, but this is what happens when you go out to sail in actual wind: you go fast.

As afternoon came on, we began going even faster. The already good wind picked up, and the waves all around us swelled like a freshly punched face, changing color with the light of day and continuing to puff, puff, puff. We were about fifteen nautical miles offshore and would draw nearer only when we actually approached Cabo San Lucas. The trip from Mag Bay to Land's End is a straight line from point A to point B. There are no suitable anchorages anywhere along the way. This is why it's inarguably a 160-mile trip. So, this was it for us. We were close to as far away from land as we ever got, going in one direction only, for as long as it took. No alternatives, no turning back. Onward.

Based on our experience around Cape Mendocino, and the general effect any cape or *punta* we'd passed had had on the wind and seas around it, we both believed that things were going to be *real fucked up* around the tip of Baja. This was the queen mother of western capes. It is the first pronounced change along the western edge of North America, the first place since the Bering Strait where water takes over, the place where the coast breaks off—literally comes to a terminus. *Finisterra.* The end of land.

Naturally, we were concerned about this, and we didn't think it a bad idea to stand off a bit, give Cabo a wide berth. So, that's where we were around sundown: well offshore, wind building, main reefed, headsail down. Still going at least four knots. Waves growing.

As this situation showed no signs of abating—in fact, it was escalating—we, of course, started to entertain other options. We knew there were no anchorages, though, and sailing back into this wind wasn't even entertained. Even if we could turn around, the only place to end up was back in Mag Bay, with no money or supplies. So, we checked our available resources.

Charlie's Charts, we discovered, mentioned the possibility of "less seas" along a more inshore route. After mulling it over, we decided it couldn't hurt, this far away from the actual *cabo*, to head a little more inland. *If we get in close enough*, we thought, *we might be shielded a bit by the preceding headlands.* We examined our GPS, the map in *Charlie's Charts*, the whole of Baja in our Moon book, looking for supporting evidence. There was none. You'd have to go *incredibly* close in to experience the lees of the Mag Bay bump and another very minor protrusion farther south (a formation so inconsequential I can't even find a map that names it). Reluctantly, we gave up on Charlie's suggestion and headed back out.

By sundown, conditions had intensified enough that—for the first time ever—we were sailing under storm jib alone. It was something we probably *should* have tried around Mendocino, but we were feeling a little more seasoned and capable these days, at least enough to try things we knew actual sailors would do. So, storm jib it was.

(Actual sailors also do something called "heaving to." Heaving to involves fixing the helm and sails in a way that lessens forward progress; it also makes it so the boat doesn't need to be actively steered, giving sailors an oft-needed time-out. It's a common strong-weather tactic. Though we experimented with this briefly on the Columbia River, it was trickier with a fin keel, and we never quite got the hang of it.)

With just the storm jib, we were still going three and a half knots, running up to hull speed on the forward-rushing waves and falling back slower into their troughs. The waves were boss. They pushed ever under and past us, toward Cabo, alternately boosting us up on salt-sea pedestals and cradling us in folded blue-gray valleys. We were merely along for the ride.

For the next twelve hours, we basically sat, quite terrified, wishing the wind would lighten. But the sea just kept building and building, and the gusts had come to howl in our rigging, a sound I hadn't heard since Punta Gorda, and one I wasn't pleased to revisit.

Earlier, when the sun had set, the sky and sea were entirely saturated in a deep pink glow, like looking through a giant glass of ruby red grapefruit juice. One of us noted, hopefully, "Red sky at night . . . sailors delight?" No, no it wasn't.

In fact, it was the opposite. The wind was strong, growing stronger; the waves large, growing larger; and the "what-if" was only amplified by the fact that we didn't even know what we had started out with—we had no figures with which to quantify our environment.

We continued to take hourly barometer readings and monitor the sky. Low stratus clouds slowly dissipated, allowing patches of bright stars to peek through—a tear in the garment of the heavens. Even as we sought information, though, we knew that we couldn't change whatever we thought we'd found out, that we were ultimately the weather's bitch. But taking observations was something to do, which is comforting in itself. It gave the impression of control, a thing to grasp onto. Through all this, the wind grew.

⚓ ⚓ ⚓

One of the best people we met on our journey was a guy named Dave Trumble. He was sailing aboard *Andiamo* (Italian for "Let's go!") with his wife, Maureen. They were an older couple, longtime sailors from San Francisco, and they had an undeniable air of badassery about them. We would eventually have them over to *Cotton* and stay up talking late into the night, getting drunk on—what else?—cheap red wine. During this unusual occasion, Dave remarked: "Sailing is just like Vietnam. It's totally boring until you're about to die."

His words often come to mind when I consider our trip. I'll have to take his word for the Vietnam part, but I know he's right about sailing. So much of what you do is sit there, coast along, ho-hum, but when the shit's on, it's *on*. And the night we sailed to Cabo, it was. Nothing so dramatic as waves crashing *onto* us took place, but the seas were *so* big, and when they started nipping at our little planet-home more aggressively, I was sure as hell afraid for my life. Again.

As the waves moved faster and faster, grew taller and closer together, the most ferocious ones started catching up to us, smacking flat into the stern and spraying the cockpit with water. The storm jib gave us enough power to run with one wave, but we couldn't keep up with a series of them. We'd rush up onto the first wave in a set and then get hit, squarely on the butt, by subsequent ones.

It occurred to Jimmie to run the outboard for an added boost of forward momentum. JB could keep us on top of the waves, right? Yes. He did. Right when we'd normally slide down and get bumped by the nastiest of bumper cars, James Brown hefted us up, his furiously spinning props coming out of the water a little each time, a small but essential cog in the wheel of our world.

Once the moon set under some impenetrable clouds, we had to sail in complete darkness. It lasted only about an hour and a half, during which we just sat, listened, looked at nothing. We were on the Space Mountain of the sea, riding up and down hill after hill in blind blackness.

"Light Winds."

We really, really wished we could get some weather news. Back in Oregon or California, when we expected things were turning for the worse, we could tune into the NOAA, and our computer-voiced buddy would either confirm our fears (usually the case) or predict a change. Now, we had nothing. Even a *horrible* official answer to "What next?" is better than your imagination's answer.

Suddenly, we saw the light of another boat farther offshore. Jimmie decided to try an open call for weather, getting on the VHF and saying something like, "This is sailboat *Cotton*, heading south toward Cabo San Lucas, requesting weather information. Sailboat *Cotton* to any available vessels, requesting weather." We waited. Wind and water over silence.

Then, an English-speaking guy aboard *Islander* (which I misheard as "Highlander") came across the staticky line and told us he was reading fifteen to eighteen knots and that the weather for Saturday and Sunday, via a Point Reyes weather fax, was to be about the same: "Light winds," he said.

We looked at the monstrous heaps of saltwater still cascading toward us, heard our storm jib thrashing at the bow. Either things were different out where the *Islander* was or the *Islander* was enormous or we are huge wussies.

Whether it was inspired by that vessel's seemingly easier conditions or our ever-growing dread of the waters rounding Cabo, we started heading farther out to sea. On the eve of our anticipated departure from the Pacific Ocean, we worked ourselves gradually westward, deeper into it. Maybe things would get a little easier. Maybe we could skirt the worst of what Cabo had to offer. And maybe, just maybe, we would enter this magical area of "light winds" offshore, the fifteen-to-eighteen-knot paradise the mysterious *Islander* inhabited.

⚓ ⚓ ⚓

Finally, due more to the passage of time than our slight change in course, conditions did improve. The light of Saturday morning settled over our unsettled seascape, and despite the chaotic looks of things, the wind eased off. We were feeling better about our angle of approach, and the sun—its warmth and reassuring lambent glow—began to foster hope after a long, discouraging night. The waves continued to push us around like a faceless bully. But they wouldn't be mounting, a least for a little while.

We each took what Jimmie later referred to as "horror naps"—just enough sleep to make you feel even worse than before. Preceding mine, I tried for the Amigo Net and actually got the weather guy! There he was, Don Anderson, predicting fifteen-to-twenty-knot winds during the day from Punta Abreojos to Cabo Falso, the outer headland at the tip of the Baja Peninsula. "An increase to twenty to thirty knots, maybe thirty-five" was expected in the evening and overnight. Much to our validation, he said "again" after the "twenty to thirty knots overnight" remark. It felt a lot more like twenty to thirty than fifteen to eighteen, I can tell you that.

Despite the affirmation of our overnight misery, we couldn't ignore the bad part of Don's message. Like it or not, we were going just fast enough to get to Cabo Falso in the later afternoon—what we'd come to regard as the worst time of day. And getting there any later meant the possibility of gale-force winds *at* Cabo. Now that we had the weather, it was a mad dash to beat it.

We had to push through the wall of exhaustion facing us. We were so tired, so windburned, so emotionally spent from hours of worry that our sanity—that usually comforting fortress wherein a normal person can take refuge—began to crumble.

We giggled and yawned, fidgeted, spaced out. We blinked, trying to moisten eyeballs that felt like they were turning to dust in their sockets. We hung on to our wakefulness by ever-thinning shreds, knowing there was no choice but to keep going.

Around 1:00 PM, the wind started to pick up noticeably. Our brief intermission, the calm morning that allowed us to tease ourselves in and out of sleep, to boil water and eat something (queso cups!), was over. We heavy-heartedly accepted our fate of having to approach a major-ass cape in the afternoon, on huge built-up waves, during the onset of a gale.

⚓ ⚓ ⚓

Rabo-Jeeves, bless his electronic heart, had been steering like an ace for hours on end (despite the fact that he'd been rocking so hard overnight he actually popped out of his cockpit housing). Now, we needed to make a beeline for Cabo, keeping as tight a course as possible, something Rabo just couldn't do on such large waves. As conditions worsened, Jimmie took over.

The sun was high and bright now, coloring the sea a hard royal blue topped with white frosting tips, and a fierce heat was apparent despite the chilling wind. We raised the bimini in an attempt to keep from roasting our already wind-seared skin. In the distance, closer to shore, we saw men in speedboats with huge outboards racing toward the coast, hightailing it for land, getting themselves off this frothy sea ASAP. We couldn't exactly hightail it, but Jimmie aimed us in as straight a line as possible toward our ultimate goal, the Sea of Cortez.

It went on for about three hours, Jimmie steering through the heart of the afternoon as the wind got stiffer and peaks of waves collapsed in white hissing piles all around us, James Brown buzzing furiously in the background. (So much for never motor sailing!) The bone-white rocks of Baja's culmination were more perceptible by the hour. Jimmie grasped a safety line with his left hand, held the tiller in his right, and looked intensely forward, never breaking focus. I talked to him incessantly: reading GPS statistics, recalling different Mexican foods, like *papas rellenas*, we'd read about and anticipated trying in the big city ahead.

By 4:00 PM, we were actively rounding Cabo Falso, a pointed hill of barren sand with a lonely lighthouse on top. Just past this, a sprawling, fantastical display of hotels appeared, nestled in the rocks of the dwindling landmass. Embedded there, like some medieval kingdom perfectly preserved in heat and light, were rotundas and balconies and walls containing rows upon rows of windows—like giant waffles, face out—lining the beaches and cliffs. After 790.6 nautical miles (since Ensenada) of nothing but more nothing, or occasionally a small, dust-covered town, evidence of a tourist mecca assaulted our eyes. We were on the cusp.

The wind had gotten so strong around the point that Jimmie half jokingly hoped a hurricane wasn't at our backs, and I later estimated the force to be a seven, "moderate gale," on the Beaufort scale. That's twenty-eight to thirty-three knots. The Beaufort rankings are based on sea state and, if you're close enough to land to observe them, the reactions of trees, smoke, flags, etc., to the current wind. "Hurricane" is force twelve, the highest level there is (sixty-four-plus knots!). This wind may have been gusting into force eight, and that was plenty high for both of us—plenty threatening to folks who had no business rating wind forces at all.

We had to drop the bimini, and we ditched the storm jib as well. James Brown was giving us some semblance of navigational control, and we could make out El Arco and Finisterra in the distance. It would all come down soon, anyway.

We'd traveled past the western coasts of four states, over six months, covering 2,283 nautical miles; all the while, there was the sight, or at least presence, of land to our left. Now, suddenly, it ended. In a white rock arch and two towering, jagged chunks like crumbs in a massive bowl of blue, the land terminated. And there, where the Pacific Ocean and the Sea of Cortez meet, there was only water.

"Always Remembered for His Bravery and Courage."

We put Rabo-Jeeves back on for a few minutes to take photos of ourselves on deck with Land's End in the background. It was an opportunity we could not miss. Still wearing jeans and several long-sleeved tops each, we smiled, our hair—even my heavy pigtail braids—whipping in the wind, our eyes and faces a matching raw pink. In the photo, a meringue-topped sea surrounds us; we look beat, dazed, and greasy, but our faces also read amazed, relieved, happy.

We worked our way around the cape itself: Cabo San Lucas, just like the town. Glass-bottom boats and other tourist traffic zoomed about the bay, taking slack-jawed visitors up close to El Arco over armies of tropical-colored fish and onto beaches where land dissolves via tiny crystals into water. And we, fuzzily conscious after thirty-two-plus hours awake, having known nothing but Pacific for half a year, crossed an imaginary threshold and dissolved into Bahía San Lucas—into the Gulf of California, at last.

In a final you've-got-to-be-fucking-kidding-me event, the wind waves sweeping through the bay began splashing up over the port side and dousing us as we motored toward the anchorage, sending stinging saltwater directly into our scorched faces. We considered it a final "fuck you" from the Pacific—a proper send-off.

Jimmie later said, "When the ocean spits in your eye at the end of a hard day, it's just doing its job." At this point, it didn't really matter; the Pacific wasn't our concern anymore. It had been hard on us. It was what we'd asked for. Now we could let it go.

⚓ ⚓ ⚓

We were totally soaked by the time we reached the anchorage, which is nothing more than an undefined patch of water just off the wide-stretching white of Playa el Médano. Strata of commerce and nature stretched southeast across the city: hotels, bars, sand, water, and then us. It was still very windy in the bay, but we'd found a spot close in and weren't getting jostled too hard. Once settled, we peered around and saw several familiar boats: some from Turtle Bay; a fellow Oregonian aboard *Mollyhock*, an attractive blue-and-white Westsail we'd seen back in Oxnard; and *Putty Tat*, a catamaran neighbor from Newport Beach.

Putting the cabin back in order was a bit more demanding than usual. All the pitching and rolling over waves had done a number on it. And I'd stuffed all kinds of water-sensitive items—the iPod and rock module, the camera, our shortwave radio, and Jimmie's wallet—into cubbies and drawers to keep them out of the line of spray-fire. I'd also crammed various pieces of kitchen hardware into tight areas to keep their unnerving rattling to a minimum. We put all that back where it belonged; did our usual covering of sails, lashing of the boom and tiller, and cockpit straightening; then remade the dinette. All of this preceded our eventual undressing and depositing of scungy, damp pants in the cockpit. Exhaustion topped with exhaustion.

Jimmie put on a Miles Davis album and we took nips off the Mezcalito bottle while I made us a more-ghetto-than-usual Alfredo dinner using a mix-and-match assortment of what broken noodles we had left. A little booze and a meal went a long way in making us feel more human. We put our photos of the Mag-to-Cabo trip on our laptop and looked at them, bleary-eyed but proud.

A bottle of Archery Summit pinot noir remained in the tip of the V-berth. Jimmie fished it out and put it on display as a testament to our achievement. It was the final in our major-landmarks collection of fancy, non-box wines. We drank it the next night.

In other accomplishments, Jimmie would soon beat *Simon's Quest*, a video game he'd been playing since Turtle Bay. It's the sequel to the '80s vampire-hunting classic *Castlevania*, and he'd been stuck at a standstill in his quest to defeat Dracula, the big end boss. Turns out, the special boulder-disintegrating power of holy water was the key to his success. Jimmie freed Transylvania from its cursed existence and, according to the game, "will always be remembered for [his] bravery and courage." A macho boon for little boys pretending to be Simon Belmont, to be sure, but in Jimmie's case, as far as I'm concerned, it's true.

We tried for Internet and easily received several bars' worth of signal from more than one source. Hooray for civilization! We'd be able to communicate with loved ones and, we assumed, withdraw some freaking funds. All the conveniences of Cabo lay just a front yard of water away.

"Heaven Knows What We Expected . . ."

At 5:00 AM, a month later, we were both up, navigating the channel into La Paz—which, as Steinbeck says in his *Log from the Sea of Cortez*, "grew in fascination as we approached."

It had been a "slag" getting up there, as a New Zealander friend aboard *Pisces* had put it. Turns out, going north in the Sea of Cortez at all was a slag (which is why we took our time, enjoying a weekend at Los Frailes and a more lengthy sojourn at the popular Ensenada de los Muertos).

We'd been sailing overnight in shifts, but Jimmie roused me early to help as a lookout, and we ended up doing a lap down the channel and back just to let the morning lighten a bit more. The general anchorage was littered with sailboats, a mishmash of hull shapes and sail-cover colors and home ports written in varying fonts across transoms.

The shore, La Paz's famous Malecón, was empty, peacefully lined with *palapas* and rustling palm trees, mini-plazas featuring bronze and stone sculptures, and ornate wrought-iron benches coated in white paint. Anchoring was easy: we took a spot in eleven feet of water, just off the Malecón. The wind and water were calm, and all the people aboard boats in the bay were sound asleep, the sky turning to bright pink fire above them.

In about two months, we would wake many of these same people with musical carryings-on that stretched well into morning (garnering a complaint from a neighbor about trumpet practice at 3:30 AM). We didn't care; we were tipsy and together, happy and safe. We'd been living on the boat in La Paz since we arrived and had every intention of finishing out our year there. Jimmie sang "Do You Remember Love?"

to me in English, recording the performance in case it was a keeper. Hearing those words again left me all full and tender-feeling, a perfect reminder of what had brought us here in the first place. We made love with the doors open, the fresh, damp air of dawn on our skin, and fell asleep in our triangular bed at almost eight in the morning.

⚓ ⚓ ⚓

That first sunup, though, I read Steinbeck aloud in the cockpit: "Heaven knows what we expected to find in La Paz," he wrote, "but we wanted to be beautiful for it."

So did we. With its gracefully curving waterfront walk, tiny chirping orioles and cactus wrens, giant spiky agaves, and fuchsia bougainvillea growing along muraled cinder-block walls, La Paz inspired beauty. We got gussied up, as much as we could, and went into town. It was Monday, March 9, a week and seven months after we'd left Portland. Several hours later, after some shopping and an ice cream cone, we were situated in our cockpit, a meal of sliced avocado, tomatoes, apples, Manchego cheese, and crackers awaiting us below.

Jimmie sat across from me, leaning against the cabin on a new comfort module, drinking a big gin and Fresca with tons of ice out of his Halloween skele-mug. He was wearing dark Ray-Ban–style shades and a pair of boxers with red kissy lips scattered over white cotton. He looked awesome. It was late afternoon, and the sun began to take its bright, heavy light to another part of the world. A cool breeze drifted across the anchorage. Occasionally a pod of dolphins passed by.

Our world was now, after everything we'd been through, how people probably imagined it was the whole way: all sun and tropical landscapes and cocktails and relaxing. It hadn't been easy. But if it had, delights such as gin and Fresca, palm trees and white sand—and *ice*, for God's sake—wouldn't have been so sweet. We wouldn't have known, when enjoying our paradisiacal new reality, that we had arrived. And that it was worth it.

EPILOGUE

Some sunny, warm day when the sailing was actually really nice, when we were cruising along the coast of Northern Baja and just talking, speculating about the future, I remember one of us suggesting another live-aboard mission. I guess we accurately predicted that we wouldn't be *quite* ready (or willing) to return to normalcy after our year on the boat was up. *Maybe we could live aboard a* motor *vehicle*, we thought—something that existed in a world that was more stable and unthreatening than, say, the Pacific Ocean. It wasn't until we started hanging out at the Café Quinta Avenida in La Paz during the peak heat of the day, drinking *Americanos con leche*, and surfing the Internet that we eventually found the perfect thing: a camper van. The old longing returned. We had to have one!

⚓ ⚓ ⚓

So what happened to the boat? you might be wondering. Amazingly, the Craigslist gods smiled on us once again, and we were able to sell it. (If we hadn't been able to, our plan was to give it to a guy named Antonio who'd taken us horseback riding one day.) Even more amazingly—and much to our liking—*Cotton* went to a supercool couple from Portland (whom we didn't previously know). They agreed to buy it based on the ad and a YouTube video we made. We were a little nervous that it would fall through at the last minute, but Mike and Pam sealed the deal. They flew all the way to La Paz with a friend and promptly sailed *Cotton* over to their vacation home on the mainland side of the Sea of Cortez, where I assume it still is.

And what happened to us? We stayed in La Paz, as planned, and lived at anchor until we'd been gone for just under a year. Once we had faith the boat would sell, we knew what we were dealing with, financially, and could begin shopping for a new mobile home. We did research and hunted around online, eventually locating a 1979 Dodge camper van owned by a couple in Port Townsend, Washington, not far from where we'd anchored in Sequim Bay on our ill-fated maiden voyage. Its interior was wall-to-wall wood grain and had been designed by a shipwright; it featured a pullout couch, propane stovetop (and oven— frozen pizzas on the menu!), a retractable awning, and a propane fridge (who knew?). We got in touch and agreed to buy it sight unseen.

After flying to Washington and taking a few buses, we finally met this tan, Native American–themed van—it had a Chief Seattle bumper sticker, an Indian head on the spare tire cover, and appropriately patterned curtains. We spent five months living on it, dispersed camping in National Forests (it's free!) and occasionally sleeping in a Walmart parking lot (also free). We picked up my dog, Maggie, and visited friends in Portland before driving to California, then through Utah and the Rockies over to Illinois, on to Niagara Falls, through Vermont, New Hampshire, and Maine, and down through Tennessee (hot chicken! Graceland!), Mississippi, and Louisiana before finally settling in Austin, Texas (a city I'd gotten a good feeling about when covering South by Southwest for *Willamette Week* in 2006). Keeping the Pony Canyon name alive, we wrote songs and made music videos to entertain ourselves all along the way.

Vans move a lot faster than sailboats, so even though we'd given ourselves six months, we got to Austin early, and we were ready—at long last—for a regular, stationary house with a full-sized bathroom, running water, and a regulation fridge. We were even ready to have jobs again. Miraculously, we found both.